THE
HISTORY OF
ISRAEL

D0169025

THE HISTORY OF ISRAEL

Arnold Blumberg

The Greenwood Histories of the Modern Nations
Frank W. Thackeray and John E. Findling, Series Editors

GREENWOOD PRESS
Westport, Connecticut • London

Library of Congress Cataloging-in-Publication Data

Blumberg, Arnold, 1925–
    The history of Israel / Arnold Blumberg.
       p. cm. — (The Greenwood histories of the modern nations,
  ISSN 1096–2905)
    Includes bibliographical references and index.
    ISBN 0–313–30224–3 (alk. paper)
    1. Israel—History. 2. Palestine—History—1799–1917.
  3. Zionism—History. I. Title. II. Series.
  DS125.6.B58   1998
  956.94—DC21   97–45659

British Library Cataloguing in Publication Data is available.

Library of Congress Catalog Card Number: 97–45659
ISBN: 0–313–30224–3
ISSN: 1096–2905

First published in 1998

Greenwood Press, 88 Post Road West, Westport, CT 06881
An imprint of Greenwood Publishing Group, Inc.

Printed in the United States of America

The paper used in this book complies with the
Permanent Paper Standard issued by the National
Information Standards Organization (Z39.48–1984).

10 9 8 7 6 5 4 3 2 1

To my brother Nessen,
who climbed Mount Zion
but never found Maale Adumim

To Shulamith and Azriel, Lea and Bernard,
who gave me the keys to Israel

Contents

Series Foreword

The Greenwood Histories of the Modern Nations series is intended to provide students and interested laypeople with up-to-date, concise, and analytical histories of many of the nations of the contemporary world. Not since the 1960s has there been a systematic attempt to publish a series of national histories, and, as series editors, we believe that this series will prove to be a valuable contribution to our understanding of other countries in our increasingly interdependent world.

Over thirty years ago, at the end of the 1960s, the Cold War was an accepted reality of global politics, the process of decolonization was still in progress, the idea of a unified Europe with a single currency was unheard of, the United States was mired in a war in Vietnam, and the economic boom of Asia was still years in the future. Richard Nixon was president of the United States, Mao Tse-tung (not yet Mao Zedong) ruled China, Leonid Brezhnev guided the Soviet Union, and Harold Wilson was prime minister of the United Kingdom. Authoritarian dictators still ruled most of Latin America, the Middle East was reeling in the wake of the Six-Day War, and Shah Reza Pahlavi was at the height of his power in Iran. Clearly, the past thirty years have been witness to a great deal of historical change, and it is to this change that this series is primarily addressed.

With the help of a distinguished advisory board, we have selected nations whose political, economic, and social affairs mark them as among the most important in the waning years of the twentieth century, and for each nation we have found an author who is recognized as a specialist in the history of that nation. These authors have worked most cooperatively with us and with Greenwood Press to produce volumes that reflect current research on their nation and that are interesting and informative to their prospective readers.

The importance of a series such as this cannot be underestimated. As a superpower whose influence is felt all over the world, the United States can claim a "special" relationship with almost every other nation. Yet many Americans know very little about the histories of the nations with which the United States relates. How did they get to be the way they are? What kind of political systems have evolved there? What kind of influence do they have in their own region? What are the dominant political, religious, and cultural forces that move their leaders? These and many other questions are answered in the volumes of this series.

The authors who have contributed to this series have written comprehensive histories of their nations, dating back to prehistoric times in some cases. Each of them, however, has devoted a significant portion of the book to events of the past thirty years, because the modern era has contributed the most to contemporary issues that have an impact on U.S. policy. Authors have made an effort to be as up-to-date as possible so that readers can benefit from the most recent scholarship and a narrative that includes very recent events.

In addition to the historical narrative, each volume in this series contains an introductory overview of the country's geography, political institutions, economic structure, and cultural attributes. This is designed to give readers a picture of the nation as it exists in the contemporary world. Each volume also contains additional chapters that add interesting and useful detail to the historical narrative. One chapter is a thorough chronology of important historical events, making it easy for readers to follow the flow of a particular nation's history. Another chapter features biographical sketches of the nation's most important figures in order to humanize some of the individuals who have contributed to the historical development of their nation. Each volume also contains a comprehensive bibliography, so that those readers whose interest has been sparked may find out more about the nation and its history. Finally, there is a carefully prepared topic and person index.

Readers of these volumes will find them fascinating to read and useful in understanding the contemporary world and the nations that comprise it. As series editors, it is our hope that this series will contribute to a heightened sense of global understanding as we enter a new century.

Frank W. Thackeray and John E. Findling
Indiana University Southeast

Preface

This book is directed to readers seriously interested in the origins and development of the modern State of Israel, and the half century of war between Israel and its neighbors which defines that history. As scholars, we apply the rules of logic to a battle which has outlasted most of the quarrels which convulse humanity. This history directs readers to the causes of that struggle. Most observers find, however, that logic seems to evade the issue. If these pages offer any encouragement to suffering humanity, they will lead us to those rare rifts in the cloud of hatred and misunderstanding which a careful study of history may occasionally reveal.

These pages open upon the earliest thousand years when a series of Jewish kingdoms ruled independently. The reader will then explore the centuries during which, under alien rule, a Jewish population held stubbornly to the land; an unbroken presence. The greater part of the narrative describes the circumstances under which the State of Israel was created.

To derive benefit from such an uninterrupted drama, the reader need not be immersed in Jewish history. It suffices that those who examine these pages will recognize the phenomenal accomplishment of a people who, through thirty-five hundred years have maintained the evolution of the Hebrew language and the reality of their residence in the land of their ancestors.

Israel, today, is changing rapidly. The Zionist founders of the state would scarcely recognize the universities, the sports stadia, the scientific laboratories, the stock markets, the advanced military structure and the government of a modern state. Even the deeply pious fathers of Israel's religious citizens would find it hard to conceive their relationship to muscular pioneers who labor to build Zion in a religious model, though bearing little resemblance to their brethren continuing the unchanging life style of pietists. Indeed, Israel today houses some Jews who conceive themselves as having nothing in common with Jews outside Israel; latter day Canaanites. Anyone who attempts to describe modern Israel in simple terms is either a fraud or a fool. It is the difficult task of trying to describe and explain these historic contradictions to which the writer has set his hand.

In 1948 the modern State of Israel was born. In the fifty years of its existence, it has known constant war. Only a few of its friends recognize the boundary line claimed by the state. The origins of that unique uncertainty go back to the fact that there was no orderly transmission of legal claims when the British mandate for Palestine was terminated on May 14, 1948. What transpired, instead, was a war between the Kingdom of Trans-Jordan, the Kingdom of Egypt, the Syrian Republic, and a newly emerging State of Israel.

By November 1949, as the war ended temporarily with a series of armistices, Israel received boundaries which were simply cease-fire lines. Where the soldier lay down to sleep was the boundary of his country, the next day. Trans-Jordan became the Kingdom of Jordan digesting the Jordan Valley, the Samarian and Judean mountain heights, and a gash in the coastal plain carrying the enlarged kingdom within nine miles of the Mediterranean; capable of cutting Israel's industrial heart in two. The newly enlarged Jordan annexed its conquests two years later, but only Great Britain and Pakistan recognized its claims. Most significantly, Jordan while retaining Amman as its capital, occupied the eastern sector of Jerusalem, including the ancient walled city, holding many of the religious shrines of Jews, Moslems, and Christians. Jews were strictly barred from residing in or even visiting those precincts.

Egypt's spoils from the war were those territories ultimately known as the Gaza Strip. The Egyptians made no attempt to annex the "Strip," and its Arab residents received no citizenship rights. The only benefit extracted from the "Strip" was as a base for Egyptian raids against Israel.

Syria received nothing from the War of 1948–1949, but it fed the goals of a series of Syrian dictators prepared to use war with Israel as a means of strengthening dreams of a greater Syria.

Israel was acknowledged to possess only the lands encompassed by the armistice agreements squeezed from Jordan, Egypt, and Syria by Dr. Ralph Bunche, serving the United Nations. This carried within it a perpetual ticking bomb because none of the Arab participants in the armistice negotiations admitted that Israel had any claim to any part of Jerusalem. Thus, even though Israel's capital city since 1949 has been West Jerusalem, the greater part of the city which Israel had seized when the war had raged, the long forgotten 1947 internationalization of the holy city still returns to haunt the modern state.

Almost all the nations which recognize the independence of Israel still station their embassies in Tel Aviv though their ambassadors must travel the highway to Jerusalem to carry on business. In that strange diplomatic cotillion, even a nation as great as the United States supports two consulates in Jerusalem. One, in western Jerusalem, carries on its business quite routinely through the embassy in Tel Aviv. The other, in eastern Jerusalem, directs its official reports to Washington, D.C., as though it is not located in Israel. The United States Congress has passed a non-binding resolution urging that the embassy be moved from Tel Aviv to West Jerusalem. The State Department continues to allege that this would prejudice American diplomatic relations with friendly Arab states.

To quote the words of Gilbert and Sullivan, "Things are not always what they seem; skimmed milk still masquerades as cream."

Acknowledgments

I am fortunate in having colleagues who are not merely helpful but genuinely collegial. J. Garry Van Osdell and Mark Whitman, chairs of the history department at Towson University, made every effort to arrange teaching schedules that allowed adequate time for writing and research without slighting the needs of students. Dan Jones, dean of the College of Liberal Arts at Towson University, responded promptly to all my requests, giving me the feeling that my contributions were genuinely appreciated. Karl Larew and Harry Piotrowski of our history department showed exceptional interest in my work and applied their specializations to my needs. Eleanore Hofstetter and Susan Mower welcomed me to the Towson University library and provided materials that I had not found for myself. If I asked for an answer within a few weeks, their usual response was help within minutes. Professor Steven Grossman, my mathematician friend, translated meters to miles with an almost supernatural ease. Emily Daugherty, our departmental secretary, in the midst of a year marked by terrible personal loss, was always prepared to repair my inadequacies. My five student research assistants, Yehoshua Goldfinger, Arthur McGreevey, Thomas Moroney, Herbert Poledna, and Matthew Poteet, worked untiringly to find bibliographical sources.

Matthew Wynd of the university's Micromedia Services completed the maps required for this book. I am convinced that his map showing the lands under debate in the Oslo peace process combines a level of clarity and simplicity that no other publication I know of has achieved. My friend and neighbor, Ernest Bravmann, regularly found the latest news from Israel on the Internet for me. Samuel Back, who was once a volunteer serving the infant Israeli air force during the war of 1948–1949, shared recollections that books do not offer.

My children—Raphael and Mona Blumberg, and Eva and Noam Livnat, who are comfortable with colloquial Hebrew, as I am not—provided insights into the realities of Israeli life that cannot be learned from newspapers. Most of all, however, this book owes whatever vivacity it possesses to my wife, Thelma Alpert Blumberg. She listened as I read my chapters to her and did not hesitate to tell me whenever there was something inadequate about the work. Happily, she was ebullient when I hit just the right note.

In the long run, however, a writer must take full responsibility for his own work. I lay it before you in hopes that it will win your praise.

Timeline of Historical Events

539	Cyrus the Great of Persia permits resettlement of Judean exiles.
515	Second Temple is completed; Jerusalem is restored.
458	Ezra the Scribe restores Torah Law and expels pagan interlopers. Oral Law develops through the Men of the Great Assembly.
331	Alexander the Great peacefully annexes Judea; Greek dominance begins.
168	Antiochus IV, Greek king of Syria, desecrates the Temple and attempts to wipe out Judaism. Maccabean revolt erupts.
165	The Temple is rededicated; the battle to expel Antiochus continues; the Maccabean family assumes kingship.
67	Civil war erupts between rival Maccabean claimants to the throne.
63–39	Roman generals assert dominance in Judea and make their own choice of Maccabean kings.
37–4	Herod the Great, an Idumean Roman client, becomes king of Judea, launches a massive building program, and enlarges and beautifies the Temple.
29–4	Evidently insane, King Herod murders his wife and three of his sons; Herod also begins a persecution of the Pharisaic rabbis. Hillel and Shammai survive to become dominant voices of Jewish legal tradition.

COMMON ERA
C.E.

1–67	Roman procurators govern Judea. Descendants of Herod are recognized as puppet princes.
66–73	Jews revolt against Rome.
67	Vespasian is named Roman commander.
69	Vespasian surrenders supreme command in Judea to his son Titus so that he (Vespasian) may seize the Roman imperial crown.

70	Titus conquers Jerusalem and allows the Temple to be destroyed.
73	The last Jewish resistance is stamped out at Massada.
90	Rabbinical leadership makes the rabbinic school Yavneh the intellectual heart of Jewish religious survival.
132–135	Jews revolt, led by Shimon Bar-Cochba and supported by Rabbi Akiva. Romans crush the rabbinic leadership and sell Jewish rebels as slaves, thereby unwittingly spreading Jewish communities throughout the Roman Empire.
135	Jewish residence in Judea continues, but the center of Jewish religious thought is transferred to Babylon-Parthia. Romans invent the term *Palestine* to indicate that Judea is again Philistine.
311–313	Constantine the Great makes Constantinople the center of the Roman Empire. The triumph of Christianity marks a steady deterioration of the social and religious security of Jews.
637	Arab Moslems conquer Palestine. Their earliest relationship with Jews is one of tolerance; Jewish rights to holy places at Jerusalem and Hebron are recognized. Jews are also freed of legal restraints that had been imposed by the Zoroastrians and Christians.
644–764	The security and prestige of the religious academies in the Moslem-held Tigris and Euphrates Valleys transmit disciplined authority to the entire Jewish world.
8th century	Emergence of post-Koranic oral traditions marks a diminishment of Jewish religious claims in Palestine— notably to Jewish possession of the Temple Mount in Jerusalem, and the Tombs of the Patriarchs at Hebron.
1095–1099	The First Crusade, marking the European Christian conquest of Palestine, features the slaughter of all the Jews of Jerusalem and a threat to Jewish survival in all of Palestine.

1187	Saladin, a Kurdish Moslem, reconquers Jerusalem. Saladin, who is personally tolerant of Jews, employs the Jewish intellectual giant Maimonides as his physician. Jewish residence in Palestine makes a rapid recovery.
13th century	European Jewish emigration to Palestine increases as persecution in western Europe witnesses massive expulsions.
16th century	Jewish residence in Palestine increases dramatically in Jerusalem, Safed, and Tiberias. Joseph Nasi subsidizes it.
1701	Yehuda Ha-Chassid (Judah the Pious) attempts to build an Ashkenazic community in Jerusalem. His premature death delays its growth. The Jewish community remains overwhelmingly Sephardic.
18th century	The general population of Palestine declines, and government interest in the land declines.
1811	The first large Yiddish-speaking Lithuanian Jewish community is established in Jerusalem, submitting itself to the authority of the Sephardic rabbinate.
1833–1841	Mehmet Ali, viceroy of Egypt, attempts to assert his independence of the sultan of Turkey. Though ultimately frustrated in that goal, he manages briefly to assert control of Syria, Lebanon, Palestine, and the Sinai Desert.
1838	Mehmet Ali opens Jerusalem to permanent residence by foreign non-Moslems and particularly to foreign consuls with capitulatory treaty rights.
1841	After the Turks had succeeded in expelling Mehmet Ali, they retained his reforms. This meant that foreign consuls were particularly anxious to build lists of "protected" residents, giving each consul the power to advance the ambitions of his own government against those of the Turks.
1849	As part of Russia's imperial ambitions, the Russian consuls make themselves the defenders of all Orthodox Christians in Palestine but surrender jurisdiction over stateless Russian Jews in Palestine to the British consul.

1825–1855	The persecution of Russian Jews by Czar Nicholas I greatly increases the numbers of Russian Jews moving to Palestine. By the end of the Crimean War in 1856, Jews constitute a clear majority of the population of Jerusalem, and possibly of Safed and Tiberias.
1873–1879	Though not recognized officially, the Ashkenazim gain the right to name their own chief rabbis, who enjoy control of the Ashkenazic Jewish community.
1881–1882	The murder of Czar Alexander II of Russia creates an anti-Semitic reaction designed to drive out the Jews. Seven thousand arrive in Palestine in 1882, more than had arrived in any year since the fall of a Jewish state in 70 C.E.
1882–1896	The Russian Haskala movement profits from a religiously well-educated Jewish elite that forms a natural heart for Zionism, as early nationalism comes into being. During the same period, BILU and Hovevei Zion make Jewish labor on the land central to their philosophy.
1882–1922	Eliezer Ben-Yehudah spearheads the movement to make Hebrew a viable modern language suitable for a Jewish state.
1895	Theodor Herzl is moved by the French trial of Captain Alfred Dreyfus to conclude that only in a Jewish state could there be an end to anti-Semitism. Herzl publishes *Die Judenstaat* in 1895–1896.
1897	First World Zionist Congress is held in August.
1908–1911	The kibbutz movement is founded. A. D. Gordon spearheads the *kibbush avoda* philosophy.
1882–1904	The First Aliya lays the foundation for a Zionist "New Yishuv."
1904–1914	The Second Aliya; impelled by the Kishinev pogrom, Russian Jews adopt Zionist self-defense.
1917	The Balfour Declaration of November 1917 constitutes Britain's pledge to recognize Zionism and to assist in the establishment of a Jewish homeland in Palestine.

1919–1939	The Third, Fourth, and Fifth Aliyoth succeed in building Palestine's Jewish population to 400,000 by the eve of World War II, May 1939.
May 1939	The British attempt to win Arab support during the anticipated war by abandoning their pledges to Zionism under the Balfour Declaration. The White Paper of 1939 proposed that all Palestine become an Arab state.
1939–1945	The Palestinian Yishuv attempts to support Britain's battle against Nazism while battling Britain's betrayal of Zionism.
1945–1948	The Yishuv, aware of the consequences of the Nazi Holocaust, struggles to rescue as many European Jewish survivors as possible. Moderate Jewish resistance consists of evading the British blockade to bring European Jews to Palestine. Extremist Jewish resistance resorts to terrorist actions against the British.
1947–1948	The British announce their intention of abandoning the Mandate as of May 1948.
1948	The Yishuv prepares for war against Arabs who are determined to make Palestine an all-Arab state.
1948–1949	Birth of the State of Israel on May 14, 1948; large-scale rescue of Jewish refugees from Europe and the Arab lands.
1948–1956	The numbers of Arab refugees fleeing the new State of Israel are matched by Jewish refugees fleeing persecution in Arab lands. Israel absorbs all Jewish refugees. Arab refugees remain in refugee camps in Arab states, which assure them that they will ultimately recover their lost homes once Israel has been destroyed.
1956–1957	Israel conquers the Sinai and agrees to withdraw in 1957 only if the major world powers issue assurances that the Egyptians will be barred from aggression against Israel.
1967	Precipitating the Six-Day War, the Egyptian army enters the Sinai and imposes a blockade on Israel's Red Sea coast. Israel requests fulfillment of the pledges of 1957. Receiving none, Israel launches an attack on Egypt in June, seizing the entire Sinai Desert. At the conclusion of the Six-Day War, Israel holds the Sinai Desert, the Gaza Strip, the Jordanian West Bank, and the Syrian Golan Heights.

1968	The Palestine Liberation Organization (PLO) endorses a charter pledging the destruction of Israel through the use of terror and war.
1970	King Hussein of Jordan expels the PLO. Most of the terrorists flee to Lebanon.
1971	Israel and Jordan open trade and tourist passages across the Jordan River. Israel and Jordan cooperate against terrorist attacks across the border.
1973	Anwar Sadat of Egypt launches the Yom Kippur War, ultimately suffering defeat but winning the diplomatic struggle by forcing the major world powers to place pressure on Israel to retreat in the Sinai.
1977	In November, Anwar Sadat accepts the invitation of Israel's Menachem Begin and flies to Jerusalem. In an address to the Knesset, Sadat presents uncompromising demands for Israel's surrender of all Arab lands seized by Israel in 1967.
1978	Under President Carter of the United States, the Camp David agreements of September create an Israeli-Egyptian peace treaty pledging the return of the Sinai to Egypt. Egypt abandons Gaza, although Israel had not annexed it.
1968–1992	Both Labor and Likud governments sponsor and encourage Jewish settlement in the Golan Heights, Judea, and Samaria.
1982	The government of Menachim Begin launches an invasion of Lebanon to end PLO terrorism against the north of Israel. The PLO is forced to abandon its Lebanese bases, evacuating its leadership to Tunisia.
1982–present	Hafez el-Assad, Syria's dictator, regards Lebanon as an enlargement of Greater Syria and maintains pressure on Israel without involving Syrian troops, by supporting native Lebanese factions or imported Iranian terrorists to continue the pressure against Israel. Israel constructs a "security zone" in southern Lebanon to protect northern Israel.
1982–1992	Following Begin's abandonment of power after the Lebanese fiasco, Israel is governed by a Likud government under Yitzchak Shamir and by attempted coalition or unity governments sharing power between Labor and Likud parties. Disunity results.

1992–1996   Prime Minister Yitzchak Rabin, dominated by Shimon
                   Peres and the Meretz faction, accepts the Oslo peace
                   agreements with the PLO.

1995   On November 4, Yitzchak Rabin is assassinated.

1996   Labor loses the election in May when 55 percent of
                   the Jewish voters support the election of Benyamin
                   Netanyahu of Likud. The Arab voters, almost entirely
                   for Peres, narrow the Likud victory to 51 percent.

1996–present   Netanyahu fulfills some of the terms of the Oslo Ac-
                   cords but yields nothing to Yassir Arafat as long as
                   the Palestine Authority fails to fulfill its own pledges,
                   chiefly Yassir Arafat's pledge to oppose terror. In-
                   stead, he has continued to incite terror and to en-
                   courage violence against Israel.

Present   Netanyahu attempts, without success, to put pressure
                   on Arafat by refusing to allow free passage into Israel
                   from the territories held by the Palestine Authority,
                   and by withholding tax money owed by Israel to the
                   Palestine Authority.

Prologue

LAND AND CLIMATE

Within its borders established in 1949, Israel claims 20,700 square kilometers (7,992 square miles). The Golan Heights represents 1,156 square kilometers (446 square miles). Judea and Samaria (the West Bank) count 5,948 square kilometers (2,296 square miles). The Gaza District holds 361 square kilometers (139 square miles). For comparative figures, the State of New Jersey has 8,224 square miles (21,300 square kilometers), the State of Delaware has 2,376 square miles (6,154 square kilometers), the Irish Free State (Eire) has 26,582 square miles (68,847 square kilometers), and Ulster has 5,237 square miles (13,564 square kilometers).

The distance from Metulla, the northernmost town in Israel, to Eilat, the southernmost city, is 469 kilometers (291 miles). The greater part of the country's Mediterranean coast is flat and close to sea level. From north to south, mountain ranges form the country's rocky spine. In the north, close to Rosh Hanikra and Haifa, the mountains are close to the sea. South of Haifa, the flat lands called the Sharon Plain steadily widen. The Yarkon River, which runs to the sea through Tel Aviv, marks the end of the Sharon Plain and the beginning of the Shefela Plain. There, the sea-level coastal strip achieves its widest stretch, continuing through Gaza and on into Egypt.

The mountainous heart of the country features Mt. Meron, the highest in Israel at 1,208 meters (3,963 feet). Beyond the ridges of the mountains, the land descends dramatically into the Jordan Valley, which is part of a great gash in the earth that includes the Red Sea and continues into East Africa. Sodom is the lowest point on the face of the earth, at 395 meters (1,296 feet) below sea level. Israel has always thought of the Jordan Valley as the biggest tank trap on earth. Conventional military wisdom has held that Israel must never surrender the Jordan because its possession would prevent an enemy invading from the east from climbing the mountains and piercing Israel's heart at the seacoast. From certain lookout points in the mountains it is possible to see simultaneously the Mediterranean, the Sea of Galilee, and the lands in the Kingdom of Jordan. Anyone who questions Israel's preoccupation with guarding the Jordan River frontier must understand that.

In terms of climate, the one central and dominant fact is that rain is probable only from October through April. The north receives the heaviest yearly precipitation with 1,000 millimeters (39 inches) at Metulla, whereas only 20 millimeters (0.8 inch) may fall at Eilat. Some Israelis take it as a bad omen if it rains at all in June, July, or August. Thus, the greatest problem to face the modern state has been the need to make the best use of limited water resources. This will be discussed later.

In the mountains, winters are cold and damp with occasional snow and ice. Numerous brooks and streams become lifeless wadis or dry streambeds, during the summer. In the Sharon and Shefela plains, snow is almost never seen, but cool, damp conditions are normal. In the mountains, the summers are mild. However, the extremely dry atmosphere may cause perspiration to evaporate so rapidly that individuals who are unaccustomed to the climate may face dehydration unless they drink liquids constantly. The nights are pleasantly cool. On the seacoast, however, both day and night are hot and humid, so that residents there regard air-conditioning as a necessity. Occasionally, for mercifully short periods, the *hamsin* or *sharav* (a hot, dry desert wind) blows across the entire country.

NATURAL RESOURCES

A popular joke alleges that Moses erred in leading the Israelites to the only country in the Middle East that has no oil. That is not quite true. In 1955 oil was found at Helets near Ashkelon on the Shefela coast. Occasionally new oil wells have been tapped elsewhere. In 1996 the newest find was reported at Arad, and it is currently being explored. However, Israel has never found enough oil within its borders to satisfy its domestic needs. Of course, the search continues, but Israel has had to look abroad for that vital resource. That search will be discussed later.

For centuries the minerals carried by rains and by the waters of the Jordan River have been deposited in the Dead Sea, which has no exit. That body of water, shared by Israel and Jordan, is thus a rich source of potash, which is useful for fertilizers, and other minerals. Both Israel and Jordan have industrial complexes engaged in extracting the minerals for export. Moreover, the mineral baths of the Dead Sea have caused it to become a luxurious tourist vacation center and a medical attraction, especially for persons with a variety of skin conditions. The salts are packaged and sold to be enjoyed in bathtubs all around the world.

Israel possesses superior glass sands, and glass products are produced by small artisans as well as by large commercial factories. The production of cement is a major industry. As all tourist guides point out, Israel has stone in unlimited quantity and does not object to tourists taking it home with them. In Jerusalem, all buildings must be at least faced with stone. In the rest of the country, stone structures are much more common than wood. Stucco, concrete blocks, and varieties of plastics are other materials used in construction.

Before World War II, Dutch Jews had made diamond cutting their monopoly. Israel has created a diamond center at Natanya and in other coastal cities, and today Israel is a world center for polished and cut diamonds.

The Israelis have become pioneers in all sorts of aircraft construction. The Israel aircraft industry, often in cooperation with American producers, has become important in creative research for the production of unmanned drone planes and a growing panoply of defensive weapons.

Israel has done remarkably well in becoming self-sufficient in agricultural basics. Its foreign exports in citrus fruits, flowers, and other crops directed to European markets during the winter have made its role both lucrative and competitive. The country is self-sufficient in poultry and egg products. It imports meat, much of it from Argentina. Israel has done pioneering work in "fish farming," creating large ponds in which freshwater and saltwater fish can be bred and harvested. The country would be self-sufficient in its fishing needs except that Israeli consumers have grown sophisticated and demand such imports as Nile princess fish from Africa, and all the fishes of the North Sea.

The development of viticulture has grown steadily since 1882, when

France's Baron Edmond de Rothschild planted French grape vines in Turkish Palestine and proved that the land could produce palatable wine. It was the Israeli occupation of the Golan in 1967, however, that enabled European-trained viticulturalists to produce wines that could compete with some of the best European vintages. Today, even very selective wine connoisseurs find an occasional Israeli wine worthy of boasts.

From the beginning of the Zionist movement, reforestation has been a priority. Zionism has always emphasized the necessity of rescuing the land from centuries of neglect. The restoration of woodlands destroyed by centuries of neglect and spoliation became a symbol of Israel's goals. Tree planting is central to that effort. Politically motivated arson and spontaneous combustion during the long, rainless summers have made the task seem insurmountable. When, in the summer of 1995, fire swept through a large part of the Jerusalem Forest on the western approaches to the capital, travelers on the superhighway connecting Jerusalem and Tel Aviv had an opportunity to see all the resources of the nation poured into saving as much of the forest as possible. The Arabs in the village of Abu Ghosh were prepared to fight the fire side-by-side with the Jews of Motza.

The Society for the Preservation of Nature in Israel has worked closely with the Jewish National Fund to restore as much of Israel's native flora and fauna as possible. Once again gazelles inhabit the forests and ibex roam the mountains. The Biblical Zoo at Jerusalem has searched the world to find rare or endangered species that once had roots in Israel. In the less densely inhabited mountains, hyenas, jackals, porcupines, hedgehogs, mongoose, and many other native and imported species maintain themselves without protection. Even the crocodile once again breeds, close to the shores of the Sea of Galilee.

As Israel is on one of the major flight paths of birds that winter in Africa but spend the summer in Europe, Israelis are especially careful to avoid any step that might inhibit their migration. When the United States reached an agreement with Israel to construct a Voice of America (VOA) radio station capable of broadcasting to the USSR, a national debate was precipitated by the fear that the facility would disturb the flight of birds. The fall of communism and the breakup of the USSR terminated the necessity for a new VOA station and ended the debate. When Israel abandoned the Sinai Desert to Egypt, the Israeli air force was obliged to relocate its bases to the Negev. The press was full of stories offering assurances that the new air bases posed no threat to migrating birds. As far as is known, they have not.

POPULATION

It will be the principal goal of later chapters in this book to describe the circumstances under which the Jewish population of Israel grew. Therefore, that will not be discussed here.

In 1994 Israel had a population of approximately 5.3 million: 81.5 percent Jewish, 14.1 percent Moslem, 2.7 percent Christian, and 1.7 percent Druse and others. In 1996 Israel's Central Bureau of Statistics reported that the population stood at 5,716,000. Jews constitute 4,620,000 (80.8%), Moslems count 835,000 (14.6%), Christians claim 166,000 (2.9%), and 95,000 (1.7%) are Druse. The population increased by 141,000 from September 1995 to September 1996, or by 2.5 percent compared to 2.6 percent from 1994 to 1995. The percentage of new immigrants in 1996 dropped from 42 percent of the increase in 1994–1995 to 40 percent in 1995–1996. The great majority of non-Jews are Sunni Moslem, although Shi'ites can be found in the north.

As in all religious communities in Israel, matters of marriage, divorce, inheritance, guardianship of minors, religious membership, and burial are settled by the clergy of that denomination, whose salaries are paid by the State of Israel. Moslem *sharia*, or religious courts, issue judgments concerning Moslems that are binding under state law. The Waqf, or Moslem religious endowment, controls all mosques and other religious property. In certain areas, notably in Jerusalem, a debate rages among Moslems as to whether Yassir Arafat's Palestine Authority or the King of Jordan may designate such supreme Moslem authorities as the grand mufti of Jerusalem. This is very important because the grand mufti controls the wealth of the Waqf. The Israeli government has chosen to abstain from taking sides in that politically sensitive dispute.

Although all Israeli Jews are subject to compulsory military service, Arab Moslems have been exempted to spare them any conflict of conscience in a war against Arab neighbors. Individual Arabs may volunteer for service if they choose to do so. Many Bedouin tribes have volunteered collectively to accept military service and have earned a reputation for courage and effectiveness as Israeli soldiers. Ironically, the Israeli government has undercut the alliance with the Bedouin by its attempts to persuade them to abandon their nomadic lifestyle and to become villagers with a fixed residence. In the Negev Desert and in the Galilee, travelers can see the neat houses subsidized by the government standing adjacent to the black tents of the Bedouin; the two lifestyles are placed side-by-side. The arrival of urban Arabs serving as teachers in the new schools for Bedouin children may cause the Bedouin to convert from their tradition as loyal citizens of Israel to the somewhat uncertain attitudes of many Israeli Arabs.

The Christian minority is mostly Arabic in speech, but it represents thirty denominations. As in the nineteenth century, Jerusalem is the seat of the resident Greek, Latin, and Armenian patriarchs as well as an Anglican bishop of Jerusalem. The ancient quarrels between these congregations still persist. To this day, a Moslem family whose ancestors have performed the duty for many generations, nightly locks itself into the Church of the Holy Sepulchre so that no Christian denomination can claim to possess the keys of that most sacred Christian shrine. Similar compromises persist at the churches in Nazareth and Bethlehem. Because the Israeli Christian citizenry speak Arabic, their publicly expressed sympathies have been pro-Arab. Indeed, many leaders of the Palestine Liberation Organization (PLO) were Christians by birth, notably Dr. George Habash. Nevertheless the rise of Moslem fundamentalism has been much more threatening to the Christian minority than to the Jewish majority. Thus, the Christian population of Jerusalem and Bethlehem has fallen sharply. Today, for the first time, Bethlehem has a growing Moslem majority. Israeli Christians have taken refuge in the Jewish-dominated parts of Israel proper, and many have emigrated, chiefly to the United States.

The Druse are a sect that broke away from Islam in the tenth century. The precise principles of their faith are known only to a circle of initiated clergy. They believe they are descended from Jethro, the father-in-law of Moses. His tomb in the Lower Galilee is the site of a mass annual pilgrimage by Israeli Druse. There are approximately 60,000 Druse living in eighteen villages concentrated near Haifa and in the Galilee. From the birth of the State of Israel, the Druse have participated fully in the duties as well as the privileges of citizenship. They have collectively accepted compulsory military service. They have also made important contributions as policemen in Arabic-speaking areas of the country. They have sometimes faced conflict with Moslem Arabs who resent their participation in Israeli life. Nevertheless they have remained steadfast. On the other hand, most of the Druse living in the Golan Heights have remained loyal to Syria and refused Israeli citizenship. The Druse in nearby Lebanon have been among Israel's most fanatical enemies.

In a land that never entirely renounces any part of its past, numerous small minorities hold tenaciously to their traditions. About six hundred Samaritans form two communities, one living in Shechem or Nablus near their holiest shrine at Mt. Gerizim. The other lives at Holon, Israel. They meet, annually if possible, to observe Passover at Mt. Gerizim. The Samaritans regard themselves as the true Jews. They are the offspring of Jews who were expelled from Jerusalem by the biblical Ezra, for having taken pagan wives. The Samaritans accept the Five Books of Moses but reject the Oral Law and most of the Bible. Their Torah is contained in scrolls written in Aramaic rather than Hebrew.

Another minority, the Circassians, are a small Moslem community living in two Galilean villages; they emigrated from imperial Russia in the nineteenth century. Their young men voluntarily accept Israeli military service. Haifa houses the world center of the Baha'i religion, yet another minority.

TRANSPORTATION

Most Israelis make use of an excellent bus system run by two companies: Dan and Egged. Arabs have their own bus companies connecting large areas of Arab population. At selected centers in large cities *sherutim*, or service vans, take as many as eight passengers at a time to specific out-of-town destinations. Hotels typically arrange *sherut* service to the airport at a set rate, paid for in advance. Taxis also serve the public.

The railroad system is antiquated and slow. Most persons taking the train from Tel Aviv to Jerusalem, or from Tel Aviv to Haifa, do so in order to enjoy the magnificent scenery. Today, however, Israel is beginning to refurbish its railroads; if plans are fulfilled, it will ultimately have rapid and efficient service. Haifa offers the *carmelit*, a clean, rapid, and efficient rail system on the slopes of Mt. Carmel. Tel Aviv has just begun the groundwork for its first subway.

Israelis are well equipped with automobiles, but the big cities have not kept up with the automobile age. Consequently there are serious traffic jams. Some effort is being exerted to build access roads for the big cities. Because of the political problems created by the transfer of Arab-inhabited cities to the Palestine Authority, bypass roads connecting Jewish-inhabited areas have been constructed. This has resulted in somewhat improved travel time. New government regulations require attendance at special instruction classes for drivers who are guilty of careless or dangerous driving.

EDUCATION

A large proportion of children between 2 and 4 years of age attend a *Gan*, which provides preschool education. It is neither free nor compulsory, but a great many citizens organizations strive to make it available for poorer children. The Ministry of Education sets aside funds to extend it to children in development towns and those designated as urban renewal areas.

Kindergarten for 5-year-olds is free and compulsory. School attendance is compulsory to age 16 and is free to age 18. About 10 percent of the school-age population over age 12 attends boarding schools. Schools are divided into four categories: state schools, state religious schools, Arab and Druse schools, and independent Torah schools. The last group, though receiving government support, seeks additional public financial support to maintain a longer school day and more study of religious subjects. In the fourth grade, children are given an opportunity to study a second language. Most Jewish children study English. Few study Arabic. Many Arab children study Hebrew as a second language, but English is growing in popularity.

Because Israel is a country of immigrants, great attention is given to adult education in Hebrew. The system, known as *ulpan*, consists of using only Hebrew to teach the class. This intensive approach, though sometimes difficult for older students, hastens the moment when the student can make functional use of the national language. The fact that three years after a new immigrant accepts citizenship he or she faces military service typically makes a knowledge of Hebrew necessary.

Almost 100,000 students attend the twenty institutions of higher learning. These include fully developed universities, those offering only bachelor's degrees, and regional colleges supervised by one of the universities. The minister for education heads a Council for Higher Education, which is appointed by the president of the State of Israel on the recommendation of the Ministry of Education.

The universities (in order of age) are as follows. The Technion, or Israel Institute of Technology, actually originated in the era when Turkey still held Palestine, at which time it was patronized by German philanthropists and the language of instruction was German. Subsequently, even before World War I the students insisted on the use of Hebrew. The official birth date of the modern Technion is 1924. Described as the MIT (Massachusetts Institute of Technology) of Israel, it emphasizes scientific studies, engineering, and industrial development. Faculties for medicine, the life sciences, the social sciences, economics, education, computer science, engineering, architecture, and agriculture are among later additions to the Technion's programs.

The Hebrew University of Jerusalem was officially founded in 1925. It includes schools of medicine, dentistry, pharmacy, veterinary medicine, agriculture, and almost every other graduate and undergraduate endeavor except engineering, architecture, and physiotherapy. It is also the home of Israel's National Library—Israel's equivalent of the U.S. Library of Congress, France's Bibliothèque Nationale, or the British Museum.

The Weizmann Institute of Science, founded in 1934, was originally known as the Sieff Institute. It is a postgraduate center for research in physics, chemistry, mathematics, and the life sciences. The Institute promotes excellent high school science teaching and the development of new curricula for that level. The campus includes a museum containing the memorabilia of Dr. Chaim Weizmann, a major Zionist leader and the first president of independent Israel.

Bar Ilan University was established in 1955 and integrates the spiritual values of Judaism with a modern liberal education. It offers fields of studies in law as well as the social sciences, humanities, business administration, economics, psychology, library science, the arts, social work, education, mathematics, computers, and the natural sciences. Bar Ilan has built a branch in the city of Ariel, the first university-level institution in Samaria, beyond the Green Line, the boundary for territories once ruled by Jordan or Egypt before the Six-Day War of 1967.

Tel Aviv University, founded in 1956, actually was created when three existent institutions were joined to form a university for the Tel Aviv area. Today it is Israel's largest university. Tel Aviv encompasses schools of medicine, dentistry, law, engineering, physiotherapy, and nursing. It places great emphasis on applied research, strategic studies, health systems management, technological forecasting, and energy studies. Tel Aviv offers fields of study in the humanities, social studies, business administration, economics, psychology, the arts, social work, education, mathematics, and computers.

Haifa University, established in 1963, features a school of law as well as departments of the humanities, social sciences, business administration, economics, psychology, library science, the arts, social work, education, mathematics and computer science, and the natural sciences. The university has become a center for the study of the kibbutz as a unique Israeli social institution. The kibbutz, to be discussed later in more detail, is a collective community in which all residents share equally in personal wealth and self-government. It is also concerned with the enhancement of Arab-Jewish cooperation and understanding. With 30 percent Arab enrollment, Haifa probably has the largest Arab student presence of any Israeli university.

Ben-Gurion University of the Negev, founded in 1967, is located at Be'er Sheva, where it specializes in the unique conditions engendered by life in the desert. Be'er Sheva is today a major medical center, and the university's medical school has pioneered community-oriented medicine in the country. Schools of nursing and physiotherapy complement that effort. The university also offers a full set of courses in the humanities, social sciences, business administration, economics, psychology, social work, education, mathematics, computer science, the natural sciences, and engineering. The university also maintains a campus at Kibbutz Sde Boker, where David Ben-Gurion (Israel's first prime minister) lived his last years and where he is buried. He had made it one of his life's priorities to develop the resources of the Negev Desert. The university's campus there is devoted to research touching his life and interests.

HEALTH

All Israeli residents have access to a health fund (Kupat Cholim). There are four principal organizations to which gainfully employed persons pay dues. Each has its own staff of physicians and other medical personnel. A National Health Insurance Law of January 1, 1995, guaranteed all Israeli residents medical services including hospitalization. The Ministry of Health supervises the degree to which beneficiaries and employers must make financial contributions to the fund. Persons requiring emergency surgery or other vital care receive priority. Persons with less urgent needs may have hospital visits deferred. Persons wishing to receive immediate care for elective medical services may seek it from private medical practitioners. Dentists, also, offer their services on a private-care basis. Persons affiliated with Histadruth, the giant labor union, have access to sanatoria where they may enjoy recuperative rest following hospitalization. Mothers with newborn babies typically are allowed a longer stay in the hospital than is common in other countries. Special rest homes for newly delivered mothers are also available at inexpensive rates. Volunteer organizations such as Yad Sarah lend persons medical equipment for extended periods of time, without charge.

THE ARTS

The publication of books, in a startling variety of languages, has always been a preoccupation with Israelis. Because it does not rain in the summer, public parks become ideal locations for book fairs. It is estimated that biblical Hebrew contained only 8,000 words, but modern Hebrew encompasses an estimated 120,000 words. The work of Eliezer Ben-Yehudah will be discussed elsewhere in this book, but he must be mentioned in any discussion of language. Hebrew prose, much of it translated into English and other modern languages, includes the work of Yosef Haim Brenner, Shmuel Yosef Agnon, A. B. Yehoshua, Amos Oz, Yaakov Shabtai, Aharon Appelfeld, David Grossman, Alexander and Yonat Sened, David Shahar, Hanoch Bartov, and Shulamit Hareven.

The Haskala, to be discussed later, proved to be particularly significant in fostering modern Hebrew poetry. Among the most representative names in that large school are Haim Nachman Bialik, Saul Tchernichovsky, Abraham Shlonsky, Natan Alterman, Lea Goldberg, Uri Zvi Greenberg, Yehuda Amichai, Natan Zach, David Avidan, and Rahel Blaustein.

Theatre

For so small a nation, Israel has been extraordinarily creative in the theatre. Although located in specific cities with their own stages, many companies tour the country and a few have gone abroad, especially to large cities with audiences likely to appreciate Hebrew-language drama. Among the leading troupes today are Habimah, established in 1931; the Cameri, established in 1944; the Haifa Municipal Theatre, established in 1961; the Be'er Sheva Municipal Theatre, established in 1974; the Khan Theatre, a repertory company founded in the mid-1970s; and the Children's and Youth Theatre, sponsored by the Ministry of Education and founded in 1970. Some of the theatres offer ear phones, making it possible for English-speaking patrons to follow the dialogue through translation.

Music

First-rate classical music has dominated the Israeli cultural scene. The Palestine Orchestra, today known as the Israeli Philharmonic Orchestra, has had its seat at Tel Aviv since 1936 but regularly tours the country. Distinguished ensembles have their seats in Jerusalem, Be'er Sheva, Haifa, Natanya, Holon, and Ramat Gan. Choruses, dance groups, folk dance ensembles, and specialized musical groups are well established. Fine music schools as well as music departments at the universities have built a vital music culture in Israel. The arrival of numerous Russian Jews immigrating to Israel has brought a large body of competent musicians, only a small part of which has been able to find employment. It is hoped that all the truly talented performers will find a niche for their creativity.

Music at a popular level draws huge and enthusiastic audiences. Rock concerts and other youth-based performances have become routine. In the popular music area, foreign performers find Israel very receptive.

Museums

In a land with thousands of years of history, museums of every variety have proliferated. Jerusalem's Israel Museum has many departments that cover every aspect of history, archeology, and ethnography. The Shrine of the Book, housing the Dead Sea Scrolls, is one of its sections. The Haifa Museum is almost as ambitious as the Israel Museum, and it includes a large collection of Arab and Druse materials. In that area, the Institute for Islamic Art in Jerusalem emphasizes that important facet of Israeli society. Beit Hatefutzot, or the Diaspora Museum, at Tel Aviv University specializes in all aspects of Jewish history and culture throughout the world. Yad Vashem is a national institution devoted to documenting all aspects of the history of the Holocaust.

SPORTS

Israelis are sports enthusiasts. The most popular sports are soccer, basketball, swimming, tennis, volleyball, track and field, gymnastics, sailing, weightlifting, and fencing. Team sports, led by soccer, enjoy mass support in large stadia. Major sports organizations such as Maccabia, Betar, Hapoel, and Elitzur stir up enthusiastic fan support. Every four years Israel has its own "Jewish Olympics," the Maccabia Games. Israel belongs to the Asian Games Federation and is involved with a European sports federation for basketball, volleyball, and soccer.

GOVERNMENT

Israel is a democratic republic. It has never ratified a constitution, so its legal system contains elements of Ottoman and British law as well as statutes passed by the Israeli Knesset, or parliament, since the attainment of independence in 1948. Marriage, property inheritance, and many elements of self-identification remain entrusted to the clergy of the many religions in the country.

The president of Israel is usually a distinguished scholar, or a widely popular politician or soldier with enough support in all parties to be above partisan politics. He or she is chosen by a vote of the Knesset. The president fulfills the same ceremonial role as the king or queen of a constitutional monarchy. However, the president can and does speak out if he or she feels that the government is guilty of error. The president usually—though not always—can speak Hebrew, English, and Arabic, the three official languages of the country. When a president is deficient in Arabic, he or she appoints an Arabic representative to speak to the non-Jewish citizenry, some 18 percent of the population.

Until 1996 the prime minister was chosen by the largest single party in the Knesset, if it was capable of forming a coalition. Beginning with the election of May 29, 1996, however, the electorate has been allowed to choose the prime minister by direct vote. This has opened Israel to the potential for political crisis that might be precipitated if the new prime minister did not belong to the largest party in the Knesset. To form a coalition capable of winning a confidence vote, the parties that have formed a coalition must be able to count on a minimum of sixty-one votes.

Israeli voters cast their votes for complete party lists, rather than for individual candidates. The party lists were once chosen by party bosses in the fabled "smoke-filled room." Today, however, the principal parties construct their lists through primary elections involving all registered members of the party. Attention is given by the party leadership, however, to constructing a list that will appeal to all elements of their voting public. This often means that candidates who are women or members of religious minorities may be assured safer seats, high on the list. On election day the proportion of the popular vote for the party determines the proportion of the list that will be inducted into office. Thus, the more important leaders of a party are usually assured of a "safe" seat high on the electoral list.

Because no party has ever won 61 seats, and the Knesset has 120 members, all Israeli governments have been formed by coalitions. Before 1996, immediately following an election, the president called on the leader of the most numerous party to try to form a government. Since 1996, the popularly elected prime minister has had the task of opening negotiations with the leadership of other ideologically compatible parties. Written agreements are signed between all coalition partners, setting forth the conditions for cooperation and allocating the number and kind of cabinet and subministerial posts to be shared with the smaller parties.

When an assured sixty-one members have committed themselves to the
new government, a vote of confidence is taken in the Knesset. In that
situation, victory for the government is ensured. If a "no confidence"
vote of sixty-one or more results in the government's defeat, both the
prime minister and Knesset must face new elections. If, however, a dis-
satisfied Knesset desires the prime minister to resign, a minimum of
eighty hostile votes is necessary.

Another innovation adopted in 1996 is known as the Norwegian Law,
based on a model used in that country. Under its terms, persons named
to hold cabinet posts must immediately abandon their seats in the Knesset. Their replacements are the persons immediately following them on
their party's electoral list.

The seat of the government is in Jerusalem, the capital. The Knesset
meets in a building located a short walk away from Kiryat Ben-Gurion,
where three buildings house the prime minister's office, the Ministry of
the Interior, and the Ministry of Finance. Other ministries are scattered
around the city. The Ministry of Defense has always maintained its
"command center" at Tel Aviv, simply because security demands that it
be at a distance from the frontiers.

The Foreign Ministry operates at a peculiar disadvantage. Most of the
nations that recognize Israel and maintain embassies in the country have
never recognized the annexation of west Jerusalem to Israel in 1948 or
the annexation of east Jerusalem after the Six-Day War of 1967. The pretense is still maintained that the United Nations, in recognizing the independence of Israel in 1948, declared Jerusalem to be an international
city. Nevertheless all of Israel's government business is conducted in its
capital, where the president and the prime minister have their official
residences. Thus, the greater part of the world's nations maintain their
official embassies in Tel Aviv but staff very large consulates in Jerusalem
that carry out many of the functions that would ordinarily be borne by
an embassy. Ambassadors and their staffs must divide their time between the two cities. Thus, Israel has a foreign ministry building in Tel
Aviv and a foreign ministry complex in Jerusalem.

Israel possesses a very independent and securely tenured judiciary that
has served as a bulwark for the guardianship of the civil rights of minorities. This refers, for example, to suspected Arab terrorists threatened
with the loss of their freedom or property after the alleged commission
of heinous crimes; or to right-wing Jews urging civil disobedience in
protest against government policy. As a heritage of the British Mandate,

1919–1948, administrative detention may still be imposed, without trial, on persons suspected of incitement to sedition. Such persons have found the judiciary to be a valuable ally in struggles with overzealous bureaucrats.

1

A Survey of Zion's Earlier History

GEOGRAPHY AND HISTORY

The land called Israel, today, is at the center of the Fertile Crescent, a band of relatively productive land stretching from the Tigris and Euphrates Valleys in the north to the Nile Valley in the south. Within the crescent of that verdant circle lie the torrid heat and barrenness of the desert. Throughout history, armies mounting war against Babylonia or Assyria to the north, or Egypt to the south, have marched across this land called Zion. Hittites from the north, Semitic tribes from all directions, and Philistines from the islands of the Mediterranean have pursued their military ambitions, settling in the Fertile Crescent. The Jews have lived in that difficult neighborhood for more than 3,500 years.

Three thousand years ago David, king of Israel, captured a fortified hilltop called Jerusalem from the Jebusites. Previously his capital had been at Hebron. In approximately 973–933 B.C.E. his son Solomon built a temple there (this became known as the First Temple). The glory of the ancient Kingdom of Judea was destroyed by the Babylonians in 586 B.C.E., and part of the Judean population was forced into exile. After seventy years of exile in Babylon a remnant of the exiles was allowed to return to Zion by Cyrus the Great of Persia, who had conquered Babylon.

From 538 to 515 B.C.E. a modest Second Temple was erected at Jerusalem by Ezra the Scribe and by Nehemiah, whose work is detailed in the biblical accounts bearing their names.

Ezra's greatest work, however, lay not in building but in establishing social institutions that were meant to insulate Jews from the destructive practices of pagan neighbors. It was Ezra who expelled members of the community who were irrevocably committed to paganism. It was Ezra who ordained the public reading of the Torah, the Five Books of Moses. It was he who brought together the Men of the Great Assembly, a self-perpetuating body of scholars who determined which books belonged in the Bible as divinely inspired, and which books were worthy of study but lacked the divine stamp and had to be consigned to the Apocrypha. Most important, the Great Assembly provided the foundation for the interpretation of Jewish Law, generation after generation, which created the Oral Law. The Oral Law would someday become Mishna, and ultimately Gemara or Talmud, the great body of law governing every aspect of Jewish life.

CONSEQUENCES OF THE BABYLONIAN EXILE

One result of the seventy-year exile in Babylon was the abandonment of Hebrew as the vernacular tongue. Thereafter Hebrew remained the language of prayer, study, and law, but the common folk spoke Aramaic, a kindred Semitic language. The encroachments of the new language are exemplified, however, by the fact that the biblical book of Daniel is in Aramaic rather than Hebrew. Hebrew was never forgotten as a means of communicating with Jews speaking other tongues, but it would become a colloquial tongue again only in the nineteenth century.

In 334–331 B.C.E. Alexander the Great passed peacefully through Jerusalem and annexed Judea, having conquered the Persians. His behavior toward the Jews was so benign that the Talmud states that every boy born that year was named for him, and "Alexander" became a Hebrew name. After Alexander the Great's death the Jews of Judea found themselves ruled by his lieutenant, Seleucis, who founded a line of Greek kings in a Syrian-Palestinian kingdom.

The Greek adoration of nature and of beauty for its own sake was inevitably at war with Judaism, which denies any physical form to divinity. The Greek tendency to idealize the lusts, and even the perversions, of their physically perfect gods and goddesses proved dangerously subversive to the Jewish concept of a perfect, omniscient, incorporeal divinity. To traditional Jews, the spectacle of young men standing naked in the amphitheater represented lewdness, especially if the athletic contest or the dramatic presentation was dedicated to the Greek gods.

Matters came to a head when a Seleucid king, Antiochus IV, usurped the throne in 175 B.C.E. His excesses, and especially his insistence on being worshipped as a god, finally led the Jews to full revolt. The Maccabean or Hasmonean rebels ultimately achieved independence from Syrian control in 142 B.C.E. The new dynasty was not descended from King David, but its kings built a Judean monarchy as large and powerful as that which David had built. Moreover, the Hasmonean kings were also members of the hereditary priesthood descended from Aaron, the brother of Moses. The possession of kingship and priesthood in one family spelled self-destruction through an excessive abuse of power.

IMPORTANCE OF THE PHARISEES

The new rebellion against the abuse of power came not through the sword but through the book. The Hasmonean priestly party, or the Sadducees, rested their authority on a narrow, literal interpretation of the Torah. The peaceful rebels were those Pharisees who turned to the *rabbi*, the "master" or "teacher" who knew the Oral Law and could apply it to the needs of each new generation. The Great Sanhedrin (supreme court), the Lesser Sanhedrins (courts of appeal), and local rabbinic law courts made the Pharisaic system work.

It was fortunate for Jewish survival that the Pharisees created a Judaism capable of surviving bitter persecution. The new threat was Rome, which succeeded in displacing the Maccabean kings and enthroning a puppet, King Herod. Herod was undoubtedly insane. He has become known throughout history as Herod the Great because he was an imaginative builder. He enlarged both the Temple Mount and the Temple so that it rivaled or outshone the First Temple in magnificence. Its massive retaining walls form the Kotel, Judaism's most holy shrine today. His work can be seen at Herodian near Bethlehem, in the walls of the Tombs of the Patriarchs and Matriarchs at Hebron, and in the fortress of Masada near the Dead Sea. When he died in 4 C.E., the last remnants of Jewish independence were gone.

The last kings of Judea were Roman puppets. In 66 C.E. Emperor Nero went too far, profaning the Temple courtyard with pagan images. Revolt flared up. Although the fighting went on for seven years, the end result was inevitable. The Temple and Jerusalem were destroyed in the year

70. The last resistance was crushed in 73. Fortunately the Romans tolerated the construction of a school at Yavne, which ensured the triumph of rabbinic authority now that priestly and royal authority were defunct. From 132 to 135 a last revolt against Roman rule was led by Shimon Bar-Cochba. At its destruction, the triumphant Romans sold thousands of Jews into slavery, slaughtering rebels caught with arms in hand. In the aftermath, Jews were a minority in Zion. Quite unwittingly, by selling Jews into slavery, the Romans helped to build strong Jewish communities all over the empire. The Romans invented a new name for Zion, calling it Palestina as though it were once more the land of the Philistines. The Romans imagined that by executing the rabbis who had supported Bar-Cochba, they had finally eliminated a stubborn foe.

Instead, the Pharisaic leaders merely built new schools in the Galilee, centered at Tiberias, one of the four Jewish holy cities to this day. Between 170 and 217, Yehuda Ha-Nasi (Judah the Prince) supervised the codification of centuries of judicial decisions in the Oral Law, constituting the Mishna.

IMPACT OF CHRISTIANITY

The founding of Christianity, at first, was not threatening to the Jews. Christians were merely regarded as observant Jews who believed that the messiah had already arrived. It was only after St. Paul offered the hope of salvation and eternal life to Gentiles who had not accepted the 613 commandments binding on Jews that the two faiths split irrevocably. The Christian concept of Holy Trinity was anathema to Jews, who defined deity as incorporeal. In the fourth century the formerly persecuted Christians triumphed when the Roman emperor Constantine the Great declared Christianity to be the state church. Julian the Apostate, who succeeded Constantine, made an ineffective effort to return to paganism. He even allowed the Jews to begin to rebuild the Temple at Jerusalem. However, after his death Christianity permanently triumphed, the Temple was not rebuilt, and Palestinian Jewry went into eclipse. Jews continued to live in Palestine, especially in the Galilee, but the center of the Jewish world shifted eastward to Babylon, or Parthia.

IMPACT OF ISLAM

In 637–638 Palestine was conquered by the Arab Moslems sweeping up the Mediterranean coast and across North Africa. They arrived in Palestine only five years after the death of their founder, Mohammed, in

632. Their faith, newly revealed to them through the Koran, made it plain that conquered pagans could accept conversion or die. Christians and Jews, however, were to be spared—provided that they behaved humbly, paid a head tax in exchange for protection, and renounced the right to bear arms. The Ahl Ud-Dimma, or "Protected People," were conceded to be "Peoples of the Book" who possessed an authentic, divinely revealed Bible, even though they rejected the final revelations of Mohammed. Thus, the Semitic Arabs (newly converted themselves) welcomed the easy conversions of Greek-and Aramaic-speaking Christians and Jews, leading to the gradual adhesion of a majority of the population to Islam and the Arabic tongue.

For Jews who remained true to Judaism, their first generations under Moslem rule were marked by tolerance. The earliest generations of newly converted Moslems were perfectly willing to designate Jews as the "custodians" of the Temple Mount. Only a post-Koranic tradition later caused the Temple Mount to rank as the third most holy Moslem shrine after Mecca and Medina. It was held that Mohammed and his horse had leapt from the Temple Mount in a mystic night journey to heaven. Thereafter Jews were only allowed access to the Western Wall of the Temple Mount, the Kotel as it is called today. At Hebron, the second holiest Jewish shrine (the burial place of Abraham, Sarah, Isaac, Rebecca, Jacob, and Leah), Jews and Moslems shared custody of the tombs. Abraham, after all, was the father of both Jews and Arabs. Herod the Great had covered the burial caves with a magnificent structure of heavy stone, still visible today. Jews were allowed to build a synagogue next to the shrine. It was only in later centuries that the Arabs barred Jews from exercising their ancient pious practices at the tombs.

Jews continued to live in all the fair-sized towns of Palestine. There were occasional Moslem persecutions of Jews and Christians by relatively rare Moslem bigots such as the early eleventh-century Fatimid caliph Al-Hakim, but he was an exception.

In 1071, however, the Seljuk Turks took Jerusalem—from the Arab Moslems, who held it—as part of their drive against the Christian Byzantine Empire. Thereafter the Turks, newly converted to Islam, renewed the drive against Christian Europe that had been dramatically successful at the hands of the Arabs in the seventh and eighth centuries.

THE CRUSADES

All Christendom responded to the call for help issued by the threatened Byzantines. The result was the First Crusade, 1095–1099, the most disastrous for the Jews. When, in 1099, the largely French and German Crusader army captured Jerusalem, every Jew in the holy city was burned alive in the devastated synagogues. Similar scenes of horror were duplicated throughout Palestine. For Jews, the beginning of the twelfth century was the low point in the long Jewish bond with Zion.

The second and later generations of Crusaders resident in the Holy Land began to adopt the costume, social habits, and speech of the natives. Invariably the Italian merchants were more interested in buying the products of the East than in crushing the native faiths. In 1187 the great Kurdish Moslem sultan Saladin had reconquered Jerusalem. Indeed, Richard the Lionhearted of England, on the Third Crusade in 1189, became warmly friendly to Saladin. Holy Roman Emperor Frederick II of Hohenstaufen, on the Sixth Crusade in 1229, worked out a settlement in friendly conversation with Saladin's nephew, who bore the same name.

Slowly the Jewish population, which had been much reduced by the First Crusade, began to recover. Indeed, the greatest Jewish philosopher of the Middle Ages, Moses Maimonides, settled briefly at Acre in 1165 before continuing on to Egypt, where he served as Saladin's physician. He was ultimately buried at the Jewish holy city of Tiberias. In 1211 three hundred rabbis from France and England immigrated in a group, settling in Acre and Jerusalem. The great Spanish Jewish scholar Nachmanides lived at periods of his life in Acre, Shechem (Nablus), and Jerusalem. When England's Jews were expelled in 1290, and France's Jews a century later, many went to Palestine, thereby hastening the recovery of the Jewish community that had been so decimated by the Crusades.

In 1291 resurgent Islam conquered the last Christian base at Acre. Thereafter the Latin or Roman Catholic patriarch of Jerusalem (1291–1847) was usually an Italian prelate who never saw Jerusalem. Roman Catholic interests were handled by the Franciscan monastic order, which was designated as Custodia Terra Sancta. The title is still borne by them to this day. The Greek Orthodox patriarch of Jerusalem continued to preside over the affairs of his church, under Moslem rule.

For the Jews, notwithstanding occasional friction and even persecution, the restoration of Moslem rule in Palestine meant rapid recovery from the blows suffered during the Crusades. In 1335 a Roman Catholic monk on pilgrimage referred to the Jewish quarter of Jerusalem as being at Mt. Zion, where it still thrives today.

SEPHARDIC JEWS

In 1453 the Ottoman Turks finally conquered Constantinople and caused the downfall of the Byzantine Empire. When Spain expelled its large and creative Jewish population in 1492 and the Portuguese followed suit in 1497, the Turks welcomed the refugees. In Hebrew, the name of Spain is *Sepharad*. Hence, Jews of Spanish origin are called Sephardim. The term has been extended to include oriental Jews whose Hebrew pronunciation or religious customs are similar.

So many Spanish and Portuguese Jews settled on all of the hospitable shores of Turkey's Mediterranean realm that the native Jewish communities were absorbed by the newcomers. Ladino, a fifteenth-century Spanish dialect written in Hebrew letters, is still in use among Mediterranean Sephardim today. Until recently Israeli radio broadcast the news in Judeo Espanol, for the convenience of a declining but still considerable population that speaks Ladino. That service, however, may be on the verge of abandonment. There is much demand for Russian language programs to accommodate one million Russian immigrants.

From 1250 to 1517 Palestine was ruled by the Egyptian Moslem Mamluks. In 1517 the Ottoman Turks, a non-Arab people, added Palestine to their vast realm. Their rule in Palestine was to last exactly 400 years.

THE PALESTINIAN JEWISH COMMUNITY

The "Old Yishuv" refers to the Jewish community of Palestine that existed before political Zionist settlement began. Under the benign rule of the Turks, the Jewish community of Palestine thrived. Joseph Nasi, a Portuguese Jew, served Sultans Suleiman II and Selim, making himself indispensable as a financial advisor until the death of Selim in 1574. He was awarded the title Duke of Naxos, which gave him possession of several Mediterranean islands. Most relevant to this topic, he was given permission to settle Jews in the Palestinian Jewish holy city of Tiberias and in seven nearby villages. He hoped to make Sephardic Jewish settlers self-sufficient by training them to cultivate mulberry trees and silkworms, with a view to producing Palestinian silk. Unfortunately the largely urban Jews were ill-adapted to rural life, and most of the immigrants ultimately made their way to the towns. However, once again the Galilee became the center of Palestinian Jewish life. The great religious scholar Joseph Karo would do his most important work there. In 1631 a French Christian visitor reported Jewish communities in Jerusalem, Hebron, Tiberias, Safed, Gaza, Haifa, Acre, Shechem (Nablus), Ramla, and Sidon.

In 1701 Rabbi Judah the Pious (Yehuda Ha-Chassid) arrived in Jerusalem from Poland with a large band of students and their families. He intended to build an Ashkenazic synagogue in the Jewish Quarter. *Ashkenazic* refers to Jews speaking German or Yiddish, which is derived from German. In the Bible, Ashkenaz is identified as Noah's great-grandson, and Jewish tradition identifies him with Germany. The dominant Jewish population of Jerusalem were Ladino-speaking Sephardim. Unfortunately Rabbi Judah died only three days after he arrived. His disheartened followers began the building of the synagogue, but discouraged and burdened by debt they abandoned Jerusalem and by 1720 had moved to the more hospitable Galilee. Thus, for 150 years Rabbi Judah's synagogue was called the Hurva (ruin). It continued to bear that name even when in the 1850s Congregation Beit Yaakov (the House of Jacob) built a magnificent domed structure, which stood until the Jordanian Army destroyed it in 1948, during the Israeli War of Independence. Even today, with the Jewish Quarter once again in Israeli hands, only a stone arch stands to remind the visitor of the Hurva.

In 1811 a band of Lithuanian, Yiddish-speaking Jews intruded into the Sephardic-dominated community of Jerusalem. To this day their descendants, still speaking Lithuanian Yiddish, wear their East European costume under the oriental costume of the Sephardim. However, at the beginning of the nineteenth century Palestine did not offer much hope of development. The Bedouin roamed a desolate land. It was hard to perceive any hope for a great Jewish community in the future.

2

The Old Yishuv, 1833–1880

NINETEENTH-CENTURY JEWISH PALESTINE

The Hebrew word *lashev* means "to sit" or "to dwell." The word *Yishuv* refers to a community. This chapter, and those that follow, will compare the Old Yishuv, which was deeply religious and nonpolitical, with the new Zionist Yishuv that ultimately grew secular and highly political.

It has been estimated that in 1832 there were less than a quarter of a million inhabitants in the land between the Jordan River and the Mediterranean Sea within the boundaries that Israel held until 1993. As foreign non-Moslems could not purchase land in Jerusalem, or live there permanently, only very determined pilgrims made the effort to visit the shrines that were sacred to Judaism or Christianity. Few ships made a stop in Palestinian ports to load or unload goods. Small exports of grain, sesame, and oranges or such exotica as the products of Hebron glass rarely warranted specifically planned voyages. As the native forests had long since been destroyed, wealthier inhabitants anxiously awaited imports of European charcoal and other consumer goods, especially during the winter. There was not a single road in all the land. Pilgrims and merchants visiting the principal towns followed the well-worn paths through the mountains, traced by centuries of passage by horses, camels, and mules.

A traveler could disembark dry shod and walk ashore on a pier in the two principal ports at Gaza and Acre. Haifa was merely a small fishing village across the bay from Acre. However, pilgrims or merchants planning to visit Jerusalem or Hebron preferred to come ashore at Jaffa, where the only means of reaching shore involved plunging into the surf and wading to the beach within the shelter offered by an ancient jetty, the Andromeda Rocks. The once-great port from which the biblical Jonah embarked on his famous voyage had long been closed by the shifting tides of the sea, and oranges grew where vessels once had sailed. In spite of all the difficulties encompassed in such a landing, Jaffa was preferred because it opened the shortest route to Jerusalem—only 60 kilometers away.

To make any journey in Palestine in 1832 it was necessary to buy protection. Most typically, foreign consuls in the port cities held the key to security for travelers. Less typically, wealthy native merchants mastered the art of buying protection. *Cicerones*, or travel guides, offered the least dependable assurance of safety for the traveler. Experienced foreign consuls usually spent years in winning the friendship of the sheiks of Bedouin tribes, and the headmen (or *mukhtars*) of villages, by sponsoring extravagant feasts at which the consul, the sheik, or the *mukhtar* negotiated the fees that would have to be paid for the safety of travelers.

A pilgrim or merchant traveling under the protection of a consul who had firm agreements with all clans and villages along the trail to Jerusalem could rest secure if led by a 10-year-old boy from the clan or village. Any reckless traveler who attempted to undertake the short 60-kilometer journey without buying safety imperiled his life, without hope of redress.

When the Arab Moslem invasion of 637 had conquered the land, two major Arab clan groups settled in what had been a Byzantine Christian province with a large Jewish minority. These were the Kais, descended from tribes originally residing in the northern Arabian peninsula, and the Yeminis, descended from south Arabian tribes. Almost 1,200 years later the two clan groups had erected barriers of hatred and jealousy, buttressed by memories of centuries of real and imagined injuries. No traveler could risk being seen as an ally of a hostile clan.

NON-JEWISH RESIDENTS

All the larger towns were walled. Turkish soldiers barred the gates at nightfall, and no one entered or left without their consent. Reliable population figures are unavailable, but it is estimated that in 1832 Jerusalem had only 12,000 inhabitants. Even thirty years later, when some population statistics became more certain, Hebron had only 5,000–10,000 residents; Nablus or Shechem had only 8,000; Jaffa, Safed, Bethlehem, and Nazareth had 3,000 each. Gaza had 15,000–16,000 residents. Even at the end of the century Haifa, today Israel's largest port and naval base, had only 6,000 inhabitants and was overshadowed by nearby Acre. Small, unwalled Arab towns clustered for security on hilltops, not daring to fence in their wells and springs because wandering Bedouin tribes regarded all natural water sources as open to their use. At the approach of Turkish soldiery, the villagers hid everything of value because these often irregular soldiers, or *howari*, had a very liberal definition of taxation. The *howari* were often local Arab villagers pressed into military service by the Turks.

Most of the Moslem Arab population were Sunni. In the far north, some Arab villages were Shi'ite. The adherents of these two great branches of Islam were often at war with one another. Druse clans were resident near Haifa, and periodically the Druse from the area south of Beirut raided the area of what is now northern Israel.

The Christian population of Palestine cannot be accurately counted before 1850. By that date, in Jerusalem there were 3,500 communicants of all denominations. Of these, 2,000 were Greek or Russian Orthodox Christians recognizing the leadership of a resident Greek Orthodox patriarch. Approximately 1,000 were Roman Catholic, but no Latin patriarch resided in Jerusalem until 1847. Catholic interests were handled by the Custodia Terra Sancta, an arm of the Franciscan monastic order. The remainder was divided among smaller sects, the largest of which was the Armenian Church headed by a resident patriarch. There were clear Christian majorities divided neatly between Greeks and Latins in such towns as Bethlehem, Nazareth, and some smaller villages.

JEWISH CENTERS BEFORE 1880

The Jewish population, or *Yishuv*, was concentrated in Judaism's four holy cities: Jerusalem, Hebron, Safed, and Tiberias. There were viable Jewish communities in all the larger towns, and even in some of the Galilean villages. Jews constituted a plurality of Jerusalem's religiously splintered population. Some Jewish families boasted proudly that their ancestors had never left the Land of Israel. The Jews with ancient roots in the land had been inundated by waves of immigration by refugees from the Spanish and Portuguese Inquisition during the fifteenth and sixteenth centuries. Thus, the dominant language spoken by Jews of all origins was Ladino, a tongue derived from ancient Spanish and heavily mixed with Arabic, Hebrew, and Turkish words. The language was written in Hebrew letters, however. Of course, all native Jews also knew Arabic, and a minority had a functional use of Turkish.

Beginning in the seventeenth century, the Palestinian Jews began to designate a chief rabbi, known as the *Rishon l'Zion* or "First in Zion." It was not until 1842, however, that the Turkish authorities recognized him as the official spokesman of the Jewish community and afforded him the same dignity extended to Christian patriarchs. This concerned, in a practical sense, the right to employ a *kawass*, or armed Moslem guard, who could strike Moslem troublemakers with impunity.

Yiddish-speaking Jews of eastern European origin maintained an uneasy coexistence within the Old Yishuv. Their rabbis enjoyed no recognition unless they were prepared to submit themselves to the authority of the *Rishon l'Zion*. He alone had the right to approve burial in Jewish cemeteries, to certify the authenticity of kosher meat, to regulate the inheritance of property, and to settle disputes between Jews. Ashkenazic, or German-and Yiddish-speaking, Jews had no legally recognized religious status unless they were prepared to become "honorary" Sephardic or Spanish Jews. For some, that even meant the adoption of oriental costume.

MEHMET ALI AND PALESTINE'S CHANGING FACE

For the entire Middle East, May 1833 marked a watershed date. Mehmet Ali, the viceroy of Egypt, was theoretically subject to Mahmoud II, sultan of Turkey. That very able soldier, an Albanian peasant by birth, had gambled for high stakes in 1832–1833. His Egyptian armies had marched north through the Sinai Desert, Palestine, and Syria and had penetrated the territories inhabited by ethnic Turks. In 1832 he had seemed to be in a position to overthrow the sultan and perhaps even seize his crown. However, Russia, England, and France intervened to save the sultan. Thus, on May 5, 1833, Mehmet Ali gained a lesser although glittering prize through the Treaty of Unkiar Skelessi. He was persuaded to moderate his ambitions and content himself with becoming the viceroy of what is today Egypt, Israel, much of Jordan, Lebanon, and Syria. Though still theoretically subject to the Turkish sultan, Mehmet

Ali became the virtually independent ruler of the eastern Mediterranean coastal lands.

Able, efficient, and ruthless, Mehmet Ali spent the following years in preparation for his next gamble. In 1838 he was ready for the next throw of the dice. He sent his Egyptian army—40,000 men strong—marching northward for a second attack on the Turks. This time, the French emerged as his open ally. The government of King Louis Philippe envisioned French hegemony in the eastern Mediterranean. The British, however, concentrated their navy in those waters, and it became a question of who would blink first. In the end the British bombarded Beirut, landed marines at Beirut and Acre, and effectively closed off the supply lines of Mehmet Ali's army commanded by his son, Ibrahim Pasha. Mehmet Ali lost his gamble by depending on the French. He was forced to abandon all of Syria, Palestine, and the Sinai Desert. He gained only the consolation prize: recognition as hereditary viceroy of Egypt.

The reforms introduced by Mehmet Ali, however, could not be scrapped by the Turks, even as they recovered sovereign power in the lands lost by the Egyptians. With regard to Palestine, this meant that for the first time since the Crusades, foreign non-Moslems could reside permanently in the holy city of Jerusalem. For the first time foreign consuls could be stationed there as well. In 1838, while Mehmet Ali still seemed securely in power, the very first consul took up residence in Jerusalem when William Tanner Young opened a British consulate. Somewhat more hesitantly the other major European powers—and even, ultimately, the United States—did the same. With them, a flood of Christian missionaries and church prelates took up residence as well.

For the Jews, the return of the Turkish authorities in 1841 meant an opening to settlement such as they had not dared to attempt before the reforms of Mehmet Ali. Nicholas I, czar of Russia, had tried every possible expedient for the forcible conversion of Jews in that country. What he succeeded in doing was to precipitate Jewish flight from Russia. Young Jews typically fled to other, more liberal European states. Moreover, the invention of the railroad, the steamboat, and the telegraph made possible a modest but significant migration to Palestine. A Jew leaving for Palestine usually had no intention of ever returning to Russia. However, he did not dare to lose even the fragile protection that a passport offered. Consequently Jews leaving their inhospitable homeland were given a visa that was good for one year. There was no Russian consul in Jerusalem, but the vice-consul at Jaffa would renew the visa if it suited him to be generous.

SEPHARDIM AND ASHKENAZIM

The majority of the Ashkenazic Jews who suddenly found themselves in the Sephardic-dominated Jewish holy cities of Palestine were determined to spend the rest of their lives in prayer and religious study. They were organized in *kollelim*, or corporate bodies, through which funds were distributed to married men devoting full time to pious exercises. The *kollelim* sent out *meshullachim*, or emissaries, to Europe to raise money for the support of the *kollelim*. Thus, the rapidly growing Yiddish-speaking Ashkenazic Jewish population crowded into the Jewish holy cities of Jerusalem, Hebron, Tiberias, and Safed, slowly outnumbering the native Sephardim but subordinated to the authority of the *Rishon l'Zion* and his corps of Sephardic rabbis and judges.

For the Ashkenazim, the most vital question was personal security. Theoretically, as Russian subjects, they could look to the Russian vice-consul at Jaffa for protection. However, a growing majority of those émigrés had neglected to renew their visas, which had originally been granted for a one-year absence from Russia. If they were to lose their passports they would become stateless persons, abandoned to the justice dispensed by a *kadi*, or Moslem judge, in a religious court where only Moslems could give sworn testimony as witnesses. In any quarrel with another Jew they could seek redress in a rabbinic court, or *beth din*; but as the judges were Sephardim, appointed by the *Rishon l'Zion*, a Russian Jew often feared discrimination as well.

FOREIGN CONSULS

The emergence of a foreign consular corps at Jerusalem, with jurisdiction in Hebron as well, offered some relief. The consuls possessed, by right of treaty with Turkey, the peculiar system known as capitulatory rights. This meant that every consul was authorized to serve as judge and jury in all disputes between persons of his own nationality. In the event of quarrels between two or more Europeans of different nationalities, the consuls of two or more nations could serve as judges *en banc*.

For the mass of Russian Jews, it was a matter of great importance that in 1849 the Russians decided to transfer to the British the jurisdiction over Russian Jews who had neglected to renew their visas. For the Russians, the abandonment of stateless Jews to the British served a triple purpose. First, it freed them from the necessity of defending Jews in

Palestine when the official policy of Czar Nicholas's government was blatantly hostile to Jews. Second, it permitted Russia to present itself to the Turks as the defender of all Russian and Greek Orthodox Christians in the Holy Land. Third, it permitted Carl Nesselrode, chancellor of the Russian Empire, to pursue an alliance with Britain against the ambitions of France in the Middle East.

The British also found the assumption of responsibility for thousands of stateless Jews useful for their own imperial goals. Instead of serving as protectors of a few dozen English, Dutch, Scandinavian, and Prussian Protestants in Palestine, Britain suddenly could claim thousands of Jewish protégés. A consul had the right to accompany a protégé into a *kadi*'s court to act as his advocate, though neither the consul nor the Jewish defendant could offer sworn testimony. A *kadi* was ill-advised to treat a foreign consul with contempt. (Everyone remembered the British success against Mehmet Ali in 1841.) Of course, a British consul such as James Finn (1846–1862) found the sudden increase in strength through the increased numbers of protégés a very useful tool for his personal goals. Consul Finn was an active missionary who imagined that a grateful Jewish population would be receptive to Protestant conversion.

In the end, the Russians and the British failed to get what they had sought through the transfer of stateless Jews. The Russians did not gain a British alliance against France. James Finn won very few sincere Jewish converts. Nevertheless the sudden thrust of consular influence into the equation changed the history of Palestinian Jewry. Primarily the presence of the European Great Powers at Jerusalem made it possible for the Ashkenazim to gain independence from the dominant Sephardic rabbinate. Their own rabbis mastered the fine art of maneuvering between the *kadi*'s court, the Sephardic Beth Din (or rabbinic court) and the arbitrary decisions of the Turkish pasha (the appointed governor of the administrative district known as the *Sanjak* of Jerusalem).

THE GROWTH OF SECULAR CHARITIES

From 1853 to 1856 the Crimean War saw France, Great Britain, Turkey, and the Italian kingdom of Sardinia-Piedmont aligned against Russia. It was an alliance that could hardly have been predicted a few years earlier. No fighting took place in Palestine. Nevertheless the war had tremendous consequences for the Jewish community of the Holy Land. While the war raged, no money could leave Russia for the hard-pressed and poverty-stricken Russian Jews dependant on the *kollelim* for support. Russian Jewish emigration almost came to a halt. Thus, a new force entered the picture.

This was the entry of western European Jewish charities. Great philanthropists such as Sir Moses Montefiore of Britain; the Rothschild families of Austria, France, and Britain; and numerous other donors sent relief to their impoverished Russian kinsmen. The traditional *kollelim* had emphasized the support of a purely religious society. The western charitable donors emphasized the building of secular schools for both boys and girls, the construction of hospitals, and the training of Jews for performing manual labor and learning useful trades. The Sephardic rabbis, who had never experienced the destruction of Jewish religious loyalty that secularist assimilation posed, tended to be more permissive about accepting these gifts. The Ashkenazic rabbis, however, were quite familiar with the dangers of spiritual nihilism. They feared total alienation from Jewish tradition and ultimate assimilation. Nevertheless, no one was prepared to refuse generous gifts even if they might have potentially dangerous consequences.

With the end of the Crimean War, the old order seemed to have been restored for Russian Jewry. The steamboat brought increasing streams of Jewish reinforcements to the four Jewish holy cities of Palestine. Jerusalem had a Jewish majority by the end of the war. It is probable that Safed and Tiberias had Jewish majorities as well. At Hebron, the Jewish population had swelled, although it was still a minority. Even in such towns as Gaza and Nablus, Jewish numbers had grown.

WESTERN EUROPEAN JEWS AND THE OLD YISHUV

Moses Montefiore established the first Jewish suburb outside the walls of Jerusalem in 1860. Clustered near his windmill, which is still standing, Sir Moses built Mishkenot Sheananim (the Habitations of Delight), designed to house twenty-four industrious Jewish families who were prepared to take up a life of useful labor. It was to be a few years more before he found families bold enough to leave the security of walled Jerusalem and venture into the open countryside. It should be remembered that there was no Turkish land registration law until 1858, and that until 1867 the purchase of land by foreign non-Moslems was prohibited without specific permission embodied in a *firman*, or imperial decree, from the sultan. Even Sir Moses Montefiore required the intervention of the British embassy at Constantinople to obtain such favors.

Albert Cohn, an agent of the French Rothschilds, had to receive imperial permission to establish Misgav Ladach, the first Jewish hospital in Jerusalem, in 1854. Mea Shearim, founded in 1875, was the second Jewish suburb just outside the city walls; it was built by devoted pietists who constructed a walled enclave where they could be free of the secular distractions that they found offensive as Jerusalem grew to its 1880 population of 30,000. In 1878 a third population explosion from Jewish Jerusalem resulted in the creation of Petach Tikva, a religious farming community, which nearly foundered in the marshy land near Jaffa but survived to become the city bearing that name today.

In 1867 the Turks constructed the first road in Palestine, connecting Jaffa and Jerusalem. In 1870 a second road connected Jerusalem and Shechem or Nablus. In 1865 a telegraph line was completed, connecting Jerusalem to Europe. However, the Old Yishuv, even as it grew, was devoid of Jewish nationalist impulse. The constructive work of European philanthropists remained straightforward charity designed to improve the lot of poverty-stricken Jews. Zionism did not yet exist in a political sense.

In October 1875 Rabbi Zvi Hirsch Kalischer and his son, of Thorn, Prussia, bought three dunams of land near Rachel's Tomb near Bethlehem. They intended to create a Jewish farming colony there. The entire transaction was accomplished without the Kalischers leaving Germany. The German consul-general, Baron Thankmar von Münchhausen, handled the purchase as a service to a Prussian national. The land was transferred to the custody of the Perushim Congregation in Jerusalem, the occupants of the splendid Ashkenazic synagogue ironically still called the Hurva, or "Ruin." To contemporaries, Kalischer's work seemed to be simple charity with a German label. Similarly, in 1871 when the French Alliance Israélite Universelle had built an agricultural school called Mikve Israel, the enterprise seemed to be charity with a French label. The language of instruction was to be French. The only purpose of the school was to train young urban Jews to become self-supporting farmers.

EMERGENCE OF AN ASHKENAZIC CHIEF RABBINATE

It is ironic that the greatest milestone in the development of Ashkenazic and western-oriented dominance in the Jewish community grew out of what appeared, superficially, to be a petty quarrel. Ashkenazim had always resented the dominance exercised by the *Rishon l'Zion* in supervising the preparation of kosher meat. The Turkish government interested itself in kosher animal slaughter because a tax was paid to the authorities for each animal. At the same time, the Sephardic rabbinate imposed a small communal tax to support Jewish charities. However, Ashkenazic butchers traditionally sold the hindquarters of animals to Arab butchers, because their rabbinate held that few men had the skill to remove the specific categories of fat, veins, and sinews that were not to be eaten by observant Jews. The Sephardic butchers, however, had always performed that task themselves, confident in the surgical skill required. Thus, Sephardim consumed the entire animal whereas Ashkenazim sold the hindquarters to non-Jewish butchers. The Ashkenazim argued that they should not have to pay the Turkish tax and the communal tax because the greater part of the meat was sold on the public market, and because only through such a dispensation could the poorer class of Ashkenazim afford to eat red meat at all.

The *Rishon l'Zion* regarded these claims as a subterfuge to avoid paying a fair share of communal expenses by Ashkenazim, who formed a majority of the Jewish community. Repeatedly, in 1853, 1862, 1866, and 1867, the united Ashkenazic rabbinate had attempted to attain independence from Sephardic control by invoking the intervention of the British, Austrian, and Prussian consuls. The Ashkenazim brought legal action to end Sephardic monopoly of the communal tax on meat. In each case the Turkish pasha of Jerusalem declined to disturb the status quo—ironically, on the grounds that Turkey could be accused of religious persecution if he did so. There was also the secondary matter of the fact that Islam regards the Jewish method of animal slaughter as acceptable according to Moslem religious law. The Turkish authorities did not choose to become involved in the question of whether the Ashkenazim were as authentically Jewish as the native, Sephardic, Turkish Jews.

However, in January 1873 a way was found to circumvent all the thorny questions so as to satisfy everyone but the *Rishon l'Zion*. The first mayor of Jerusalem, as distinct from the pasha of the *Sanjak* of Jerusalem, was an Arab merchant, Joseph al-Khalidi. The municipal council imposed its own tax on carcasses sold by butchers. The mayor was prepared to allow the Ashkenazim to open their own slaughterhouses and to sell the hindquarters to Arab butchers, provided that both parties paid the municipal tax. At that moment a newly elected Sephardic chief rabbi (named, ironically, Abraham Eskenasi) either could not or chose not to pursue the matter further. Baron Karl von Alten, the German consul-general, undertook to serve as guarantor that Ashkenazic butchers would be supervised by him and obliged to pay the tax.

Out of this strange quarrel an independent Ashkenazic chief rabbinate grew. After 1878 and until his death in 1909, Rabbi Samuel Salant was unofficially the Ashkenazic chief rabbi. To the very end of Turkish rule in Palestine in 1917, however, only the *Rishon l'Zion* enjoyed an official position recognized by the government. It was only after the establishment of the British Mandate after World War I that Rabbi A. I. Kook was installed as the official Ashkenazic rabbi, recognized as the equal of the Sephardic chief rabbi or *Rishon l'Zion*. Rabbi Kook became the philosophical ideologue of religious Zionism.

EMERGENCE OF SECULARISM

Even while the Old Yishuv labored single-mindedly in its pious mission of prayer and study, the contacts with western Europe were preparing the way for the future growth of a Zionist New Yishuv. Joshua and David Yellin, father and son, dared to give their children a secular education. They were consequently thrust out of their *kollel* and deprived of their share of *haluka*, the financial support dispensed by the rabbinate. David Yellin, a teacher in secular schools, composed textbooks in Arabic for the use of Arabic-speaking Jewish children. He was unique among the small band of Ashkenazic secularists in the Old Yishuv, because he interested himself in Sephardic culture and was one of the first Ashkenazim to study Moslem ideas in a systematic way. As the Yellins favored agricultural settlement, they became a link between the Old Yishuv and the New Yishuv.

Although few people thought of it in those terms, the practical experience that the Old Yishuv gained in dealing with western European philanthropists and diplomats was to provide the foundation on which the New Yishuv could build.

3

The New Yishuv and Zionism's First Two Aliyoth, 1881–1914

THE RUSSIAN HASKALAH AND ZIONIST ORIGINS

In 1855 Czar Alexander II mounted the Russian throne; he was the first and only Russian emperor to show comparatively liberal tendencies. During his reign certain "privileged" Jews were allowed to settle outside the old Pale of Settlement, including cities such as Moscow or St. Petersburg, which had previously been closed to Jews. Catherine the Great, who seized much of Poland from 1772 to 1795, forbade Jews to live in Russia proper. The geographic limits, thus created, locked Jews into a Pale, or huge ghetto, which subsisted until the reign of Alexander II. After the German duke of Hesse Darmstadt made Joseph Günzberg a baronet in 1871, the czar granted him the title of hereditary baron in 1874. In so doing (albeit reluctantly) the czar gave recognition to a Jew— one who had been in the forefront of the construction of Russian railroads and the growth of commerce. Most significant, the czar opened the universities to Jews at the same time as their faculties were forced to examine new ideas. Jews were admitted to the legal profession in 1864; and as other fields opened, Jews experienced an intellectual revolution.

Prior to the reign of Alexander II all Jewish males of normal intelligence were sent to the *cheder*, or one-room school, where boys age 3 to 13 learned to read, write, and translate biblical Hebrew. Thus, almost the entire Russian Jewish male population could understand the Hebrew of their prayerbook and the Bible. Yiddish, the language spoken in the home and streets, is a Germanic dialect written in Hebrew letters. It was learned incidentally, and as a result the male population could write the language that most east European Jews spoke. Whereas careful attention was given to teaching boys proper Hebrew grammar and spelling, Yiddish spelling was "catch-as-catch-can." In the Pale of Settlement, to which Jews had previously been confined by law, many towns had a Jewish majority. All Jews spoke the local language, whether it was Polish or one of the Russian dialects. However, almost no Jews considered it worthwhile to become literate in those languages. Jewish parents dreamed that their sons would display such scholarly progress that they might pursue studies in Gemara and Talmudic Law, the mastery of which would lead to rabbinic ordination. Only through the *yeshiva*, or rabbinic seminary, could a young man attain scholarly distinction.

The opening of the universities to Jews shook the old order of Jewish life in the Pale to its foundations. With disconcerting speed, young men who would have sought mastery of the great body of Talmudic Law known as the Gemara sought instead to enter the professions of law or medicine. Motivated to achieve success, these newly secularized scholars found, however, that their fellow students—and more than a few of their professors—still harbored feelings of anti-Semitism.

The young Jewish intellectuals resolved their problems in a unique way. In 1863 Baron Joseph Günzberg founded the Society for the Spreading of Enlightenment among the Jews of Russia. In Hebrew, the word for "enlightenment" is *haskalah*. Those who accepted the new enlightenment were called the Maskilim. Both terms had been used in eighteenth-century Germany when Moses Mendelssohn started the Haskalah movement. Mendelssohn had been an ordained orthodox rabbi who believed that Jews could attain full civil rights if they became Germans culturally, abandoned the social customs of the ghetto, and became simply "Germans of the Jewish faith." This first Reform Jew expressed his doubts about the divine inspiration of all the Bible but remained a conforming traditional Jew throughout his life. However, the two generations that followed witnessed a race to the baptismal font.

The Russian Maskilim differed markedly from the Germans who had identified with that title. Very few of the Maskilim glorified the Russian language to the extent that Mendelssohn had elevated the German tongue as a key to cultural assimilation. Russian was rejected because it was the language of oppression. Indeed, most educated Russians took pride in the elegance of their French. Although some Russian Maskilim were willing to regard Yiddish as the means whereby Jews could become equal participants in the brotherhood of nations, most rejected it as the language of the Pale of Settlement, the tongue of the ghetto. Thus, ironically, the Russian Maskilim turned to the one language they had learned in *cheder* and *yeshiva*: Hebrew. Most such men knew biblical and Mishnaic Hebrew, but among religious Jews the holy tongue could not be used in vulgar conversation. The Maskilim, however, set themselves to reviving Hebrew as a language equal to the other languages of the world. New terminology had to be invented to describe the mysteries of science and technology. The poet Judah Leib Gordon, writing in Hebrew, urged his readers to adopt the culture of enlightened men.

Not all the Maskilim had the same goals. A few aimed at the dissolution of Jewish separateness; they wanted to use Hebrew to bring Jews into the brotherhood of European culture. This would have brought an end to Jewish history through the use of the one language that had nourished Jewish uniqueness for three millennia. Other Maskilim, such as Peretz Smolenskin, wanted to preserve the Jewish hope in redemption by the Messiah; but Smolenskin seems to have viewed the Messiah in abstract and even poetic terms, far from the supernatural expectations of religious Jews. Some traditional orthodox Jews, such as Rabbi Israel Lipkin of Russian Lithuania, founded the Mussar movement, which emphasized religious morality as opposed to dry legalism. Lipkin accepted the use of a secularized Hebrew to advance the accommodation of religion and the technological culture of western society.

Most of the Maskilim could be described as socialists. They believed that only state ownership of the means of production and distribution could end the gap between rich and poor. They blamed the inequities of capitalism for anti-Semitism. Very few of the early Maskilim regarded Jewish nationalism as a solution to the Jewish problem. As early as 1862, however, Moses Hess in Germany had published *Rome and Jerusalem*. Hess, who had been an anarchist, a socialist, and a communist in turn, had finally convinced himself that the only solution to the Jewish problem would be Jewish residence in Palestine. In a totally unanticipated development, however, the Haskalah changed its direction and meaning.

THE FIRST ALIYA

Persecution of Russian Jews

On March 13, 1881, assassins in St. Petersburg murdered Czar Alexander II. His son, who ascended the throne as Czar Alexander III, was a committed reactionary who believed that liberalism had contaminated Russia. In his eyes, the urban and cosmopolitan Jews became the embodiment of the devilish forces that had killed his father. He believed that Holy Mother Russia could be redeemed only by himself, the Church, and the uncontaminated peasantry. Constantine Pobedonovstyev, the czar's lay procurator of the Holy Synod of the Russian Orthodox Church, spelled out the new Jewish policy clearly. One-third of the Jews were to be converted, one-third expelled, and one-third starved.

In May 1882 the so-called May Laws were enacted as the "Temporary Rules." Jews were confined to towns with more than 10,000 inhabitants so that they would be denied contact with the peasantry. By that decree, thousands of Jews were driven to severe poverty and, perhaps worse, deprived of the sight of open fields, green trees, and unpolluted nature that soothes the human spirit. Even Alexander III could not push back all the Jews into the Pale of Settlement from which Czar Alexander II had released them. However, he could reduce the number of Jews allowed to enter universities and other state schools. Indeed, in 1889 Jews were barred from practicing law. As early as 1882 the number of Jewish surgeons serving in the army was drastically reduced. Worst of all, on April 10, 1882, the first *pogrom*, or massacre of Jews, occurred in the commercial town of Balta. Historians still debate the extent to which the government was responsible for inciting the slaughter. There can be no doubt, however, that the government was not averse to the incitement of *pogroms*. Usually the army intervened to stop the bloodshed only in response to foreign protest, and only after much delay.

Suddenly the Maskilim were forced to reevaluate their entire philosophy. A small minority opted for support of violent revolution. The majority preferred the adoption of Jewish self-assertion. It would be misleading, however, to label the dominant spirit of the Maskilim after 1881 as "Jewish nationalist." Nevertheless a definite determination arose to leave Russia and to live assertively as Jews somewhere else. Palestine was one obvious choice—although Argentina and Vineland, New Jersey, were regarded as alternatives if the urban Jew was to be "normalized" as a farmer. In the autumn of 1881, Moses Loeb Lilienblum called for mass emigration to Palestine. (It must be noted, however, that he was very hostile to traditional Jewish religious practice. Nevertheless he felt an attachment to the empty, semi-desert land of Palestine as more than a randomly chosen refuge.) In 1882 Leo Pinsker published a pamphlet, *Auto-Emancipation*, urging Jews to save themselves either by moving to Palestine or by fleeing to any land that would receive them. The masses of Russian Jews did not need the inspiration of Lilienblum or Pinsker to flee Russia. Indeed, the persecution under Alexander III's government expedited their departure. By the hundreds of thousands they swelled the American and British Jewish communities and reinforced Austro-Hungarian and German Jewish numbers in all the years until World War I.

Pre-Zionist "Zionism"

Before Pinsker could sound his call, a group of Jewish university students at Kharkov founded BILU, a group whose name is an acronym for *Bais Yaakov Lechu Unel'cha* ("House of Jacob come ye, and let us go"). They attracted only a few hundred members in Russia, but their importance was measured by the symbolism of their efforts. Only forty members of BILU actually went to Palestine immediately. Harsh reality was a shock to them. They had imagined that Jewish landowners would gladly employ them. They found instead that most Jewish farmers preferred to hire Arab laborers, who were accustomed to the climate and who could be paid modest salaries. The BILU pioneers faced malaria, which was still widespread. Many of them died. Some returned, disheartened, to Europe. The survivors found employment at the Mikve Israel colony founded by the Alliance Israélite Universelle and at another Jewish colony at Rishon L'Zion.

If the agricultural pioneers of the New Yishuv were cursed by failure, Jews nevertheless crowded into Palestine. The year 1882 saw seven thousand Jewish immigrants. Most of these simply enlarged the Old Yishuv; their philosophy was religious rather than nationalistic. They crowded into the four Jewish holy cities at Jerusalem, Hebron, Safed, and Tiberias, devoting themselves to prayer and religious study. Nevertheless the arrival of so many Jews at once, whether their motives were religious or nationalist, began to change the face of the land. A second nationalist organization, the Hovevei Zion, or "Lovers of Zion," enjoyed the support of Rabbi Samuel Mohilever of Bialystok, who brought many religious Jews into alliance with young Maskilim. The new organization succeeded after 1884 in founding several farm communities, creating a firmer foundation for the New Yishuv.

Revival of Vernacular Hebrew

In 1882 a 24-year-old Lithuanian dropout from a French medical school was one of the seven thousand new arrivals. His name was Eliezer Ben-Yehudah. On the boat bringing him to Zion, he vowed to speak only Hebrew for the rest of his life. Fortunately he found a wife and raised a family that was equally committed to reviving Hebrew as a modern, spoken language. An account (perhaps mythical) avers that when his mother came to visit him, she could not get her son to relax into a Yiddish conversation. His religious neighbors were constantly shocked to hear the Ben-Yehudahs using the language of the Bible to discuss the vulgarities of daily life. Nevertheless only a single-minded eccentricity bordering on the anti-social could have accounted for Ben-Yehudah's success as the father of modern Hebrew. By 1910 he had begun to publish a thesaurus of modern Hebrew, into which he thrust words derived from ancient sources to describe new technologies or ideas. Although modern Israelis have rejected many of those newly invented terms, it was Ben-Yehudah who made Hebrew a language ready to receive the twentieth century.

The Dreyfus Trial and Theodor Herzl

On October 15, 1894, an event occurred in France that at first glance might seem to have no relationship to Palestine. Nevertheless it was to carry the seed out of which Zionism sprouted. Captain Alfred Dreyfus, the first self-confessed Jew named to the French Army General Staff, was arrested and charged with revealing French military secrets to Germany. Condemned by a court-martial, he was transported to Devil's Island, a French prison colony located off the coast of South America. However, his brother and his wife would not let the matter rest. All of France joined in the debate as it became obvious to honest observers that Dreyfus had been the victim of deliberate forgeries. His innocence or guilt became almost incidental as monarchist, clerical, and conservative France condemned him, refusing to admit that the army had erred or that French officers had been guilty of dishonesty. Equally, republican, liberal, and anti-clerical France defended Dreyfus. Emile Zola, Anatole France, and the future prime minister, Georges Clemenceau, risked their professional careers and even their personal freedom to defend Dreyfus. Hanging over all was the specter of anti-Semitism, as French mobs coursed through city streets shouting "Down with the Jews." However, the evidence of Dreyfus's innocence was so overwhelming that in 1899 he was pardoned by the president of France. In 1900 the Court of Cassation declared him innocent. Restored to rank, he lived to enjoy promotion to the rank of general and to command the garrison of Paris during World War I.

One observer in the courtroom during Dreyfus's long trial had been a reporter representing Vienna's *Neue Freie Presse*. In 1895, Dreyfus was 36 years old. The reporter, Theodor Herzl, was 35. All that bound the two men together was their youth and the accident of Jewish birth. Neither man took his religion very seriously. Indeed, Theodor Herzl had once written an essay arguing that the problem of anti-Semitism could be easily solved if on a given day all the Jews of Vienna would submit peacefully to baptism.

Birth of Political Zionism

However, the crisis that split France in two served to unify Herzl's disparate outlooks. In 1895, knowing nothing of Moses Hess or Leo Pinsker, he wrote *Die Judenstaat*, which was published in 1896. Anyone reading *The Jewish State* or Herzl's diaries, which have also been translated into English, would conclude that the author was a hopeless dreamer. However, as Herzl himself said, "If you will it, it is no dream." He predicted that a Jewish state would exist within fifty years. He was wrong by only two years.

Herzl preferred Palestine, but he would have settled for Argentina or any land where Jews could achieve self-government under a democratic monarchy or an aristocratic republic. He believed that a moderate socialist economic system was necessary, and he proposed a flag bearing seven stars representing a seven-hour working day. He also believed that the Zionist dream would not be fulfilled until most of world Jewry had moved to the new Jewish state. He regarded Great Britain as the world power freest of the taint of anti-Semitism, and he proposed that Britain be entrusted with arranging the sale of Jewish property for those moving to the new state. He also imagined that only £50 million would pay for the project, and that the sum could be raised by popular subscription.

Following the publication of his book, Herzl devoted the rest of his short lifetime to travels across Europe and the Near East in pursuit of his dream. Herzl met Emperor William II of Germany at Jerusalem and received encouragement but no concrete aid. King Umberto of Italy received him kindly but declined to become involved. The French republic had its own Jewish problem to solve—the Dreyfus Affair. The Austro-Hungarian government was friendly but detached. Herzl promised the Turks that he would pay off their national debt if they yielded Palestine to Jewish sovereignty. It may have been just as well that Constantinople refused the offer, because there was no way that the infant Zionist organization could have fulfilled Herzl's pledge. Pope Pius X granted Herzl an audience but repulsed him by offering to convert all Jews setting foot in Palestine. Herzl even went to Russia to meet the enemy. The ultra-reactionary minister of the Interior, V. K. Plehve, assured him that Zionist activity in Russia would be tolerated as long as it expedited Jewish emigration to Palestine, but that Jewish nationalist propaganda would not be tolerated. Herzl had hoped that Russia would exert its diplomatic influence to persuade the Turks to encourage Jewish settlement in Palestine, but he could not obtain Plehve's support for the venture.

On a less flamboyant but much more practical level, important foundations were laid by successive, annual World Zionist Congresses convened by Herzl. The first World Zionist Congress was planned to meet in Munich, but the chief rabbi of that city informed Herzl that he would not welcome the Zionists lest he appear disloyal to Germany. Thus, the congress was moved to Basel, Switzerland. Herzl received very little support from western European and American Jews, who were comfortable in tolerant states. Wealthy Jews, such as Baron Edmond de Rothschild of France, gave generously to the establishment of Jewish farming ventures in Palestine but had no interest in supporting Jewish nationalism.

Throughout Herzl's life, the heart of his support came from Russian Jews for whom a Zionist refuge had become a matter of life and death. The only American delegate to the First World Zionist Congress in 1897 was Dr. Schepschel Schaffer of Baltimore's devoutly orthodox Congregation Shearith Israel. Very shortly thereafter, Rabbi Schaffer regretted having supported so secular a nationalist movement and broke with Zionism.

The First Congress began consideration of a Jewish National Fund, which was not actually implemented until 1901 at the Fifth Congress. Indeed, as early as 1884—before Herzl conceived of political Zionism—the plan for a Jewish National Fund had been proposed. Professor Hermann Schapira, at the Hovevei Zion conference convened at Kattowitz, Germany, had proposed the creation of a fund to buy land in Palestine. It was to be the "inalienable property of the Jewish People." The conference had approved the idea, but it remained merely a paper plan until Herzl's Zionism made it a reality. As originally conceived, the Jewish National Fund (JNF) was to buy land that would belong to it in perpetuity. It was to be leased to Jewish farmers. Another cornerstone of JNF land management—one that is no longer maintained rigidly today—was that no paid laborers were to work on the land. As Herzl had been unsuccessful in persuading wealthy philanthropists to support Zionism, the successive congresses emphasized fundraising through the pennies of the Jewish masses. The little blue-and-white collection box remains a Zionist symbol to this day. In 1903, a year that was to be marked with tragedy, one very positive development was the founding of Mizrachi Zionism by Rabbi Isaac Jacob Reines. Previously Zionism had been shunned by religious Jews as secularist, if not anti-religious. Mizrachi contributed balance to Zionism by recruiting middle-class capitalists to a movement that previously had been almost uniformly socialist.

Rejected Alternatives to Palestine

In August 1903, at Basel, Herzl surprised the Sixth World Zionist Congress by revealing that the British colonial secretary, Joseph Chamberlain, had offered the Zionist colonization rights in Uganda. The British had previously offered a strip of the Egyptian Sinai that they controlled. However, the Egyptian government had objected to the necessity of piping Nile River water to the proposed settlement, and the idea was dropped.

The Uganda proposal actually involved land that would become modern Kenya, but what emerged is still called the Uganda Plan to this day. The British offered autonomous self-government under the British flag, if the Zionist Congress chose to accept their invitation to settle the fertile Kenyan highlands that possess a temperate climate. Of the five hundred delegates at the congress, a majority seemed willing to accept the British offer. They regarded it as a first step toward the fulfillment of the Zionist goal of possessing Palestine—a temporary shelter. Menachem Mendel Ussishkin, a leader of the Hovevei Zion and a strong opponent of the Uganda Plan, referred to it contemptuously as *eine Nachtasyl*, or a "night's rest." The Russian delegates were unwavering in their insistence that Zionism should only seek rights in Palestine. After all, they argued there is a 3,500-year record of Jewish residence in Zion; Jews had no historical claim to East Africa.

After furious debate, the congress broke up as 185 delegates walked out of the hall. The dissidents then met in Kharkov, Russia, and sent an unnegotiable demand to Herzl to drop the Uganda Plan. Herzl tried to prove his long-term devotion to Palestinian settlement by reopening negotiations with the Turks. He was then deserted by some western Zionists, notably the distinguished British author Israel Zangwill. Those, like Zangwill, who would have settled for an African refuge called themselves the "Territorialists." With his organization in disarray and the very existence of Zionism threatened, Herzl died suddenly on July 3, 1904, at 44 years of age.

Following the premature death of the great visionary, the future of Zionism seemed dim. The movement split as the Territorialists and the eastern European Zionists exchanged insults. It seemed a harbinger for the future when Israel Zangwill, an affectionate exponent of Jewish folklore, quit the Zionists and ultimately rejected involvement in Jewish life. In Palestine, the children of the BILU and Hovevei Zion pioneers were leaving the land and either gravitating to the cities or moving back to Europe.

KISHINEV AND THE SECOND ALIYA

However, an unrelated disaster proved to be the salvation of Zionism. On Easter Sunday, 1903, which coincided with the last day of Passover, the worst of all the long series of pogroms erupted. At Kishinev in Russian Bessarabia, close to the Rumanian border, a government-orchestrated slaughter of Jews was perpetrated. The Russian army did not intervene to stop it until the third day. At the end, 45 Jews were dead, 86 had suffered serious injury, and 500 had experienced light injuries. Women were raped, babies thrown from windows, and all Jewish property destroyed.

The Christian nations of Europe and North America reacted with revulsion. Even a tiny minority of Russian Christians condemned their government for its evident complicity in the pogrom. Count Leo Tolstoy, the great novelist, had the courage to condemn the czar's government for the atrocity. Loans that the Russian government had negotiated with western financiers were denied. Most significant, however, Jews felt not only fear but self-loathing and shame because so few of the victims had attempted to defend themselves.

Thus, a sort of rip-tide was created as some Jews saw Zionism as their best hope to recover self-respect, whereas others rejected Zionism in the aftermath of the Uganda Plan and the death of Herzl only a year after the disaster at Kishinev. The great poet of the Maskilim, Chaim Nachman Bialik, portrayed the pain of the Jewish dilemma in his Hebrew-language poem *A Tale of Slaughter*. It was almost coincidental that Russia itself endured an agonizing disgrace when, in 1904–1905, the government of Czar Nicholas II blundered into war with Japan and was defeated under humiliating circumstances.

Thus, even while the great Russian Jewish flight to America accelerated with hundreds of thousands of terrified refugees, what came to be called the Second Aliya began to build Palestine. It would continue from 1904 until the outbreak of World War I in 1914. It is said that necessity is the mother of invention; the Second Aliya can be said to have been a singularly creative episode in the evolution of Zionism.

Origins of the Kibbutz

The most important invention of the Second Aliya was the kibbutz. Meaning "gathering," the kibbutz is a community whose members are pledged to communal living, sharing all income and property. In 1911, following several failures dating back to 1908, ten men and two women founded Kibbutz Deganya on the southern shore of the Sea of Galilee. The new experiment solved the greatest riddle that faced Zionism: How could an urban population of young, intellectual idealists be transformed into effective farmers?

As early as 1855, Sir Moses Montefiore while visiting Palestine had entrusted an evangelical Christian, Colonel Charles Henry Churchill, with money to buy land on which Jewish farmers could be settled. James Finn, British consul at Jerusalem from 1846 to 1862, had bought land on which he employed hundreds of Jews to perform manual labor. He was an active missionary who failed in his primary goal, ultimately converting very few of his employees. He did, however, teach many of them such useful trades as stone cutting, building construction, and the rudiments of agriculture. In 1871 Charles Netter was commissioned by the French Alliance Israélite Universelle to found Mikve Israel as an agricultural school to train Jewish farmers. Rabbi Zvi Hirsch Kalischer of

Thorn, Germany, bought land for Jewish farmers and worked closely with Netter to settle them. Moreover, work had been done by the Palestine Jewish Colonization Association, or PICA, founded by Baron Edmond de Rothschild of France incidental to his work in creating a wine-producing industry.

Nevertheless the greater part of the experimental farms for Jews rested on the idea that Arab hired labor was essential to success. BILU and the Hovevei Zion had utterly failed in their attempts to persuade Jewish farmers to hire Jewish laborers.

The new Kibbutz Deganya set out to find a means whereby Jews could perform essential labor on Jewish land. Schemes for collective farms had been proposed in the early nineteenth century by Robert Owen in Britain and Charles Fourier in France. Both had failed because neither British nor French farmers were motivated to renounce individualism and to "bury" themselves in a collective entity. In the New Yishuv, however, the collective farm was the perfect answer to the question of how inexperienced city-bred Jews could become productive farm laborers.

The kibbutz established certain principles that are still held to this day. Members are admitted only after a trial period. Members share personal property; for example, either all members own a television set, or all must have equal access to a set owned by the kibbutz. All labor is shared, although some members may specialize in a particular function. (As a case in point, when Golda Meir—the future prime minister of Israel—opened the first Israeli embassy in Moscow in 1948, all members of the staff from the ambassador down to clerks and maintenance personnel took turns washing dishes.) The executive of a kibbutz is its secretary, democratically elected by all its members. Any profits earned by a kibbutz are disbursed with the approval of all voting members. Kibbutz members' children with special talents or ambitions may be sent to universities or specialized schools, but only with the consent of the collective membership. It is increasingly rare today, but for the first generations of the kibbutz movement, infants were tended as a group in the kibbutz nursery and saw their parents only at certain times. All dining and cooking was carried on as a collective activity in the classic kibbutz. Decisions about religious practice, or the lack thereof, were also collective choices.

Today less than 3 percent of the Jewish population of Israel live on fully collective kibbutzim. Nevertheless left-wing Israeli politicians still find it useful to refer to their kibbutz origins, as American politicians used to refer to their origins in a log cabin. Today the kibbutzim are often in debt, faced with competition from privately owned Jewish and Arab farms. Nevertheless, without the kibbutz, it is doubtful that Israel could have become self-sufficient in basic agricultural products.

A. D. Gordon and the Conquest of Labor

Side-by-side with the kibbutz, a new philosophy was conceived. Aaron David Gordon, usually known by the names of the Hebrew letters that are the initials of his name, has gone down in history as Aleph Daled Gordon. He was almost 50 years old when he reached Palestine in 1904. For twenty-seven years his uncalloused hands had been employed as a manager on one of the Russian estates of Baron Günzberg. The metamorphosis that he underwent when he reached Palestine remains a mystery. However, he became the advocate of the philosophy associated with his name: *kibbush avoda*, or "conquest of labor." He believed that hard manual labor ought to be sought as a joyous experience. He taught that there would never be a Jewish state unless Jews were prepared to do every kind of necessary work. (Putting the statement facetiously, Achad Ha-Am is supposed to have remarked that he would know that Zionism had succeeded when he heard that a Jewish thief had been apprehended by a Jewish policeman, tried by a Jewish judge, and jailed in the custody of a Jewish warden.) *Kibbush avoda* is probably the hardest battle ever fought by an urban, highly intellectual people who had been barred from peasant labor by their historical experience. *Kibbush avoda* made the kibbutz possible. The kibbutz made *kibbush avoda* necessary.

Other Giants of the Second Aliya

Along with the necessary but painful transition was the need to protect oneself in a hostile environment. The earliest Jewish farmers in the new Palestine hired Arab guards. They proved unsatisfactory, as they were sometimes in collusion with the thieves they were supposed to deter. In 1907 the first armed Jewish guards made their appearance. These young men called themselves *shomrim*, which means, simply, "watchmen" or "guards." They were haunted by the deep sense of shame and frustration felt by Russian Jews when the victims of the pogroms of 1903–1904 had died without offering effective resistance.

From the beginning, the *shomrim* were highly disciplined and required all new recruits to serve a trial period before being accepted. They would accept service only on farms employing Jewish labor exclusively. Ultimately the *shomrim* were to provide a part of the tradition and the organization out of which would develop the Israel Defense Forces.

Closely bound to the tradition of self-defense was the purchase of land for settlement. The most famous of the land purchasers was Joshua Hankin [Chankin], originally from Kremenchug, Russia. He had come to Palestine with the BILU. He learned to speak fluent colloquial Arabic and eventually earned the friendship and respect of the rural Arabs with whom he negotiated. Like any good Levantine merchant, negotiation for him was an enjoyable game, a peaceful sport to be pursued for its own sake. Hankin lived to a ripe old age, but his greatest work belongs to the Second Aliya. Besides buying the lands for numerous colonies, he purchased the lands that became the first Jewish suburbs overlooking Haifa. As an agent for Arthur Ruppin of the World Zionist Congress he bought the first stretch of sand dunes north of Jaffa, on which was built the all-Jewish city of Tel Aviv.

In 1907 the World Zionist Congress met at The Hague in the Netherlands. That congress established the "Palestine Department" and sent Arthur Ruppin to develop the country with funds supplied by the newly created Jewish National Fund and the Jewish Colonial Trust. Ruppin asked for a quarter of a million dollars. All that the congress could afford to give him was $25,000, or £5,000 British. In spite of grandiose ambitions, the Zionist Congress and the JNF still relied on the small donations from victims of persecution. The well-financed experiments of Baron Edmond de Rothschild's PICA had little interest in the Zionist goals of the conquest of labor, collective farming, or the revival of Hebrew. Nevertheless the idealism of the Zionist pioneers enabled Ruppin to establish dairy farms and to plant groves of fruit trees, using only Jewish labor.

Ruppin appeared at first to be an unemotional bureaucrat, a most atypical Zionist. Born a German subject in East Prussia, he did not seem ideologically bound to the goal of creating a Jewish homeland in Turkish Palestine. Nevertheless he probably contributed as much as any of the highly verbal Zionists whose ideals brought them to Palestine before World War I. He was the first agent of the World Zionist Congress who made practical use of the Jordan and Yarmuk Rivers to generate hydroelectric power. Moreover, he had the prescience to recognize that any successes for Jewish nationalism would indirectly foster Arab nationalism.

By 1914 there were 70,000 Jews (constituting about one-tenth the total population of Turkish Palestine), west of the Jordan River. Within the

Jewish community a majority was still deeply religious and nonpolitical. Indeed, the Old Yishuv was still dominant. Among Moslems, Jews, and Christians, self-definition was still determined by religion. There was no sense of Palestinian nationalism. Arab nationalism, like Jewish nationalism, was just coming to life.

- Nasif Yazeji and his son Ibrahim had founded the Syrian Scientific Society at Beirut and Damascus in 1868.

- A select group of eight Arab students conspiratorially reciting fiery Arab nationalist poetry did not seem threatening to the Turkish government.

- Arab notables who seemed too ambitious to build a political following among Turkey's Arab subjects were invited to Constantinople as "honored guests." There they were treated as men of distinction but kept under discreet surveillance.

- Some Arabs of note were given posts in the sultan's government.

- An honor guard composed of Arab recruits was on duty at the imperial palaces.

Indeed, at the time when Turkey was losing European lands, the Ottoman ensign was advancing into previously unsubdued portions of the Arabian peninsula.

Most early Arab nationalists were products of Western universities or Christian mission schools in Lebanon. Because Christians were at the vanguard of the modest and nascent Arab nationalism, the Ottoman government consciously promoted pan-Islamic revivalism. Sayyed Jamuluddin al-Afghani, residing in Egypt from 1871 to 1879, had enjoyed support by Arab intellectuals as he evoked images of a revival of the Moslem Golden Age from the seventh century, when the Islamic world had been united under one caliph. Even Sultan Abdul Hamid II, 1876–1909, had had the common sense to win the support of the sherif of Mecca, Mohammed's descendant who was the guardian of the Moslem holy cities of Mecca and Medina.

Thus, the Zionists building their foundations in Palestine saw no reason to fear Arab hostility. To use a popular analogy, Palestine was a mansion with many rooms, capable of accommodating all the residents of Palestine without conflict.

Arthur Ruppin, however, who was busy building the Zionist structure, became acutely aware of the first voices raised against Zionism in Arab publications. Arab hostility was still moderate and confined to a small portion of the Arab press. Nevertheless Ruppin urged all his employees to learn conversational Arabic. By the end of World War I, Ruppin had become one of the Zionists who despaired of creating a Jewish state. He had become a binationalist. He believed that power would have to be shared between Jews and Arabs.

Nevertheless the Second Aliya had done its work well. The foundation had been laid for a Jewish homeland.

4

The Third, Fourth, and Fifth Aliyoth, 1919–1939

WORLD WAR I

The outbreak of World War I in 1914 represents a hiatus in the history of the New Yishuv's growth. Russia's attack on Turkey in October 1914 brought the Ottoman government into the war as an ally of Germany, Austria-Hungary, and Bulgaria. Great Britain, France, Serbia, and ultimately Italy, Greece, Rumania, Portugal, China, and Japan— and finally the United States—formed the alliance opposed to the Central Powers.

Russian belligerence proved to be disastrous for Palestine generally, but particularly for its Jews. Russian-Jewish money and numbers had fueled the first two *aliyoth*. Now the Turks viewed anything Russian as subversive, including Jews who had fled Russian persecution. Turkish Jewish subjects (even if Russian-born) who served in the Turkish armed forces—such as Moshe Shertok (later to become Israeli foreign minister Sharett)—were not molested. However, young Zionist activists were expelled for sedition. David Ben-Gurion, who would someday be Israel's first prime minister; Yitzchak Ben-Zvi, a future president of Israel; and Rabbi Y. L. Fishman, later to become Israeli cabinet minister Maimon, spent the war years in the United States.

Exile in the United States

The circle of Zionist exiles in America were not impressed by the American Jews as potential supporters. These children of Russian refugees were too busy earning a living and raising their American-born children. They were not prepared to uproot their families for a second time in one lifetime. Ben-Gurion and the others visited most of the major Jewish communities on speaking tours and were usually disappointed by the poor turnout and the lack of enthusiasm of their audiences. However, all the exiles absorbed valuable lessons about the United States that would serve them well when the State of Israel was born a generation later.

Henry Morgenthau, U.S. minister to Turkey until the United States entered the war in April 1917, performed yeoman service in saving Palestinian Jewry from expulsion and severe poverty. Through his good offices, American charities sent food and money. Captain Decker of the U.S. cruiser *Tennessee* became a hero to Palestinian Jews because he brought needed food and supplies and carried those whom the Turks expelled to safety, free of charge.

The exigencies of the war saw a serious decline in the entire Palestinian population. It is estimated that by 1918 there were only 55,000 Jews left in the country. Accurate figures are not available for the general population in 1918. However, by 1922 when the British mandatory government, which was destined to govern Palestine from 1919 to 1948, completed the first postwar census, there were 589,000 Moslem Arabs, 71,000 Christians of all origins, and 7,500 Druse. As exiles returned and immigration resumed, the Jewish population rose to 100,000.

Secret Agreements to Partition the Middle East

During those hours of the war when it seemed possible that the Central Powers would triumph, the beleaguered British, French, Italians, and Russians began diplomatic maneuvres to discuss the future partition of Turkey if, indeed, the Central Powers could be defeated. Each of the European powers had ambitious goals. The British and French made their own secret agreements for a postwar division of the Middle East. What evolved was a tangle of conflicting claims.

In 1916 Mark Sykes, a British parliamentarian and an assistant secretary to the war cabinet, was named the British negotiator. Charles Georges Picot, formerly the French consul-general at Beirut, represented

France. Perhaps to keep the entire proceedings secret, the two allies had designated agents of modest stature. What emerged was a very complex agreement known as the Sykes-Picot Accord.

Stated simply, France was to have virtually sovereign authority in the coastal and northern regions of Syria, and Britain was to have similar rights in Iraq, trans-Jordanian Palestine, and the ports of Haifa and Acre. They deferred until a later date a discussion of those parts of Palestine that would be placed under some unspecified form of international rule. Consultation was to take place with the Russians and with the Emir Hussein, sherif of Mecca and the hereditary claimant to be protector of the Moslem holy cities. Sykes and Picot did not draw precise maps. They were not alert to the necessity of studying the river systems and water supply of the region. As a result, a crucial area such as the Golan Heights, which supplies about 33 percent of the water in the Sea of Galilee, was first assigned to the proposed British zone and then transferred to the French Syrian sphere of influence. (The implications of such carelessness haunt the area to this day.)

British Plans for Postwar Palestine

While the Sykes-Picot Accord was being designed, the British pursued two other sets of territorial negotiations, one with the Arabs and one with the Zionists. Emir Hussein, sherif of Mecca, being a descendant of Mohammed and the hereditary defender of Islam's holy cities, aspired to the creation of a great Arab kingdom stretching from the Persian Gulf on the east to the Mediterranean and the Red Sea on the west. At the onset of war in 1914, Hussein had sent his son Feisal to Cairo to meet Lord Kitchener, the British high commissioner in Egypt. Hussein assured the British that he could stir up a great Arab revolt against the Turks if his dream of becoming king of the Arabs could be realized. Kitchener was warmly receptive, and on October 24, 1915, Sir Henry McMahon, Kitchener's successor at Cairo, wrote officially to accept the sherif's proposals.

McMahon made one major exception to Hussein's blueprint, indicating that he would not receive those portions of Syria lying to the west of the districts of Damascus, Homs, Hama, and Aleppo that could not be said to be purely Arab. It may be supposed that McMahon was attempting to reserve those areas for a future imperial settlement, but at that date the Sykes-Picot Accord did not yet exist. Sherif Hussein took the exceptions to mean that Britain did not regard the Christian and Druse population of Lebanon and Syria as Arab. However, he did not make the British reservation of the coastal districts a subject for debate. He certainly did not break off negotiations on that account.

Another area of negotiations in conflict with the other two involved the Zionists. As long as czarist Russia was in the war, the sympathies of east European Jews and their American coreligionists were pro-German. When Emperor Franz Josef of Austria died in 1916, New York's Jewish East Side went into mourning. As German and Austro-Hungarian soldiers entered Russian Polish towns, the Jews greeted them as liberators. In 1916 the Germans seemed everywhere triumphant. Their submarines were decimating the British merchant marine. French troops on the front line were attempting mutiny. The British were forced to suppress rebellion in Ireland. Under those circumstances the British opened negotiations with the Zionists. After all, the largest and most Zionist-inspired Jewish community in the world lived in that portion of Russia where the Germans were triumphant.

Therefore the British began a double-pronged set of negotiations to discover the sort of role that the Zionists might play after the war. It must be remembered that the Sykes-Picot talks and the correspondence with Sherif Hussein were in progress at the same time.

Origins of the Balfour Declaration

The voice of Zionism in Britain was that of Dr. Chaim Weizmann. He was Russian-born, German-educated, and a naturalized British subject. Holding a Ph.D. in chemistry, he had rendered crucial service to wartime Britain through his development of underwater explosives. His years of life and research in Britain had made him an enthusiastic Anglophile. Though he ultimately became the first president of Israel in 1948, his critics have always alleged that he put too much trust in British promises.

At the moment when the first "feelers" were proposed to Dr. Weizmann, the British cabinet approached the Board of Deputies of British Jews and the Anglo-Jewish Association. The latter two organizations represented the highly centralized voices of the Jewish establishment. These wealthy, very assimilated British Jews were concerned lest they be accused of double loyalty. For them, Zionism was an embarrassing foreign loyalty.

Thus, Lord Arthur James Balfour, the British secretary of state for foreign affairs, found himself in a peculiar position. He was an evangelical

Christian who believed that it was part of the messianic program that Jews should restore Zion. He found himself making proposals to an Anglo-Jewish aristocracy that was embarrassed by any suggestion that it was less British than Lord Balfour himself. Indeed, Edwin Montagu, the only Jew in the cabinet, was hostile to the proposed declaration. Lord Balfour also found the Zionists with whom he dealt—notably Dr. Weizmann and Nahum Sokolow—prepared to settle for something less than a sovereign Jewish state in Palestine.

In February 1917 the czar was overthrown and a moderately socialist republic came into being, headed by the first democrats ever to rule Russia. Since the government of Professor Kerensky and Prince Lvov proposed to continue the war as Britain's ally, there was every reason to expect that Jews would rally to the support of the war against Germany. No one had any inkling that in Russia Lenin was about to overthrow Kerensky and surrender to Germany. For the moment, the British government regarded a concession to the Zionists as merely a small capstone to the agreement already made with France and Sherif Hussein.

Thus, on November 2, 1917, the so-called Balfour Declaration was issued in the form of a letter addressed to Lord Rothschild of the Board of Deputies of British Jews. It read:

> I have much pleasure in conveying to you, on behalf of His Majesty's Government, the following declaration of sympathy with Jewish Zionist aspirations which has been submitted to, and approved by, the Cabinet.
>
> His Majesty's Government view with favor the establishment in Palestine of a national home for the Jewish people, and will use their best endeavors to facilitate the achievement of that object, it being clearly understood that nothing shall be done which may prejudice the civil and religious rights of existing non-Jewish communities in Palestine, or the rights and political status enjoyed by Jews in any other country. . . .

The British Conquest of Palestine

The anticipated great Arab rebellion against the Turks, promised by Sherif Hussein, never fulfilled expectations. Colonel T. E. Lawrence, the British agent sent to coordinate Arab efforts, accomplished little. The colonel, who became known as Lawrence of Arabia, proved to be a much more effective self-promoting publicist than a Napoleonic exemplar. His *Seven Pillars of Wisdom*, published after the war, became a popular book and made its author a popular hero.

However, with regard to Palestine, Colonel Lawrence's untrained Arab volunteer troops did make one great contribution. By capturing Aqaba at the north end of the Red Sea, they precluded the possibility of German submarines establishing a base there. They also expedited the movement of regular British troops under General Allenby as they conquered Palestine. On December 16, 1917, Allenby entered Jerusalem. It required the rest of the war until November 1918 for the British to drive the Turks out of northern Palestine. In the last part of the campaign Ze'ev Jabotinsky, a Russian Jew residing in England, succeeded in raising and arming a Jewish Legion in England and the United States. It rendered service fighting as a unit, several battalions strong, in Allenby's army. Its men constituted the first Jewish army unit to fight in the name of an anticipated Jewish state since the defeat of Shimon Bar-Cochba at the hands of the Romans in the year 135. Jabotinsky was destined to become the founder of aggressive nationalism in Zionism and is still the model for Betar and Cherut, the political movements that were the predecessors and models for the Likud Party of today.

Allenby's triumph spelled the end of those provisions in the Sykes-Picot Accord that called for some sort of international control. Britain settled down to govern Palestine on both sides of the Jordan River, as well as Iraq. The French raised their flag in all of Syria and Lebanon. Sherif Hussein, who still anticipated the great Arab kingdom to be proclaimed, informed the British that he would welcome Jews to Palestine if they intended to be his loyal subjects. Having no such intentions, Dr. Weizmann left London in March 1918, while the war still raged, and came to Jerusalem to serve as an advisor to the British as the Jewish homeland was established.

THE LEAGUE OF NATIONS AND THE BRITISH MANDATE

In 1919, the League of Nations officially recognized the British Mandate for Palestine, on both banks of the Jordan River, even as the League itself was being founded under the Treaty of Versailles. The terms of the Balfour Declaration were included in the Treaty of San Remo in 1920. In May 1920 the British named Sir Herbert Samuel, later to become the first Viscount Samuel, as their high commissioner for Palestine. He formally took office in July 1920.

The new high commissioner suffered from a heavy burden of conflicting commitments. As a secular Jew and as a liberal he had, as early as 1915, urged the cabinet to support a Jewish state in Palestine. He was personally not a Zionist, however, and strained to avoid offending the Arabs. Of course, he ended by taking sides; and as Arab hostility to Jewish immigration grew, he attempted to keep the peace by making concessions to Arab demands. He then failed to placate the Arabs and drew Zionist resentment by eroding their expectations under the terms of the Balfour Declaration. By steadily cutting immigration quotas, he failed to win Arab support while infuriating the Zionists.

The growing conflict was further complicated by the final resolution of Anglo-French rivalries growing out of the Sykes-Picot Accord. Sherif Hussein had expected to become sovereign of a great Arab kingdom. The French, however, expected to become the mandatory power for Syria and Lebanon, whereas Britain would hold Palestine and Iraq. The Zionists had their own concept of a Jewish national home whose territorial limits would include a Palestine extending far to the east of the Jordan and encompassing the water table of the Sea of Galilee. However, no legally binding, definitive maps had been drawn. All the parties had impressive piles of documents to support their cases, but no one had reconciled the conflicting claims.

FRUSTRATION OF ARAB HOPES FOR A HASHEMITE KINGDOM

In 1921 Sherif Hussein's son Abdullah marched northward with an army to assert his father's claim to Syria. The French, at Damascus, promptly repulsed him. To compound the humiliation of the sherif of Mecca's Hashemite Dynasty, Ibn Saud (a rigidly ascetic Moslem Wahabi sectarian) seized the holy cities of Mecca and Medina, thereby depriving Hussein (a direct descendant of Mohammed) of his hereditary power base. Britain's principal Near Eastern ally was thus plunged suddenly to the status of a nonentity.

Winston Churchill, the British colonial secretary, moved aggressively to turn the defeat of Britain's Arab ally into a partial success. In 1921 London prohibited Jewish settlement east of the Jordan River. In September 1922 the League of Nations endorsed that administrative measure. In September 1923 the British completely severed the Palestinian mandate at the Jordan, creating the kingdom of Trans-Jordan under King Abdullah. Previously, in August 1921, Abdullah's brother Feisal had been crowned king of Iraq. Thus, in a display of sleight of hand, the British made kings out of the two sons of their wartime ally, Sherif Hussein. They satisfied the French by giving them all of Syria and Lebanon free of Arab control and including the water table of the Golan, which was essential to their own realm in Palestine. The Zionists were left with a cloudy claim to Cis-Jordanian Palestine, which was thereafter contested with increasing violence by the Arab clan leadership. As though a symptom of the problem, to the very end of the British Mandate the mayors of Jerusalem continued to be aristocratic, land-owning Arab effendis such as the heirs of the Nashashibi family, although Jews had constituted a majority of the city's population since 1855.

The effendi aristocracy played a dangerous but profitable double game. The absentee landlords sold land to the Zionist organizations at highly inflated prices. They then took the lead in nourishing the resentment of landless peasants against Jews engaged in new agricultural enterprises. The Arab effendi did not cultivate nationalism in a European sense. Instead, they advanced the interests of their clan in exactly the same way in which the Arab aristocracy had always striven for profitable advantage under the Turks.

The Grand Mufti of Jerusalem

Sir Herbert Samuel's greatest and possibly most tragic error of judgment was to confirm al-Hajj Amin al-Huseini as grand mufti of Jerusalem in 1921. The Moslem supreme authority in Palestine was thereby given control of the resources of the Waqf, the foundation controlling Moslem religious property. In particular, he could reassert Moslem possession of El Aqsa and Al Haram, the two central shrines sacred to Islam atop the Temple Mount, the holiest of all Jewish shrines. In the nineteenth century there had been occasional Moslem leaders in Jerusalem who had striven for compromises between the two religions claiming the same shrines. Europeans who knew the grand mufti were impressed with him as a handsome, amiable, and soft-spoken man. Yet al-Huseini would prove to be capable of brutal abuse of his position.

From 1920 to 1936 he tested the ground to see how far the British would allow him to go. He discovered that they were willing to look the other way as Arab terrorism against the Jews grew, provided that there was no direct confrontation with British authority. This was made easier by the fact that the lower ranks of the police force were overwhelmingly Arab.

ORIGINS OF JEWISH SELF-GOVERNMENT IN PALESTINE

In the face of all this evidence that Zionist skies were darkening, the World Zionist Organization continued to work as though there was no threat to "the national home for the Jewish people." The World Zionist Congresses created a Jewish Agency for Palestine that functioned like a parliamentary cabinet, speaking to the British high commissioners as the official voice of the Yishuv. In turn, the Yishuv was not content to allow the congresses, dominated by persons living abroad, to make decisions regarding the life of committed Zionists. Therefore a quasi-parliamentary body, the 314-member Asephat Ha-Nivcharim (literally, the "Chosen Assembly") became both the vital support of and the opposition to the Jewish Agency executive. It elected its own Vaad Le'umi, or National Council. All registered members of the Zionist organizations constituting the New Yishuv could vote for the Assembly. A very lively multiparty political life evolved, offering invaluable experience in democratic self-government.

Most of the people who ultimately served in the government of Israel gained their practical experience in the Jewish Agency executive or the Asephat Ha-Nivcharim. Actually, the British preferred to deal only with the Jewish Agency executive and did not even grant the Asephat Ha-Nivcharim the right to tax the Jewish community until 1927, and did not grant broad powers in that area until 1932. Much of the Old Yishuv, composed of deeply pious Ashkenazic and Sephardic Jews, tended to hold themselves aloof from the secular and sometimes highly undignified political life of the New Yishuv. After all, as many as twenty political parties contended in very lively elections. It should not be thought, however, that they were indifferent to the political struggle into which they were increasingly dragged as the Arab-Jewish-British conflict became more marked and painful.

The Arabs developed no democratic political institutions. Instead, the Arab Higher Committee was dominated by the grand mufti and the established effendi aristocracy.

HENRIETTA SZOLD

Immediately after World War I an extremely valuable recruit for Zionism made her first visit to Palestine. Henrietta Szold, born in 1860, the daughter of a Baltimore Reform rabbi, had labored for thirteen years assisting Louis Ginsberg as he published his magisterial *Legends of the*

Jews. In this she was a very competent translator. At her first visit to Palestine, which was newly taken from the Turks, she found a land in which malaria, hepatitis, high infant mortality, and disease-induced blindness were endemic. She was horrified to see children whose eyes were covered with stinging insects and who made no attempt to defend themselves. She subsequently founded Hadassah, the Women's Zionist Organization that established a network of social welfare and health organizations. Today Hadassah maintains two hospitals as well as medical, dental, and other professional schools in Jerusalem.

Henrietta Szold died in 1945, before Israel became an independent state. She did not believe that a Jewish state had a practical chance for success. She therefore was not so much enthusiastic as resigned to a binational state in which Jews and Arabs would share power. However, as a pragmatist she created a Youth Aliya, bringing young Jews out of Europe after Hitler came to power. Parents who could not (or chose not to) leave Europe at least could save their children thanks to the efforts of the elderly Baltimorean.

THE THIRD ALIYA

The years usually assigned to the Third Aliya, 1919–1924, witnessed great successes. The British had not yet renounced their commitment to the Balfour Declaration.

Human Resources

In the aftermath of World War I, the newly drawn borders of eastern Europe were still unsettled. A very aggressive Polish republic was engaged in attempts to regain the historic borders of the eighteenth-century kingdom of Poland, at the expense of a Soviet Union torn by civil war and foreign intervention. In the confusion, Jews who wished to flee the disputed lands could do so.

Britain was locked in economic depression and did not welcome immigration. The United States was enjoying prosperity but had retreated into isolation and did not welcome east European immigrants. Therefore, Palestine became a destination of choice for Jews seeking a better life.

The Third Aliya witnessed the adoption of Hebrew as the language of instruction at the Haifa Technion, which before the war had been a German-language institution. It would ultimately prepare technical professionals whose services became indispensable in founding a modern state.

The kibbutz system founded before the war proved itself during the Third Aliya. Concurrently the Moshav movement created varieties of agricultural communities in which individual members were free of collective regulation but agreed to work with other members of the Moshav in their various means of production or their marketing. Kibbutz and Moshav proved to be the means whereby an urban population learned to succeed as farmers.

Arthur Ruppin put his theories to work and began to coax hydroelectric power from the Jordan River, which rushes downward in its precipitate drop to the Dead Sea. Rapidly growing Tel Aviv invited the world to its first Industrial Exhibit, which thereafter became scheduled Levant Fairs. Because the Arab Higher Committee chose not to cooperate, the Jewish Agency established its own school system, enjoying British government subsidies from largely Jewish Palestinian tax revenue.

Origins of the Hebrew University

Spanning the Third Aliya was the development of what would become an internationally respected institution of higher learning. On July 24, 1918, the cornerstone of the projected new Hebrew University was laid on Mount Scopus, overlooking the walled city of Jerusalem. Officially founded in 1925, the university did not graduate its first class until 1931. It was years before a decent library existed. There were no dormitories, and students roomed elsewhere. Professors, who were European-educated, spoke halting Hebrew. One member of the first graduating class stated that a lecture would often be interrupted while professor and students explored the Hebrew language to find appropriate words for the professor's topic.

THE FOURTH ALIYA

What has come to be called the Fourth Aliya is usually dated 1924–1929. It was dominated by urban Polish Jews fleeing a blatantly anti-Semitic Warsaw government. In fact, as many as 34,000 Polish Jews might have entered Palestine in the course of a single year. In the absence of rigid British immigration quotas, a flood of refugees made their way to Palestine. However, the Polish newcomers were neither ideologically motivated nor emotionally prepared for Palestinian conditions. The Fourth Aliya was doomed to begin in boom and end in bust. Far too many of the Polish Jews were small shopkeepers, and there was a limit to how many dealers in dry goods or housewares the small Palestinian urban centers could absorb. By 1929 more Jews were leaving Palestine than entering it.

The Grand Mufti's Campaign of Terror

In the summer of 1929 the grand mufti of Jerusalem went to the shrine of the Nebi Musa, which Moslems believe is the tomb of Moses. There, on the edge of the Judean Desert, he preached to huge congregations on the Moslem sabbath, accusing the Jews of having forcibly seized Al-Aqsa and Al-Haram atop the Temple Mount. There was no basis to these accusations. Even before the alleged Jewish seizure of the Mount, the mufti had harangued masses of Arab villagers on the Mount itself, where mischief was bound to develop. The British did nothing to deter the grand mufti or to prevent the arrival of enraged Arab mobs in crucial urban centers.

On the Jewish sabbath of August 24, 1929, infuriated Arab mobs attacked Jewish communities wherever they could. The New Yishuv defended itself effectively. In the towns of the Old Yishuv, however, the slaughter was extensive. The nonpolitical, deeply religious Jewish communities had lived side-by-side with Arabs for centuries, usually in peace. Arab merchants knew enough Yiddish to bargain with customers who avoided speaking Hebrew. The Old Yishuv had stood aloof from the struggle between Zionists and the younger generation of Arabs.

However, on that sabbath, 133 unarmed Jews were killed and 339 were injured. Hebron suffered the most. As one of the four Jewish holy cities, the burial place of six biblical patriarchs and matriarchs, it had always housed a large Jewish community. They accepted inferior status as though it were natural. Moslems had barred Jews from entering the building that Herod had built as a Jewish shrine. Jews were allowed to climb only the first seven steps leading to its door and had to recite their prayers outside. They did not dare to show resentment.

The violence of August 24 continued for several days. At Tel Aviv, armed Jews counterattacked and killed six Arabs. Only after non-Arab police forces were rushed to the scene from other British bases in the Mediterranean could the British end the pogrom, killing 110 Arabs and wounding 232.

Neutral observers such as the U.S. consul in Jerusalem worked stead-fastly to extricate American citizens from danger. The consul also ac-cepted the official explanation that Jew and Moslem had flown at one another and had been separated only by the British police. No one seemed willing or able to blame al-Huseini for instigating the massacres. After 1929, Jews simply abandoned their homes in Hebron. A few mer-chants continued to attempt to do business there, but the last such effort ended in 1936. Jews were destined not to return to their ancient homes until after the Six-Day War of 1967.

In the aftermath of the events of 1929, the Fourth Aliya ended in fail-ure. It seemed that the Zionist experiment was doomed.

One result of the massacre of 1929 was that Jews with pacifist tenden-cies (such as Arthur Ruppin) abandoned their hopes for a binational state to be shared equally by Jews and Arabs. Zionists as different as Ze'ev Jabotinsky (on the right wing) and David Ben-Gurion (the secretary of the Socialist Labor Union, the Histadrut) concluded that Arab-Jewish armed confrontation was inevitable. Ben-Gurion may have regarded Ja-botinsky as a fascist, but he agreed reluctantly that the New Yishuv would have to defend itself by force of arms.

THE FIFTH ALIYA

World Depression

In October 1929 a great depression enveloped the industrial world. Unemployment rose to a disastrous 15 percent and became a norm in much of the recently prosperous West. Immigrants were not welcome in any depressed area. In Zionist Palestine, however, Jewish immigration was welcomed and enthusiastically supported. Financial donations from world Jewry, however much reduced, generated a modest prosperity. Thus, oddly enough, Palestine was a small pocket of economic vigor in a sluggish world economy.

At that juncture, however, the British began a steady retreat from their Balfour Declaration pledges. Increasing limits were set on Jewish immi-grants who lacked the resources to be self-supporting or who had no specific guarantees of support from Zionist institutions. In this atmos-phere of uncertainty, the Nazis came to power in Germany.

Republican Germany saw its last free election in 1932. President Paul von Hindenburg chose to form a Nazi–right wing coalition because the alternative would have been a Communist-Socialist coalition. In January 1933, Adolf Hitler became chancellor.

Hitler and Racial Anti-Semitism

Hitler made it clear that racial anti-Semitism was a cornerstone of his philosophy. His initial attitude was that Jews must leave the country. Extermination did not become a part of his policy until 1942, when during World War II Hitler found himself the captor of most of the world's Jewish population. He had spoken of sending the Jews to French Madagascar, but that was merely rhetoric.

In Hitler's Germany only about 550,000 persons with four Jewish grandparents identified themselves as Jews. Stuttgart, 6 percent Jewish, had the greatest Jewish population of any German city. Jews could be found in all the big cities and in many villages, especially in Bavaria and Wurtemberg. However, many Germans were not personally acquainted with any Jews. They were visible in the learned professions and in manufacturing and retail sales. They therefore became lightning rods for the resentment of the poor, and it seemed that German society would not be seriously disrupted if they disappeared.

Palestinian Views on Negotiating with Nazis

Palestinian Jewry was deeply divided on the question of the best policy to follow with Nazi Germany. Ze'ev Jabotinsky and his nationalist Zionist Revisionists at first considered the possibility of working with Germany against the British. He regarded Britain as committed to the Arab cause and to the betrayal of Zionism. However, he soon realized that there was no way to collaborate with a foreign state that condemned Jews as inferior, simply because of the accident of birth.

The Jewish Agency, the leadership of the Histadrut and organized labor, and the entire left wing of the Asephat Ha-Nivcharim took a pragmatic view that it might be worthwhile to deal with the Nazis in order to get Jews out of Germany and into Palestine.

In 1933 Chaim Arlosoroff, a brilliant young Socialist, was assassinated on the beach near Tel Aviv. He had been active in urging the negotiation of a settlement with the Nazis to get Jews out of Germany. It was later proven that two Arabs killed him. However, the Zionist left condemned the Revisionists, as some do to this day. In fact, one element of Israel's history is the long litany of resentments of the Zionist left and right against each other. (In later pages of this book, the conflict represented by Arlosoroff's murder will be echoed in the Season, the *Altalena* affair, and the murder of Yitzchak Rabin.) Only the persistence of common foes has kept a semblance of unity in Zionism.

The first attempt of the organized Zionist community in Palestine to rescue Jews took place in 1933, the first year of Hitler's regime. In August 1933 the German Ministry of Industry signed a formal agreement with the Anglo-Palestine Bank (today, Bank Le'umi) of Tel Aviv. Under that contract the bank undertook to act as the agent of German Jews who shipped German products to Palestine, for resale, to raise capital for themselves. The actual shipment of goods was handled by a German-Jewish organization, the Palaestine Treuhand-Stelle der Juden in Deutschland. The clearance of goods through British customs and the mechanics of the sale of the products were handled by Haavara Ltd., an instrument of the Jewish Agency. *Haavara* is a Hebrew word meaning "transfer," so the entire process was called the "transfer," or *haavara*, system.

After 1934, German Jews were limited to carrying 10 German Marks, or about $2.50, per person out of Germany. Therefore, German Jews could escape the Nazis only if they shipped goods abroad or obtained a guarantor living abroad who would support them if they had no resources. The other alternative was to risk one's life by smuggling wealth abroad. Therefore Haavara was a lifesaver. The Nazis carried legal extortion even further by imposing a "flight tax," or *Reichfluchtsteuer*, on departing Jews. Therefore many parents sent their children abroad while the parents themselves, stripped of resources, stayed in Germany.

Haavara

Thereafter, in 1936, the Jewish Agency made the decision to enter negotiations with the Nazis in order to save German Jews, rather than working through second parties. Their intermediary was Walter Döhle, the German consul-general stationed in Jerusalem. From June to August 1936 the Jewish Agency solicited two favors from the Germans. One involved permission for fifteen Hebrew-speaking Palestinian Jewish teachers to enter Germany for one year, to establish youth villages in which to train young German Jews for life in Palestine. This had to be cleared with the top level of the Gestapo. The state police made their usual noises about a group of "left-wing Marxists" coming into Germany but raised no objection if their year's stay would expedite the departure of Jews. Indeed, shortly thereafter the Gestapo raised no objection to an increase in the number of teachers.

The second favor requested by the Jewish Agency through the German consul-general was permission for two members of the Jewish Agency to enter Germany for one year, including multiple entries and exits. The two were Eliezer Kaplan, treasurer of the Jewish Agency, and Eliyahu Dobkin, of the Jewish Agency's Immigration Department. Dr. Werner Senator of the Central Bureau for the Settlement of German Jews told Döhle that their mission would involve financial advantages for Germany. The German consul-general agreed to become a friendly mediator for the Jewish Agency at Gestapo Headquarters at Berlin. The Gestapo gave its consent for Palestinian Jews who had once been German citizens to receive travel visas as foreign nationals.

Following the mission of Dobkin, Kaplan, and the German-born Dr. Werner Feilchenfeld to Germany, both sides gained advantages. The Germans enlarged their share of the pie while making the operation of Haavara easier. The financial operations of Haavara were given to the Bank der Tempelgesellschaft, which had begun as a financial organ for the German Protestant communities centered at Jaffa and Haifa. Thereby the Germans strengthened a German financial institution in Palestine. Dr. Feilchenfeld, placed in charge of Haavara, found it easier to bring goods out of Germany. The Jewish Agency found itself in the peculiar position of promoting the sale of German products at a time when most Jews were boycotting German goods.

Nevertheless by May 1938 fully 43,000 German Jews had escaped from Germany through Haavara. At least 20,000 more had come out by their own devices. Still more escaped prior to the outbreak of World War II in September 1939.

At no time did the German Jews dominate the Fifth Aliya. Russian Jews had been almost cut off from departure by the USSR. However, many victims of the other anti-Semitic states of eastern Europe, notably Poland and Rumania, sought desperately to find a refuge in Palestine. Nevertheless the Fifth Aliya is uniquely the German *aliya*. The German Jews had been successful manufacturers and retail merchants before the rise of the Nazis. In Palestine they applied their skills and experience to the new situation and began to create jobs. The net result was that Palestine developed a healthy economy and an actual shortage of workers when the rest of the industrial world was in depression.

In the Zionist parties, only Ze'ev Jabotinsky's Revisionist Betar opposed the Haavara agreement. He wanted no compromise on the boycott of German goods. Betar was willing to cooperate with the Gestapo to rescue Jews only if no financial profit for Germany was involved.

The annual convocations addressed by Dr. Judah L. Magnes, chancellor of the Hebrew University, reflect the number of German academics who were appointed to senior professorial positions. Their arrival quickly enhanced the university's reputation. The Palestine Philharmonic and other musical and artistic institutions achieved world-class prestige owing to valuable new recruits. In addition, the Germans emphasized punctuality and order.

By May 1939 there were 400,000 Jews in Palestine. Arabs were pouring into the country to take jobs as laborers, particularly in the factories and ports of the coastal lowlands. The British did not check their immigration as diligently as the arrival of Jews was monitored. Zionism was running on a treadmill, and its very success was building the Arab majority.

Contradictory British Policies in Palestine

Between 1936 and 1939 the British instituted several programs that appeared, at first glance, to be contradictory. Until 1936, as the Arab rebellion (incited primarily by al-Huseini) rose to new and threatening heights, the British had tried to keep the Jews disarmed. Even rural settlements applying to the police for permission to hire a guard were routinely refused such permission. However, in 1937–1938 the British became determined to crush Arab disorder. Colonel Orde Charles Wingate was assigned to organize and train Jewish volunteers to constitute special night squads, which were skillful in tracking Arab raiders and striking them in the darkness. These men ultimately formed the cadre of the Hagana (Defense) forces, which would later become the nucleus of the Israeli army. Wingate was an Evangelical Christian who saw Jewish settlement in the Land of Israel as prophetic fulfillment. He took the trouble to learn Hebrew. Indeed, during World War II when he was sent to fight in Burma, where he died, he left his family in a kibbutz.

As part of the new, tough policy against Arab violence, the British dismissed al-Huseini from his post as head of the Supreme Moslem Council. Fearing arrest, on October 12, 1937, the grand mufti donned disguise and fled to Lebanon, where the French gave him asylum. During World War II the grand mufti resided in Germany, regularly broadcasting anti-British and anti-Jewish propaganda. He never returned to Palestine but remained a force to be reckoned with, even in exile.

On October 13, the day after the mufti's flight, the British dismissed

Sir Arthur Wauchope as high commissioner and replaced him with Sir Harold MacMichael, who was regarded as tougher and less conciliatory to the rebels. Thereafter, while using force to quiet the Arab rebellion, an effort was begun to pacify the country from a position of strength.

The Peel Partition Proposals

In November 1936, a year before the mufti's fall, the British decided to partition the country. William Robert Wellesley, Lord Peel, was dispatched to Palestine. A grandson of the great nineteenth-century British prime minister, Lord Peel was charged to hold commission hearings to make proposals for the future of Palestine. The leaders of all factions in the Yishuv testified before the Peel Commission. The Arabs boycotted it until almost the end, in July 1937. Dr. Chaim Weizmann, known for his strongly Anglophile feelings, made a heartfelt plea for British fulfillment of the Balfour Declaration.

The Peel Commission recommended the partitioning of Palestine. It must be remembered that only a tiny minority of the land belonged to private owners. The government—whether Turkish, British, or modern Israeli—has always held title to undeveloped property regarded as public lands. Thus, the Peel Commission drew a partition map based on those areas wherein Zionist institutions had obtained legal title to the greater part of agricultural land (see Map 4.1). The commission recommended that a Jewish state be created that would include a coastal strip from south of Jaffa to north of Haifa, and all of the Galilee. Jerusalem, with a corridor to the sea, was to be continued under a British mandate. All the rest of Palestine, including the Negev, was to be Arab and placed under the crown of King Abdullah of Trans-Jordan.

For the Yishuv the offer, however inadequate, was nevertheless acceptable. It meant a chance to offer refuge to the Jews of Europe and the Arab lands, whose position was becoming increasingly perilous. For the Arabs, however, any Jewish state was unacceptable. In the face of unified Palestinian Arab rejection, the Peel Commission's partition proposal died.

British Demoralization

It must be remembered that in the years 1936–1937 Britain found itself facing demoralizing crises. The abdication of King Edward VIII dominated 1936, but far more serious matters rendered Britain's position dan-

Map 4.1. The Peel Partition Plan of 1937.

gerous. The conquest of Ethiopia by Italy had alienated London from Rome. Mussolini entered Hitler's camp and became his ally in the overthrow of the Spanish Republic. It was taken as an omen when the Oxford University Debating Union voted not to fight for King and Country.

In 1937 Stanley Baldwin was replaced by a fellow Tory, Neville Chamberlain, as prime minister. Like many of his contemporaries, Chamberlain remembered with horror what it had cost Great Britain to win World War I. He could not understand the new technologies that would place all of Europe within reach of bombers carrying total destruction. He believed that Britain might sit out a future war while the French sat securely behind the heavily fortified underground Maginot Line, even if the Nazis and Fascists took Spain, Ethiopia, Austria, or Czechoslovakia. He was prepared to buy "peace" by sacrificing those who were peripheral to his vision. For him, the sacrifice of Jews in Europe or Palestine seemed no worse than the sacrifice of the others. He was destined to lend a whole new meaning to the word *appeasement*.

In March 1938 the Germans had no trouble annexing Austria. The attitude in the British cabinet was simply that in so doing Germany had added other Germans to the Reich. It appeared, at first, as though Chamberlain meant to fight when Hitler turned his ambitions against Czechoslovakia in May 1938. However, Hitler had measured the cowardliness of the British and French accurately, and with remarkable skill he managed to get London and Paris to agree to the cession of Czechoslovakia's natural defenses in the Sudeten Mountains in September 1938. The Munich Conference agreed that Hitler would make no more demands after he had annexed the coveted territory in October 1938. However, in March 1939 the rest of Czechoslovakia disappeared: Bohemia-Moravia became a part of Germany; and Slovakia became a puppet Fascist regime.

In May 1939 the Chamberlain government, aware at last that war with Hitler was inevitable, decided that Britain needed the Arab world more than it needed the Jews of Palestine. The issuance of the so-called White Paper of 1939 provided the following:

1. Britain had already fulfilled its pledges under the Balfour Declaration and the Mandate; a Jewish homeland existed already.

2. Over the next five years, 75,000 more Jews were to be admitted to Palestine.

3. After 1944, no more Jews would be admitted without Arab consent.

4. An Arab state was to be created, including all of Palestine.

In fact, more refugee Jews were admitted to the home islands of Great Britain than to any other European country, in proportion to population. Nevertheless the closure of Palestine on the eve of World War II made Britain an accomplice to the coming holocaust of Europe's Jewish population.

Preparing for the inevitable war, Britain renewed its alliance with France and attempted to form other alliances with Turkey, the lesser Balkan states, and Poland. A joint Anglo-French delegation went to Moscow to woo the Soviets. Joseph Stalin had once been eager for an alliance against Germany. Neither Paris nor London was prepared to give him a dominant position in eastern Europe in exchange for his alliance. The Russians had just purged their army of all dissident officers, and some of Stalin's best commanders had been executed, imprisoned, or dismissed. The best Anglo-French wisdom concluded that Moscow was desperate for an alliance, and that very little had to be offered to the Soviets in order to gain their signature.

The Soviet-German Nonaggression Pact

While negotiations continued, a lightning bolt struck the unsuspecting Anglo-French delegation. In August 1939 Stalin's foreign minister, Maxim Litvinov, was suddenly dismissed. The Jewish-born Litvinov was replaced by Vyacheslav Molotov, an ethnic Russian. He then received Nazi Germany's foreign minister, Kurt von Ribbentrop. A ten-year non-aggression pact was signed, assuring Germany that it could fight a war without fear of a Soviet attack. Hitler was also thus assured that Russian oil and wheat would continue to come his way, freeing him of the fear of a crippling blockade. The secret protocols of the treaty also agreed that Germany and the USSR would divide Poland and that Russia would dominate Finland, Latvia, Estonia, and Rumania while Germany had prior rights in Lithuania.

In the blink of an eye, the entire world balance of power shifted. For six years Hitler had described Germany as Europe's defense against Bolshevism. Now he was Moscow's ally. In September 1939, Hitler attacked Poland. World War II had begun. In Palestine, the Yishuv found itself held at arm's length as the British patrolled the coast with the greatest navy in the world, to bar entry by unauthorized Jews. No one yet dreamed that Hitler planned the mass extermination of all Jews. Still, the great question before Zionism was how to fight Hitler as though there were no White Paper and how to fight the White Paper as though Hitler did not exist.

5

The Holocaust and the Struggle for Survival, 1939–1948

On September 1, 1939, Germany attacked Poland. On September 3, Britain and France declared war on Germany in fulfillment of their alliance with Poland. German tanks and dive-bombers smashed the Poles within two weeks. On September 17, the Soviet Union invaded from the east as part of the secret August agreements with Germany. By October 1, Poland no longer existed. Radio Warsaw went off the air playing Chopin's *Polonaise*. From October 1939 to May 1940, western Europe was almost silent except for an occasional air raid on easy targets such as Hamburg. Berlin was believed to be beyond reach. An air of unreality prevailed during the popularly named Sitzkrieg, or "sitting war."

HITLER AND THE JEWS, 1939–1942

Inside Poland, Hitler found himself the captor of half of Poland's more than three million Jews. He did not quite know what to do with them. For the moment, the Germans decided to evacuate Jews from small towns and concentrate them in big-city ghettoes. The Jews were to be governed by Jewish councils composed of the most respected leaders of the Jewish community. Through the Judenrat, or Jewish Council system, the average Jew never had to come face-to-face with an SS or Gestapo officer. The local German authority gave orders to the head of the Judenrat, and a corps of Jewish policemen carried them out.

The masses of incarcerated Jews never dreamed that their death might be planned. Jews were allowed the comforting illusion that this was just another ghetto like the many others that Jews had survived over the centuries. They imagined that peace would come soon, and that some improvement in their condition would surely take place.

WARTIME BRITAIN AND PALESTINE

Within Palestine, a sense of desperation set in. As part of Britain's enforcement of the White Paper, Jewish immigration was rigidly restricted. To make matters worse, Jews could buy and settle on land only in a small area of the coastal strip between Zichron Yaakov and Rehovot.

From the borders of Hitler's expanding European empire, derelict seagoing vessels continued sailing to Palestine. All the Yishuv and the Hagana were in conspiracy to land illegal immigrants, whereas the British navy and Britain's largely Arab police force worked to catch and to deport desperate refugees. Such deportees usually met a tragic fate.

At the same time, however, the Jewish Agency and the Zionist Establishment were publicly committed to supporting the British war effort. However offensive British policy might be, the need to fight Hitler was paramount.

Thus, most Palestinian Jews were sincere about seeking combat against Hitler. Volunteers numbering 136,000 fought in British uniform. However, the authorities were reluctant to allow them to form Palestinian Jewish units (such as the Zion Mule Corps or the Jewish Legion had been in World War I). Prime Minister Winston Churchill intervened in June 1940, at the crucial hour when France faced defeat and Britain was left to fight the war against Hitler, alone. Churchill urged arming Palestinian Jewry. He saw no reason why vitally needed British troops should be wasted in Palestine when they were crucially required on other fronts against the Germans and Italians. Nevertheless he was overruled by his cabinet and the top military echelons who were convinced that armed Palestinian Jews would attack the Arabs. Perhaps more significant, they feared that the Jews would unilaterally scrap the White Paper of 1939.

In fact, in 1942 the British did send 1,500 specially trained Palestinian Jewish guerrillas to fight the Germans in Libya. Known as the Jewish Rural Special Police, these soldiers eventually evolved, after the war, into the Palmach, the commando force of the Hagana, and finally into the

Israeli army. However, their small numbers and their operation outside Palestine represented no threat to the White Paper.

It was not until the end of 1944 that a Jewish brigade was finally formed and sent to Italy for the last phases of that battle. It is also to Churchill's credit that when he learned that death camps had been established to exterminate Jews, he authorized bombing the railroad lines that brought victims to the camps. Such orders were negated, however, by lesser officials. Neither the British nor the United States used air power for that purpose. As early as 1943, Churchill was attempting to get his cabinet to drop the White Paper of 1939 and to propose a partition of Palestine. Nothing came of either plan, however. Perhaps the prime minister, despite his good intentions, had other priorities as the war came to an end. Meanwhile an individual Palestinian Jewess named Hannah Senesch was parachuted behind German lines in Hungary to stir up sabotage. Her capture, torture, and execution mark a small but heroic part of the saga of Palestinian resistance to Nazism.

ORIGINS OF THE HOLOCAUST

In June 1941, having consolidated his control of conquered Poland, France, Belgium, Holland, Luxembourg, Norway, Denmark, Yugoslavia, and Greece, Hitler saw only Britain as capable of defying him. He then turned once again to the conquest of the USSR. The Germans quickly overran those territories in the Baltic states, White Russia, and the Ukraine where the world's greatest concentration of Jews lived. Sonderkommando units of the SS began the systematic slaughter of Jews who were forced to dig their own graves, stripped naked, then cut down by machine gun fire. Even the most sadistic machine gunners, however, felt some discomfort in shooting mothers holding infants. It was decidedly bad for SS morale to have such duty on a daily basis.

Therefore, in December 1941 and January 1942, the Wannsee Conference was convened at a pleasant resort near Berlin. There the top Nazis in a Christmas–New Years holiday atmosphere adopted the "Final Solution of the Jewish Question."

Put simply, this meant concentrating Jews from all parts of Europe at camps where they could be systematically gassed in sealed chambers. Gold teeth, long hair, and all objects of value could be removed from the dead. Their bodies could be cremated and their ashes disposed of easily. Slave laborers, both Jewish and non-German Gentile, could perform such grisly service in the deluded hope of saving their own lives.

Nazi scientists could perform experiments on the living before they went to the gas chambers. Overlooking nothing, the Nazis forced Jewish musicians to play sprightly marches as the victims went to their deaths.

The first reports of the death camps were transmitted to London by the Polish underground in 1942. The odor of burning bodies aroused suspicion even among the peasants living nearby. As early as 1942 the British and Americans made public announcements about mass extermination. Most people, however, dismissed the unbelievable stories as propaganda resembling the false charges invented by both sides in World War I. In Palestine, however, the leaders of the Yishuv knew the truth but were frustrated about offering remedies. Even they did not guess that the Nazis would succeed in killing 60 percent of Europe's Jews before the war ended. At the center of the Zionist leadership, a sense of desperate vulnerability prevailed as they faced the prospects of death at the hands of the Nazis or victimization at the hands of the British.

THE BILTMORE CONFERENCE

In May 1942, when the first news of the death camps became common knowledge, the national Zionist organizations in the United States convened an Extraordinary Conference at the Biltmore Hotel in New York. Six hundred of the most influential American Jews and sixty-seven Zionists from abroad attended. The latter included Dr. Chaim Weizmann and David Ben-Gurion, already conceded to be the dominant leader of the Yishuv. At the conference Weizmann's gradualism and strong Anglophilia were roundly rejected. Instead, the conferees formulated what has come to be called the Biltmore Program.

Primarily the Biltmore Program demanded the scrapping of the 1939 White Paper and the opening of all of Palestine to unlimited Jewish immigration and land purchase. It emphasized the immediate creation of a Jewish state. Only a tiny minority of influential Zionists still held the view that a binational state was possible in which Arabs and Jews might share power. These included Judah Magnes, president of the Hebrew University, and the redoubtable Henrietta Szold, founder of the Hadassah Women's Zionist Organization. As the Arabs refused to make even small concessions, and as the disasters befalling European Jewry proved even more horrifying than first reported, the irresistible logic of events drove Zionist mainstream opinion to extreme positions. In 1944 Ben-Gurion and Moshe Sharett on behalf of the Jewish Agency sent a memorandum to the British government demanding a Jewish state in all of Palestine, without partition. In 1944 the Asephat Ha-Nivcharim, through its Vaad Leumi (National Council), passed a resolution affirming the Biltmore Program and rejecting the idea of partition.

The newly aggressive spirit of the Palestinian Jewish leadership was exceeded by the British Labor Party, still out of office, which in its 1944 annual party conference urged that Arabs be induced to leave Palestine and be handsomely compensated to do so. In that stance they exceeded any position taken by mainstream Zionism. (Ironically, in 1945 Labor beat the Tories in the first election after Hitler's defeat and adopted a policy that was more hostile to Zionism than any posture previously taken by the Tories.)

Postwar Britain and the White Paper

After the Nazis had been beaten and the death camps liberated, the Yishuv expected a friendlier attitude from Prime Minister Clement Attlee's Labor government, which took office in July 1945. Instead the new foreign secretary, Ernest Bevin, crossed the line, revealing strong anti-Semitic attitudes that went beyond the previously normal pro-Arab or anti-Zionist Tory tendencies. Within the Yishuv, the years of the war had witnessed an even more dangerous phenomenon. Until 1944 the Zionist mainstream had opposed the British because of the White Paper but had desisted from violent action against them. As early as 1942, however, a small Jewish underground had developed, determined to overthrow British authority.

MENACHEM BEGIN AND THE IRGUN ZVAI LEUMI

When World War II began and Germany and the USSR partitioned Poland in September 1939, the Germans began to arrest Jews simply because they were Jews. The Soviets began to arrest Zionists known to be anti-Communist. One young man who was immediately arrested was Menachem Begin, a disciple of Ze'ev Jabotinsky and a strongly anti-Communist Zionist. He languished in Soviet prison and labor camp until Germany attacked the USSR in June 1941. At that point, the Soviets allowed Polish general Vladislaw Anders to organize a Free Polish Army and to lead its troops to British-held territory. Among the prisoners allowed to leave the Soviet labor camp and to put on Polish uniform was Menachem Begin. Upon reaching Palestine (via Iran and Iraq) with his

Polish comrades, Begin arrived in Jerusalem in May 1942, where he was reunited with his wife, Aliza, who had escaped Poland earlier. He then obtained his discharge from Anders's army in 1943 through the intervention of friends close to its commander.

As early as 1933 the beginnings of a movement for self-defense against Arab attack had been organized. These roots of the Hagana suffered from disunity even from the beginning. To the extent that the principal source of financing was offered by the Histadrut, the powerful and well-organized labor union, the Hagana was socialist. Revisionists, or Betar activists, looking to Jabotinsky's philosophy and anxious to join the self-defense movement, found themselves thrust to the sidelines by the Socialist leadership.

Avraham Tehomi, who had been a loyal Hagana leader, broke with the organization in 1933 over the issue that non-Socialists were being excluded from any meaningful share in the command. He was instrumental in founding Organization B, which soon changed its name to the Irgun Zvai Leumi (National Military Organization), widely known by the initials of its Hebrew name, the IZL or EITZEL.

Fighting the White Paper with Terror

At that point two young students at Hebrew University took control of what would prove to be the underground army. David Raziel (known by his nom de guerre, Ben-Anat) soon became the leader of IZL. Avraham Stern (known by his code name, Yair) led a second breakaway faction of the non-Socialist underground army: the Lohamei Herut Yisrael (Fighters for the Freedom of Israel). This group was known to its friends as LEHI and to its enemies as the Stern Gang. The three armed Jewish factions all agreed that the British White Paper of 1939 had to be scrapped. However, they fell into conflict with one another over the legitimacy of anti-British violence.

Toward the end of the war, when it became evident that the British would oppose Jewish immigration even though only the admission of Jews to Palestine would save lives, Hagana and Palmach reluctantly resorted to violence against the British. IZL, although not hesitating to use force against the British, usually took pride in giving warning where innocent lives were at stake. LEHI, by far the smallest and most vulnerable of the three groups, used terror as a weapon that would drive the British out of Palestine.

Many Palestinian Jews continued to think that the greatest priority had to be given to fighting the Nazis. The ideological picture was muddled by the fact that members of LEHI robbed banks and coerced ordinary Jews to support them financially, because no mainstream organization would do so. When LEHI assassinated Lord Moyne, the aggressively pro-Arab British minister-resident in Egypt, even IZL broke with LEHI for a brief period. Winston Churchill and Leopold Amery, the two British cabinet ministers who had been most sympathetic to Zionism, were revulsed by that act. Thereby LEHI lost a great deal of popular support.

On February 12, 1942, British troops and police surrounded a house on Mizrachi Street in Tel Aviv. They burst into the attic and shot dead Avraham Stern, who was hiding in a closet, as he tried to surrender after being discovered. The fallen LEHI leader became a martyr. The house where he died is now the LEHI museum and archives. Shulamit Livnat, a distinguished folk singer, is the museum's curator. Her recorded voice fills the rooms, recalling the battle anthems of the underground.

In the worst sense, the police execution of Avraham Stern reinforced the conviction of right-wing Zionists that the Socialists had become informers betraying members of IZL and LEHI to the British. These Zionists likened that behavior to dogs who lead hunters to their prey and, thus, referred to that period as the [hunting] Season. Even modern Israel has not put aside the Season, and the bitterness between the political left and right still lingers. There is a strong likelihood that the Hagana, the Palmach, and the far-left kibbutzim participated in the Season.

After Stern's death the leadership of the LEHI fell to a three-man team. This group ultimately yielded power to Yitzchak Shamir, who was later to become a founder of the Likud Party and Israeli prime minister. The leadership of IZL fell to Menachem Begin, also a future Likud prime minister. As the war came to an end, he temporarily took the IZL out of combat operations to recognize and to prepare for the anticipated struggle that would ensue if the British clung to the White Paper of 1939.

The Jewish Underground United against Britain

In June 1945, as the war against Germany ended, the Jewish Agency demanded that the British issue 100,000 new immigration certificates to provide refuge for the survivors of Hitler's death camps. In July 1945, however, the newly installed British Labor Party dealt a rude blow to that hope. Foreign Secretary Ernest Bevin's undisguised anti-Semitism had the effect of driving the Jewish Agency, the Hagana, and the Palmach into the arms of the IZL and LEHI.

On July 22, 1946, Hagana and IZL joined in a terrorist act of unprecedented proportions. LEHI had also agreed to join the plot but lacked the manpower to participate in a disciplined attack on the British, which required the efficiency of an army. The attack would involve the southern wing of the palatial King David Hotel in Jerusalem, which housed the headquarters of the British administration in Palestine.

In preparing for the attack, Hagana and Palmach entered into full partnership with their old and often-condemned rivals in IZL. Yitzchak Sadeh, commander of Palmach, laid down the only stricture that no loss of innocent life take place. Menachem Begin of IZL readily agreed. Amihai Paglin, operations officer of IZL, even went so far as to attach notes to the milk churns containing the explosive mechanisms, warning passersby not to attempt to disarm them. Just before noon on July 22, the containers were brought into the service entrance of La Regence Café beneath the hotel. They were grouped around the pillars that supported the upper floors of the hotel. With a half-hour until the expected explosion, all the kitchen staff were ordered to flee to safety. Three young women of IZL then made separate phone calls to the King David Hotel, the nearby French consulate, and the editorial offices of the *Palestine Post*. The newspaper and the consulate then made phone calls to the British military command at the south wing of the hotel. At that crucial point Sir John Shaw, secretary of the Palestine government, upon being told of the warnings by a police officer, chose to ignore the phone calls.

At 12:37 P.M. on July 22, 1946, the southern wing of the hotel was destroyed by a monstrous explosion. Two hundred casualties resulted, half of them fatal. The dead included Jewish, Arab, and British civil servants. The initial public reaction was to blame the horror on IZL. The Jewish Agency and the Hagana were willing to clear themselves of suspicion by blaming the explosion on IZL. However, just as it seemed that the Season and the wartime hostility of Jew against Jew would return, the British indirectly rescued the resistance movement from its own suicidal tendencies. General Evelyn Barker, the British commander-in-chief in Palestine, issued a public statement finding all Jews guilty of murder. Menachem Begin—in hiding, bearded and disguised in the costume of a devout religious student—saw to it that General Barker's timely "Jew-baiting" restored the unity of the anti-British underground.

"ILLEGAL" IMMIGRATION

All were now prepared to use violent resistance to the British. All the resources of what now became a rebellious Jewish populace supported an "illegal" Jewish immigration into Palestine. This movement from the European camps, which had become homes for "displaced persons," was carried out in sea-going hulks sailing secretly from French and Italian ports to Palestine. If a vessel managed to evade the watchful British navy and run aground on a Palestinian beach, the passengers were rushed to refuge in neighboring Jewish communities by all manner of vehicles, hastily recruited. In this "alternative immigration," or *aliya beth* ("immigration B"), 70,000 more Jews reached Palestine between 1945 and May 1948, the birth of Israel.

Among the many ships that formed part of this maritime defiance of the British, the one with the greatest impact on the founding of Israel was the *Exodus*. Originally built as a passenger boat designed to run between Baltimore and Norfolk on Chesapeake Bay, the steamer had a modest life from 1928 until the British purchased the vessel for a non-combat role in World War II. The *President Warfield*, as the ship was originally named, was designed to carry four hundred passengers.

In the midst of the attempt to run the British blockade of Palestine, the boat was purchased by American Zionists. It was packed beyond capacity with 4,554 desperate displaced persons ready to take any risk to reach Palestine. In mid-July 1947 the newly named *Exodus 1947* set sail from the French Mediterranean port of Sète. Immediately detected and followed by four British destroyers, the *Exodus* was boarded on July 18. The passengers offered resistance. Three were killed, and at least thirty were injured. The badly damaged vessel was escorted to Haifa and the injured were hospitalized. Photographs were taken showing British sailors with bloodstained uniforms.

It was originally proposed that the survivors be interned in British Cyprus. Ernest Bevin, however, insisted that the survivors be carried back to France. The French stated that they would give anyone asylum who asked for it, but that no one would be forced to disembark in France. Most of the passengers decided to remain on board. Eventually the British foreign secretary insisted on taking the passengers back to Germany, where they were once again placed in a British-controlled displaced persons' camp. Without intending to, Bevin thus gave Zionism the best possible public relations propaganda victory imaginable, rendering the management of the Mandate impossible.

DESPERATION BREEDS BRUTALITY

From 1945 to 1948, while the world witnessed the deterioration of Anglo-Zionist relations, it was obvious that a peaceful solution was beyond reach. LEHI and IZL now launched attacks on British soldiers, and the British began to hang captured men found guilty of such acts. Persons accused of lesser acts of violence were exiled to camps in Eritrea or were flogged. The British even cracked down on the Hagana and the Jewish Agency, largely for their support of blockade running. At that, the American Zionist leader Dr. Abba Hillel Silver initiated a mass letter-writing campaign urging U.S. citizens to press their congressmen to oppose a loan to Britain. At the dawn of 1948, it seemed that there was no end to the round of hangings and floggings that made Palestine a nightmare. Ahead lay the very uncertain prospect that a Jewish state might be born. Indeed, in the eyes of many, it seemed to have no chance of survival.

6

Birth of the State of Israel, 1947–1949

REACTIONS TO PARTITION

The Arabs Again Reject Partition

At the end of 1947 the Arab population of Palestine stood at 1,300,000, and the Jewish population had grown to 600,000. The only way in which a Jewish population half the size of its Arab neighbors could hope to achieve the Zionist dream and create a Jewish state, within those parts of the land in which Jews were a dominant majority, would be if Britain and the Arab Higher Committee agreed to partition. Still possessing the British White Paper of 1939, the Arabs were confident that they would soon possess an Arab state as well. The Jews could then either leave the country as refugees or submit to an all-Arab government with no chance of future Jewish immigration. The Arabs thus saw no reason to consider compromise.

Moreover, the British mandatory government had abandoned all pretense of even-handedness between Jews and Arabs. The British Foreign Office now anticipated eagerly the birth of an additional Arab state that could be counted on to support British imperial needs, whether in assured oil supply or military bases. After all, oil pipelines carried that precious commodity across the Hashemite kingdoms in Iraq and Trans-Jordan to the oil refineries at Haifa, secure on that great harbor.

Individual British police officers in Palestine, chafing under the humiliation they had suffered at the hands of LEHI and IZL, took their revenge through terrorist acts against randomly selected Jews. Indeed, once that form of state-sponsored anarchy began to take place, police terrorism did not discriminate between LEHI, IZL, and the Jewish Agency, the Hagana, and the Palmach. After all, the arms of the Jewish Establishment had been engaged in actions that the British regarded as terrorist. And blockade running and "illegal" immigration ranked close to forms of violence that the British regarded as criminal.

Zionism Fights for Partition

The Zionists were not as helpless as their deficiency in numbers and allies might have made them appear. In 1946, at the twenty-second World Zionist Congress in Basel, Switzerland, Dr. Chaim Weizmann approached the end of his long career as president of that organization. Threatened with blindness and seriously ill, he nevertheless spoke dramatically. He came out in favor of partition and an independent Jewish state. He had at last abandoned his long advocacy of a binational state that would share power with the Arabs. Although he was a Zionist devoted to peace, he had lost hope of working with the Arab Higher Committee. After all, al-Hajj Amin al-Huseini—even in exile, having survived the fall of Nazi Germany—was still the leader of that body. However, if Dr. Weizmann no longer believed in binationalism, he still remained an Anglophile. Furthermore, he took the occasion to condemn Jewish terrorism. In condemning LEHI and IZL, he may have been unaware that he was also condemning the Jewish Agency, the Hagana, and Palmach. It was evident to Palestinian Jewry, however, that *havlaga* ("self-restraint") was no longer valid.

Whether Socialists or disciples of Ze'ev Jabotinsky, Chaim Weizmann or Menachem Begin, David Ben-Gurion or Yitzchak Shamir, all Zionists were now committed to violent action to obtain a Jewish state. When Weizmann declined to run for another term as president of the World Zionist Organization, the office was allowed to stand vacant in deference to him. Thereafter, David Ben-Gurion became executive chairman for Yishuv Affairs. Reform rabbi Dr. Abba Hillel Silver became executive chairman in relation to America.

The British

On February 18, 1947, the British government renounced the Mandate. This startling admission of the abandonment of the White Paper of 1939 was also a confession of the repudiation of the Balfour Declaration. The move led Prime Minister Attlee's government to submit the problem to the United Nations.

The British hoped to pass on their Palestinian burden to the United Nations General Assembly, confident that partition would not be approved and that they (the British) would thereby escape the embarrassment of creating a Jewish state. London was confident that a required two-thirds of the members would not approve a Jewish state if, as seemed likely, the United States supported Britain actively—particularly by persuading Latin America to follow Washington. Eleven Moslem states, including five Arab members, would also block partition. The Soviet bloc was expected to follow. The British seemed confident that if the UN failed to support partition, the result would be a short and bloody war resulting in an Arab triumph, with Britain escaping further involvement in the Mandate issue. Thus, while the death toll between Jewish terrorists and British hangmen grew, London seemed optimistic about the ultimate settlement that might be anticipated from UN ineffectiveness.

The United Nations

During the period from April 28 to May 15, 1947, the Security Council seemed to be heading for the sort of impasse on which the British were counting. Instead, the Council threw the problem into the lap of the General Assembly. That body created UNSCOP (the United Nations Special Committee on Palestine), which was to report back to the Assembly in the fall of 1947.

The members of UNSCOP traveled to Palestine to begin their investigation on the ground in the summer of 1947. In July of that year British troops, most likely motivated by the overt anti-Semitism of their officers, headed by General Evelyn Barker, had gone on a rampage. Rankers were shooting randomly at Jews, creating a reign of terror. However painful this experience was for the Yishuv, the well-timed arrival of the ship *Exodus 1947* was a propaganda triumph that UNSCOP witnessed.

By August 31, UNSCOP had returned to Geneva and submitted its report. Seven out of ten of its members supported a recommendation that:

1. The British mandate be ended, and
2. Palestine be partitioned into Arab and Jewish states with an international zone to include Jerusalem and Bethlehem.

It was a blow to the Yishuv to be denied Jerusalem, where 10 percent of the Jews of Palestine lived and whose population contained a clear majority of Jews. The map (see Map 6.1) offered the proposed Jewish state to include the eastern Galilee, the Sharon coastal plain from Haifa to south of Jaffa, and the Negev Desert stretching down to the Red Sea at Eilat, which was then scarcely more than a village. The Arab state would include the western Galilee, including Acre; the mountainous heartland of Samaria and Judea, including Nablus and Hebron; and a strip of seacoast to the south, including the port of Gaza.

The map ensured that the Jews would retain the bulk of their industrial and agricultural complex. Receiving the barren and empty Negev Desert, they would have living space for the anticipated European and Near Eastern Jewish refugees, provided that water could be piped in to support them. For the plan to succeed, it would be necessary for the Arab and Jewish states to share control of the crossing points at the junctures of the three sections of the Arab and Jewish states. On November 29, 1947, by a vote of 33 to 13, with 10 abstentions, the General Assembly voted to accept UNSCOP's partition resolution. By a bare two-thirds majority, the proposed Jewish and Arab states were approved. To the chagrin of the British, the United States and the Soviet Union supported the resolution.

The United States and Harry S Truman

The United States had played a key role from the beginning. The State Department, being Arabists, would have gratified the British by voting against partition. President Truman, however, intervened. For him, the right of a Jewish state to exist was a simple matter of right and wrong. He was acutely conscious of the Nazi holocaust of six million Jews. Furthermore, he was susceptible to the call of personal loyalties.

Truman was strongly moved by personal appeals by his old friend and business partner, Eddie Jacobson of Independence, Missouri. He ex-

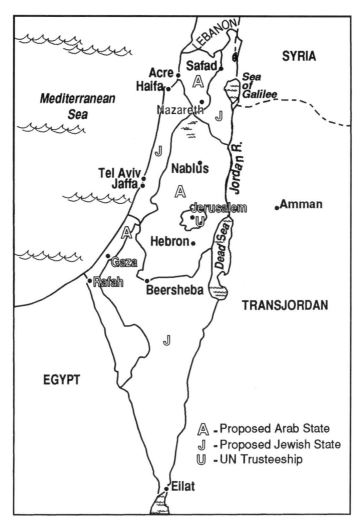

Map 6.1. The U.N. Partition Plan of 1947.

pressed his reverence for the genius of Chaim Weizmann, the veteran Zionist. It is true that he was nearly soured on the proposed Jewish state's cause by the personal hostility of the American Zionist leader, Dr. Abba Hillel Silver.

Nevertheless, when it counted on November 29, the president overruled the State Department and its British mentors, and he ordered a vote for partition. More than that, the United States now threw its weight into the battle by persuading five members of the UN General Assembly to vote for partition: Haiti, Liberia, the Philippines, China, and Ethiopia. Therefore, with as much good cheer as the Attlee government could muster, it announced that the British Mandate would end on May 15, 1948.

With the about-face engineered by President Truman, the British suddenly became acutely aware that by opposing the president, they risked too much. The United States was about to launch the Marshall Plan and make a substantial loan to Britain to revive British prosperity. Clement Attlee realized that his one-sided support for the Arabs might put British interests at risk. Thus, the British were forced to suspend their policy of arming the Arabs while refusing any aid to the Jews.

ARABS BATTLE TO PREVENT A JEWISH STATE

On the day after the partition vote, fighting broke out in Palestine as the Arabs opened attacks on Jews in the principal cities. More alarming, there were Arab riots against Jews throughout the Middle East. This launched the Jewish flight from Arab countries where Jews had lived for millennia. Indeed, even before so many Palestinian Arabs became refugees in 1948, an equally large Near Eastern Jewish refugee problem had its origins in 1947. From his refuge in Beirut, Lebanon, al-Hajj Amin al-Huseini and his Arab Higher Committee, now also in exile, publicly rejected any form of partition. Some—though not all—members of the newly formed Arab League also repudiated recognition of Palestinian partition. Most conspicuous, King Abdullah of Trans-Jordan broke with the other Arabs because, as events proved, he hoped to annex Arab Palestine.

The British, preparing to quit Palestine, withdrew to fortified strongholds. The Arabs were thus free to seize what they could, in preparation for the inevitable war. As many as seven thousand Arab volunteers from neighboring countries, notably Syria, poured into Palestine to join what was called the Arab Liberation Army. It was assumed that when May 15 arrived, the professional armies of the neighboring Arab states would invade Palestine. It was expected that they would crush any army that could be raised by the Hagana, Palmach, IZL, and LEHI. Indeed, Jerusalem was besieged and threatened with starvation months before the British withdrew from the country. They were adamant about refusing the Yishuv the right to arm itself with weaponry purchased abroad. All the odds were against the chance of survival for a Jewish state when May 15 arrived.

PROVISIONAL JEWISH GOVERNMENT

Under the guidance of the Jewish Agency for Palestine, a provisional National Council was created. This body was dominated by David Ben-Gurion and the other leaders who had been in command of the Jewish Agency ever since the end of the war, and especially since the World Zionist Congress of 1946. The National Council elected a thirteen-member Provisional Government, with Ben-Gurion acting as both prime minister and defense minister.

The Provisional Government, enjoying no recognition from the British in the last weeks of the Mandate, felt it had to be ready to act decisively should the Arab world launch its armies against the Yishuv. It was necessary, first of all, to buy the weapons that would be needed. None of that materiel could be brought to Palestine until the British departed. Money had to be raised, principally from the Jewish community of the United States. There was a vast reservoir of weapons—surplus material from the recently ended world war—but the United States would not allow weaponry to be sold to the Hagana. The Soviet Union, at that moment hoping that a desperate Jewish state would become a satellite of Moscow, made quiet arrangements to release surplus U.S. weaponry in the hands of its Czech dependents. Even that, however, could not enter Palestine until the British left. More significant, skilled foreign veterans of the recent war were recruited as volunteers to provide essential services when the moment of full-scale war arrived.

PREPARATIONS FOR WAR

In a New York hotel, the provisional Israeli government founded an organization bearing the name Land and Labor. Small groups of volunteers, recently discharged from the U.S. armed forces, were dispatched to Israel after the British left the country. Typically ships sailed under Panamanian registry, because the United States would not grant visas to volunteers who were likely to be headed to military action in Palestine.

One of the clandestine volunteers has revealed that the Panamanian-registered ship that bore him from New York to Palestine stopped at Marseilles, France, where surplus British weapons held in French warehouses were quietly "loaned" to the agents of Land and Labor.

In nascent Israel, twelve AT6 airplanes designed to be trainers for pilots were fitted with bomb racks on their wings, and thus served as

Israel's first primitive bombers. They were sent to harass the Egyptian troops centered at Gaza.

The Provisional Government also made plans to house and feed the thousands of Jewish refugees who were expected to seek entry into the country once the British left. These would include those who had tried to run the blockade and been caught and interned on Cyprus by the British navy. These would also include displaced persons still in Europe who had survived Hitler, only to discover that they were not welcome to return to hostile homelands in eastern Europe. A growing stream of Jewish refugees fleeing Arab persecution would also join them. These homeless, from whatever origin, often lacked skills, and a good number suffered from physical or emotional ills. They seemed poor raw material out of which to construct a nation, especially one that would have to fight to survive.

On the diplomatic front, the Provisional Government had to present its best diplomatic talent to win the support of other nations, especially those that might expedite the dispatch of supplies and weaponry as the battle reached its crucial point. In April and May, just before the British abandoned the Mandate on May 15, 1948, Ben-Gurion sent a delegation to see Abdullah, king of Trans-Jordan. The envoys were headed by Golda Meir, who later became prime minister. Traveling in disguise, she was charged to keep the Jordanians out of the war. The king was courteous but declined to give such assurances.

Indeed, the British were doing everything possible to encourage the king to seize all of Palestine that had been pledged to the Arabs by the 1947 partition plan. The Jordanian Legion, considered to be the best Arab army, was commanded by General John Glubb, a British officer who had converted to Islam. The Legion was British down to its bagpipes band. It is not surprising that when the Arab-Israeli War of 1948–1949 was over, Britain and Pakistan proved to be the only nations in the world that recognized the Jordanian annexation of what would be called for the next nineteen years the "West Bank."

Ben-Gurion's Plans for a War of Independence

As the anticipated date for British withdrawal approached, a heated debate broke out in the ranks of the Zionist leadership as to whether a sovereign state should be declared. Ben-Gurion had little difficulty in carrying the day in favor of that resolution. As the presumptive prime minister of that state, he had to station his limited armed forces in places where they could hold the Jewish population centers until supplies could begin to enter Palestinian seaports as the last units of the British armed forces withdrew. Jerusalem, the obvious capital of the nascent nation, would have to head the list. It was felt that the Arabs had no intention of accepting the limits set by the UN partition resolution. There was certainly no reason why the Jews should resign themselves to such a renunciation of Jerusalem, even if the UN had declared it to be internationalized.

Ben-Gurion, though not religious, was an astute Bible scholar. He had long ago discovered the route followed in ancient times between Jaffa on the seacoast, and Jerusalem. He thus emphasized preparing a road, however primitive it might be, to ensure the passage of goods to Jerusalem—even if Arab forces closed the main highway, which held to the route of the Turkish road completed in 1867. That new road, proving to be Jerusalem's deliverance, was promptly dubbed the "Burma Road," recalling General Joseph Stillwell's supply road to China during World War II.

Deir Yassin

As part of the attempt to ensure an open route to Jerusalem from the seacoast, IZL and LEHI planned to capture Deir Yassin, a strategically vital Arab fortified village about 5 miles west of Jerusalem. The Arab Liberation Army, composed mostly of Iraqi volunteers, were encamped in the midst of the village's civilian population. In light of what followed, Menachem Begin (who commanded the IZL) has said that loudspeakers were used to give the civilian inhabitants notice that a heavy weaponry bombardment was about to begin. Perhaps the announcement could not be heard above the noise of gunfire, or perhaps the Iraqis would not allow the civilians to flee; nonetheless a catastrophe followed. On April 9, 1948, more than a month before the British withdrawal, IZL and LEHI crushed all resistance at Deir Yassin.

The ensuing avalanche of Arab public relations releases concerning the massacre at Deir Yassin contributed mightily to the flight of Arabs from Palestine. Later pages will be devoted to the origins of the Arab refugee problem.

BIRTH OF THE STATE OF ISRAEL

On Friday, May 14, 1948, on the advent of the Jewish sabbath, twenty-four hours before the official end of the British Mandate, David Ben-Gurion proclaimed the independence of the State of Israel. With

Jerusalem still in danger of Arab siege, the Provisional Government was constrained to launch its career from the Tel Aviv Museum. On the next day five Arab states attacked Israel, deploying their professional armies across the borders of Palestine. Ben-Gurion delivered his first radio address from an air raid shelter as Egyptian planes bombed Tel Aviv. Ben-Gurion, who had beaten Chaim Weizmann in the battle for leadership, sent him a message: "We look forward to the day when we shall see you at the head of the State established in peace."

Standing before a portrait of Theodor Herzl, Ben-Gurion and the other officers of the Provisional Government signed Israel's Declaration of Independence. It reads, in part:

> The Land of Israel was the birthplace of the Jewish people. Here, their spiritual, religious and national identity was formed. Here they achieved independence and created a culture of national and universal significance. Here, they wrote and gave the Bible to the world. . . . We do hereby proclaim the establishment of the Jewish State in Palestine, to be called the State of Israel.

On May 15, at 6:00 P.M. Israel time and 11:00 A.M. Washington time, the British Mandate expired. Eleven minutes later President Truman announced de facto recognition of Israel. The Soviet Union followed by granting de jure recognition, a somewhat higher level of diplomatic acknowledgment implying that a nation had been born by means universally recognized under international law. De facto implies that a nation exists as an unassailable fact, in spite of the irregularity of its birth.

WAR WITH THE ARAB STATES

Israel and the Arab Liberation Army had been at war since November 29, 1947, when partition was proclaimed. Against those forces the Hagana, Palmach, IZL, and LEHI managed to set the stage for adequate self-preservation. On May 15, as the armies of Syria, Jordan, Egypt, and Iraq launched their attack, Israel prepared to fight in the most professionally profitable way.

In contrast, the five allies were disunited and hostile to one another. Christian-ruled Lebanon simply stood aside, declining to become involved. Iraq was willing to express hatred for the new Jewish state but had no intention of fighting tenaciously to advance the interests of Syria or Trans-Jordan. Egypt was willing to use its air force to bomb Israeli cities, but its army was ineffective. Only King Abdullah of Trans-Jordan possessed the military tools and the will to advance his interests. Indeed, his British patron encouraged him to take all parts of Palestine allocated to the Arabs by the UN partition of 1947. Grand Mufti al-Hajj Amin al-Huseini, still waiting to rule all of Palestine, was chagrined to discover that King Abdullah was prepared to usurp his claims. Thus, there was no love lost between the alleged champions of Arab nationalism.

King Abdullah's Jordanian Legion managed to seize and hold the greater part of what the British had called the Districts of Judea and Samaria. After a struggle, General John Glubb managed to crush Jewish resistance in the walled city of historic Jerusalem. The Israelis, however, held most of western Jerusalem, and for the next nineteen years physical barriers kept the city divided. Passage between the two parts of the city was possible, with strict military safeguards at "the Mandelbaum Gate" bridging the gap between the two Jerusalems. The heights of Mt. Scopus were still in Israeli hands when the third and final armistice brought an end to the fighting in November 1949. Thus, during the years in which Jordan held the lands east of Jerusalem (until 1967), the Hebrew University and adjacent property flew the Israeli flag and formed a small Israeli "island" surrounded by Jordanian troops. Convoys were regularly permitted to drive from Israel's advance lines through Jordanian territory to provide food and supplies as well as changes of personnel to Israelis on Mt. Scopus. This peculiar situation accounts for the fact that there are two branches of Hebrew University in Jerusalem, to this day.

Egypt, which had boasted that it would occupy Tel Aviv, failed to do so. It deployed two infantry battalions, one armored battalion, and one infantry regiment. However, a single company of Israeli troops held out against the Egyptians at the settlement of Yad Mordechai, south of Ashdod. The defense of Yad Mordechai bought five days before the Israelis had to retreat. Nevertheless by the time they abandoned the town on May 24, Israel had begun to receive new weapons because the British were no longer able to prevent their arrival. On May 29 four Messerschmitt fighter planes were ready to begin attacks on the Egyptians. The Messerschmitts, like the AT6 trainers and the other planes possessed by the Israelis, were in poor condition. Nevertheless they played a major role in halting the advance of the Egyptian army. By the end of the war in 1949, all that the Egyptians had gained was a small piece of the part of Palestine that had been destined for Arab partition—the coastal district, thenceforth called the Gaza Strip. Egypt was to occupy that territory for nineteen years but never annexed it or offered citizenship to its residents.

The Syrian and Iraqi attacks in the north, after some initial successes, gained nothing for the Arab cause. Iraqis fighting in the Arab Liberation Army centered their attacks on Jerusalem. But after their defeat at Deir Yassin, they made no attempt to make a difference. The Syrians fighting as volunteers without leadership from Damascus retreated quickly. Both Syria and Iraq saw no advantage in fighting a war which could only enlarge Trans-Jordan.

Israel's War of Independence was interrupted by three short truces. During each truce both sides surreptitiously rearmed and prepared for the next round, even though the UN had prohibited such use of truces. Certain events during the three truces had greater and more long-lasting results than anything that occurred on the battlefield. The first rose from an attempt by IZL and LEHI to recruit volunteers and to collect weapons and money abroad, on their own behalf rather than for the Israel Defense Forces per se. Ben-Gurion was no longer prepared to tolerate separate armies that were independent of his central command.

CONFLICT BETWEEN ISRAEL'S LEFT AND RIGHT

Bitter memories still prevented Zionists of the left and right from developing genuine fraternal unity. Although they could and did fight against a common enemy, there were too many words capable of sparking explosions: "Arlosoroff," "the Season," and "King David Hotel" still ignited flames of bitter emotion.

Moreover, both IZL and LEHI had been engaged in raising funds to permit them to operate independently. In fact, the American playwright Ben Hecht even produced a theatrical performance that enjoyed modest success in raising funds for Menachem Begin's IZL.

On May 28, when Israel was just two weeks old, Ben-Gurion created the Israel Defense Forces (IDF) and prohibited the maintenance of any other armed forces. However, Jerusalem had not yet been formally annexed to the fledgling state, so the smaller fighting forces still claimed the right to operate independently there. In June, however, a vessel named *Altalena* anchored boldly at Kfar Vitkin, north of Tel Aviv. The IZL had given the widest possible publicity to the fact that the ship (which bore Ze'ev Jabotinsky's pen name) was loaded with weapons that were gifts from the French government. In addition, even the newspapers trumpeted the fact that the *Altalena* had sailed openly from the French harbor of Port-de-Bouc. It seemed as though the IZL was determined to thumb its nose at the United Nations, the British, and Israel's Provisional Government.

The great mystery is why Georges Bidault, the French foreign minister, was willing to supply the IZL with arms worth $5 million taken from British surpluses stored in French warehouses. Perhaps Bidault hoped to restore French influence in the Middle East. Perhaps he hoped, as a Christian Democrat, to ensure safety for French religious institutions in Palestine. He personally was Anglophile and was hostile to Jews and Zionism. Nevertheless, for reasons not yet known, France found itself supporting the IZL in a way that was certain to shock Ben-Gurion, to alienate the British, and to infuriate the Arabs.

On Friday and Saturday, June 18–19, the agents of Ben-Gurion and Begin negotiated to determine who would receive the weaponry and the 940 IZL volunteers aboard the *Altalena*. The central question was not whether Begin recognized that IZL was to be absorbed into the IDF, but whether IZL could continue to operate independently in Jerusalem— which had not yet been declared part of the sovereign territory of the State of Israel. Menachem Begin could not put aside the rankling suspicions of Ben-Gurion and the political left, whom he regarded as having been guilty of collaborating with the British in the Season. Ben-Gurion regarded Begin and IZL as having Fascist political ambitions.

What might have been settled by prolonged negotiations degenerated into violence as Ben-Gurion and Begin, two very stubborn opponents, dug in their heels and slipped inexorably toward violence. Almost every future leader of the State of Israel, in the next generation, was ultimately involved in this tragedy. Among those involved on either side, in addition to the two chief opponents, were Ezer Weizman, Yigael Yadin, Yigal Allon, and Levi Eshkol. Even a young Palmach officer named Yitzchak Rabin threw a hand grenade against the IZL combatants in the crucial hour and was haunted by that bloodshed to the end of his life.

The conflict erupted on June 21, 1948. The IDF opened fire with a howitzer on the *Altalena*, which had moved off the Tel Aviv beach. Sixteen IZL men died and the ship was sunk. Two members of the IDF died as well. The spectacle of Jews killing Jews in the midst of a war with Arabs horrified the religious members of the Provisional Government. To the end of his life, however, Ben-Gurion never expressed regret for his decisions. He even stated that the howitzer that had fired on the *Altalena* "should be placed in the Temple." It is still called the "sacred Howitzer." Menachem Begin also revealed no regret for his behavior. He and his IZL comrades went on to found the Herut (Freedom) Party, the forerunner of the Likud Party of today. Thus, metaphorically speaking, the sons were left to continue the battles of the fathers.

NEW THREATS FROM THE UNITED NATIONS

During the same short-lived cease-fire of June 11–July 8 that witnessed the *Altalena* crisis, Israel faced an even greater threat. The United Nations Security Council had named mediators who were to attempt to negotiate a settlement between Israel and its Arab enemies. Count Folke Berna-dotte, a member of the Swedish royal family, lent prestige to the effort as chief mediator. Much more active and effective, however, was his assistant, Dr. Ralph Bunche, the first African American to achieve high diplomatic office. Both men owed their loyalty to the Security Council rather than to the General Assembly. Thus, they felt no obligation to pursue the evidently defunct partition plan of November 29, 1947, which had come out of UNSCOP, an organ of the General Assembly.

On June 27, in the midst of that crucial "truce," Count Bernadotte signed a startling, new "peace" plan that had actually been designed by Dr. Bunche, with the blessings of the U.S. State Department and the British Foreign Office. The new plan, which was unacceptable to Arab and Israeli alike, provided the following:

1. Jordan was to receive the Negev, which the 1947 plan had awarded to Israel.

2. Israel was to receive the western Galilee, which the 1947 plan had given to the Arab state.

3. Israel was to have the right to allow unlimited immigration for two years.

4. After two years, the United Nations was to control immigration into Israel.

5. All Arab refugees were to be allowed to return to their former homes in Israel.

6. Out of this new arrangement, an undefined partnership between Israel and Jordan was to emerge.

Israel could not accept the Bernadotte-Bunche Plan because it termi-nated Israel's sovereign control of its right to provide a home for Jewish refugees. Nor could the Israelis be happy to receive the western Galilee as compensation for the loss of the Negev, or half of the acreage origi-nally promised to Israel in the UNSCOP proposal. The loss of the Negev would also deny Israel a window on the Red Sea and shipping lanes to

Asia and Africa. Israeli objections to the readmission of all Arab refugees will be discussed later in these pages as a crucial, central topic.

Nor were the Arabs any happier with the new proposal, because the Egyptians, Syrians, and al-Hajj Amin al-Huseini received no compensations whereas King Abdullah emerged the big winner. Even Abdullah and the Jordanians could not admit that they approved of the plan, because it was so manifestly a benefit won by British influence at the expense of the other Arabs.

Thus, the truce expired on July 8 with everyone prepared for another throw of the dice. Fighting lasted only ten days until the second truce began. Israel widened its corridor to Jerusalem and seized sections of the Galilee as well as the previously all-Arab towns of Lydda and Ramle. It was anticlimactic that the now universally execrated Count Bernadotte was assassinated by three members of LEHI on September 17, 1948. Although world opinion turned strongly against Israel for the murder of the "gentle Count Bernadotte," few Israelis or Arabs mourned him. The most significant result of the murder was that it gave Ben-Gurion the pretext that he needed to take full control of Jewish Jerusalem and to complete the subordination of IZL and LEHI to government authority.

The Israelis realized, however, that there was still a danger that the Bernadotte-Bunche Plan might yet come to life in revised form. They therefore took advantage of two Egyptian breaches of armistice agreements, in October and December 1948, to seize the greater part of the Negev except for the Gaza Strip, which remained in Cairo's hands. Israel had now almost achieved the full extent of the armistice lines, which became the actual boundaries of the new state for the next nineteen years.

END OF THE WAR OF INDEPENDENCE

The last military episode of Israel's War of Independence occurred under unexpected circumstances. On January 7, 1949, Britain sent Royal Air Force fighter planes on a reconnaissance mission over territory on the borders of Egypt that the Egyptians had just lost to the Israelis. Israeli ground forces succeeded in shooting down five of the British planes. To the surprise of the British, the Egyptians distanced themselves from the British, declining to accept the role of British clients. At that point the Israelis, under pressure from the United States, withdrew from Egyptian territory. The enemies of Israel had been surprised and disappointed by President Harry Truman's re-election in November 1948. Israel could not afford to oppose the wishes of a president who had shown himself to be their champion, even against the Arabists in the State Department. The British, on their side, were suddenly awakened to the fact that their sacrifices on behalf of the Arab cause had not won them any friends, even in Egypt. Britain was acutely aware that only the United States could extend the financial aid that was needed to repair the war-ravaged British economy.

Thus, on January 26, 1949, Foreign Secretary Ernest Bevin, after four years of overtly anti-Jewish hostility, suffered condemnation by his own Labor Party in a House of Commons debate on his Palestinian policy. On January 29, Bevin swallowed his pride and invited Joseph Linton, Israel's unofficial representative in London, to visit him. Bevin informed Linton that Britain was about to offer de facto recognition to the new state. It must have choked the foreign secretary to tell Linton that he had never been anti-Zionist. Linton later told a journalist that he had felt sympathy for Bevin at that moment. "After all, who had done more to bring Lord Balfour's policy to final fruition?"

Ralph Bunche and the Rhodes Peace Pacts

The way was now clear for the United Nations to officiate at the negotiation of armistices between Israel and its enemies. The officiant at these marriages of convenience was Dr. Ralph Bunche, who had once been Count Bernadotte's associate. Centering his efforts on the Greek Isle of Rhodes, the mediator achieved pragmatic success by obliging the envoys of Egypt, Jordan, Lebanon, and Syria to meet face-to-face, one-by-one, with the Israelis, in his presence. He avoided obliging the representatives of the four Arab states to meet as a group, because they might have felt constrained to outdo one another in anti-Israeli rhetoric.

The Arabs were not forced to grant de facto recognition to the State of Israel. They were free to refer to the State of Israel by a variety of terms, which permitted them to pretend that a geographic boundary had been drawn, complete with maps, with a belligerent opponent, whose legal existence as a recognized state could be ignored. This deliberate vagueness made possible the creation of a map recognized internationally as that of Israel (see Map 6.2).

Dr. Ralph Johnson Bunche's work was a diplomatic triumph. It did not bring peace—because twenty-two years passed before Jordan and Israel would sign documents formulating a cooperative working relationship, and thirty years passed before Egypt would recognize the State

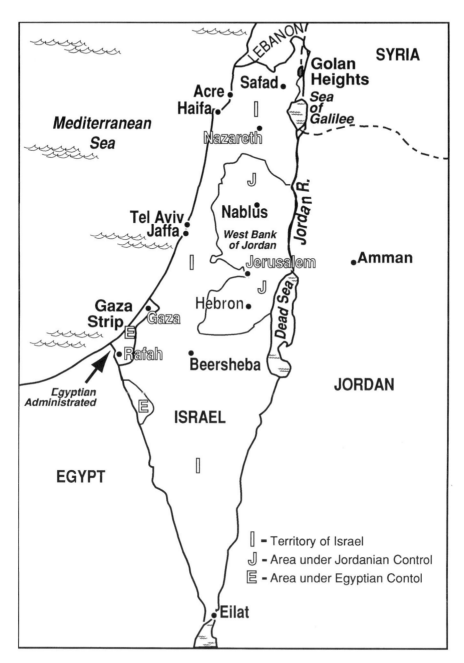

Map 6.2. Israel after the Armistice of 1949.

of Israel and open de jure diplomatic relations, complete with an exchange of ambassadors. However, within that narrow scope of achievement Bunche managed to get Arab and Israeli signatures on armistice agreements: with Egypt on February 24, 1949; with Lebanon on March 23; with Jordan on April 3; and with Syria on July 20. Iraq, which has no common border with Israel, avoided an armistice requiring a face-to-face meeting with Israelis.

Although King Abdullah's realm was now named "Jordan" rather than "Trans-Jordan," his capital was still located at Amman, east of the Jordan River. The king insisted on humane treatment for Jewish captives. However, all Jews were expelled from Jordan's borders, and no Jew could be a resident or enjoy citizens' rights or property in the kingdom. The medieval Jewish Quarter within walled Jerusalem was razed, including the historically treasured synagogues there. Although freedom of access to religious shrines for all worshipers had been pledged in the armistice agreements, that promise was not kept by Jordan. Indeed, no Jew was allowed to visit Judaism's holiest shrine at the surviving western wall of the Temple in Jerusalem or at the Tombs of the Patriarchs in Hebron. A few Jewish visitors are known to have recited prayers in silence while pretending to be tourists idly touching the ancient stones. Acres of ancient graves on the Mount of Olives, facing the eastern walls of Old Jerusalem, were ripped out and the tombstones converted to latrines. Where Jewish tradition holds that the Messiah will come to give judgment on that Mount, the Jordanians allowed the Intercontinental Hotel Chain to construct a luxury holiday spa, which stands there to this day. The Jordanians even allowed a high school to be constructed directly against the south end of the western wall, or the Kotel, obscuring that remnant of the ancient Temple.

From the ramparts of the Old City, Jordanian legionnaires would occasionally snipe at Jewish residents visible within western Jerusalem. That vast area became a "no man's land," deserted and desolate. Jewish tourists who were bold enough to do so could climb as high as possible on the Church of the Dormition on Mount Zion and catch a glimpse of the Kotel, which they could no longer approach.

In due course King Abdullah visited Jericho and was received there, ceremoniously, by all the Arab notables who would consent to welcome the king. They invited him to annex all the lands that he had seized. Thus, what came to be known as the West Bank was joined to Trans-Jordan. For the next nineteen years Judea and Samaria (the geographic nomenclature that had been universally used in Europe while the Turks ruled the country, and that the British had adopted during the Mandate) were temporarily thrust aside. In 1950 the Jordanian Parliament formally annexed the new lands to Jordan. In all the world, only Great Britain and Pakistan recognized the change.

The Arab and Jewish Refugee Questions

Throughout all this upheaval, two questions have survived and remain a haunting reality—even at this date when Israel enjoys recognition de jure by Egypt and Jordan, and recognition de facto by most other Arab states. Reference is made to the Arab and Jewish refugee questions. In 1947, prior to armed conflict, the Arab population of Palestine west of the Jordan River was approximately 1,300,000. Even before the British abandoned Palestine, the Arab population began to flee the country, headed by the wealthiest and best-educated members of the elite. These Arabs made new lives for themselves in an Arab diaspora scattered across the world but centered in the great cities of the Middle East, primarily Beirut and Cairo. Once the British left, the great exodus became a torrent, with Arabs fleeing even when there was no danger for those who stayed.

Abba Hushi, the very left-wing Jewish mayor of Haifa, sent loudspeaker trucks through the Arab neighborhoods begging Arabs to stay. He was concerned that the flight of the Arabs, who were skilled longshoremen, would end Haifa's role as a port city. The Arabs fled nevertheless. A great part of the Arab refugees believed their own propaganda promising that after the Arab armies had driven the Jews into the sea, Arabs could return and take the property of the expelled enemy. It was only as the IDF managed to gain the upper hand that there is evidence that individual military commanders actually expelled Arabs whose property was strategically essential. The only area where there is hard evidence that Arabs were expelled is at Lod, where Israel's largest international airport is now located.

In the territories that became Israel after the armistices of 1949, 700,000 Arabs had fled before the end of 1948. West Jerusalem had had 75,000 Arabs before the war. Only 3,500 remained in 1949. In Jaffa there had once been 70,000 Arabs. Only 3,600 lingered in 1949. Haifa had had 71,000 in 1947. Only 2,900 still resided there in spite of Abba Hushi's pleas that they stay.

The Jewish refugee problem became visible as early as 1946, when street mobs made Jewish flight evident. The ancient Jewish communities of Egypt, Syria, Lebanon, Iraq, Libya, Tunisia, Algeria, and Yemen fled by whatever means came to hand. In North Africa, only Morocco tried to offer assurances to Jews and to discourage flight. Sultan Mohammed and King Hassan II exerted themselves to assure their Jews of security. Morocco remains the only Arab country where a much-reduced but recognizable native Jewish population still thrives.

In Morocco, Algeria, and Tunisia, a great part of the Jews who did flee were able to claim French citizenship. As a result, most of the Jews from the Maghreb, or western North Africa, who reached Israel were the poorest and least educated; they would experience the most difficult adjustment. The Iraqis were glad to see their Jews leave and made it possible for international Jewish philanthropy to fly them out. In a similar way, the Yemenite Jews found it relatively easy to get to British-owned Aden, from which Israeli-chartered aircraft could fly them to Israel. Constituting an entire population of rich and poor, educated and ignorant, the Iraqis and Yemenites have experienced successful absorption in Israel. Whereas many Jews from Algeria have formed a part of Israel's underclass, that has not been true of those complete populations who arrived carrying their civilizations intact. A great proportion of the Jews of Syria, Lebanon, and Egypt reached the United States, assisted by western philanthropy. They have created vibrant and prosperous communities there. There was not a single Jewish refugee who needed a home after 1948. After 1948, those Arab countries which seized and profited from the property of departed Jews could have applied that wealth to the resettlement of many homeless Arab refugees, but they did not. Arab refugees continue to be promised a return to their pre-1948 homes.

The Arab refugees remain a serious problem to this day. For example, during the Persian Gulf War of 1991 hundreds of thousands of Palestinian Arabs were expelled from Kuwait simply because Yassir Arafat had committed the PLO to supporting Iraq against Kuwait and Saudi Arabia, even though these vulnerable laborers had no stake in that struggle. Ironically, Kuwait desperately needed the labor of the expelled workers.

Thus, over a half-century the United Nations Relief and Works Agency (UNRWA) has become a permanent bureaucratic fixture, feeding and housing a growing Arab population that could have been absorbed and housed by the Arab nations themselves immediately after the events of 1948. The ration cards of refugees who die are rarely surrendered, and a growing, unemployed and rootless population fills the camp-cities and feeds on resentment toward Israel.

Terrorism after 1949

The cessation of war in 1949 did not mean the return of peace. Only the border with Lebanon was quiet, as that country's Christian-led government declined to involve itself in the battles of its Moslem neighbors. Until the war of 1956, Egypt used the Gaza Strip to launch raids against Israelis in the Negev Desert. Obviously, the Israelis retaliated, helping to keep the southern front dangerous. Syria employed terror techniques ranging from artillery barrages launched from the Syrian Golan Heights on Israelis in the Galilee, to attempts at redirecting the streams that feed precious water to Israel. Israelis effectively prevented Syria from tampering with the water supply with effective artillery barrages. Jordan's legionnaires sniped at Israelis across the border. However, the armistices of 1949 gave Israel a breathing space to create a solid base for a new nation.

7

Years of Growth, 1949–1966

COALITION GOVERNMENT

On January 25, 1949, before the Rhodes armistices had been concluded, Israel conducted its first election to replace the Provisional Government that had led the country to independence. Of the 120 members of the first Knesset, 46 belonged to Mapai, the centrist and moderately socialist Labor Party. Consequently David Ben-Gurion, as the nation's first prime minister, had to form a coalition that would ensure his cabinet of a minimum of 61 votes. Indeed, no Israeli party has ever won a majority of the seats in a Knesset, with the result that all the country's prime ministers have had to seek coalition partners in order to govern.

The first coalition rested heavily on support from the religious parties. It was a partnership equally satisfactory to the socialist, secularist Ben-Gurion and his orthodox Jewish partners. By working with the orthodox, the prime minister was freed from the dictates of Mapam, the far-left Marxist party that would have made insistent demands more extreme than the pragmatic Ben-Gurion could tolerate. Ben-Gurion could accept a "status quo" agreement with the nationalist religious parties because they had limited demands. The Status Quo agreement, which survived without serious challenge for forty years, emphasized that:

1. The orthodox chief rabbinate would control questions of personal status, namely, determining whether individuals are Jewish or not.

2. The organs of the government would accept the Jewish dietary laws, the cessation of unnecessary labor on the sabbath, and the validity of marriages and divorces as they relate to official actions.

It did not particularly disturb Ben-Gurion that the orthodox parties sought to control the Ministries of Education and the Interior. The first Knesset met in Jerusalem on February 14. Dr. Chaim Weizmann was confirmed as president.

The Law of Return

On July 5, 1950, the Knesset unanimously approved a Law of Return assuring Jews of the right to enter Israel and to obtain citizenship there, except for certain categories of persons accused of crimes in other countries or behavior that Israeli judges might categorize as subversive. In that one gesture, Israel achieved the primary goal of Zionism by ending the ancient problem of homeless Jewish refugees. However, the Knesset was unsuccessful in its attempt to obtain ratification for a constitution. Thus, to this day, Israel's Supreme Court and lesser legal bodies have had to wrestle with layers of Ottoman law, British mandatory regulation, and the requirements set forth by the religious courts governing personal status in Judaism, Islam, and Christianity.

The Right of Return created unique problems for the infant state. Even as the War of Independence was fought, all the Jews interned by the British on Cyprus, and all those confined in European displaced persons camps, were free to enter Israel if they chose to do so. Those numbers were matched by the rising tide of Jews fleeing from or being expelled by the Arab states. Between 1948 and 1951, 700,000 immigrants more than doubled the Jewish population of Israel to 1,350,000. *Maabarot*, or transit camps, were hastily erected to provide shelter for these masses. From the days of the British high commissioner Sir Ronald Storrs, British mandatory decree had required that all buildings constructed in Jerusalem be built of stone, or at least be faced with stone. In the 1950s, however, in the desperate need to house immigrants, whole sections of that beautiful city were blighted by apartment houses thrown together

with haphazard building materials. In an attempt to disperse a population that wanted to live in Jerusalem, Tel Aviv, or Haifa, the new immigrants found themselves settled (often against their will) in new
development towns, some of them uncomfortably close to hostile borders. Religious oriental Jews from Arab countries found themselves
housed in secularist kibbutzim where they were under pressure to abandon a way of life that had been unbroken for generations.

The government was forced to feed and house these multitudes even
while fighting a war, and to attempt to support normal government services. Food was in extremely short supply, and rationing was imposed.
All medical services had to be mobilized because a great proportion of
the survivors of Hitler's death camps were suffering from severe physical
and mental disabilities. The American and other charitable organizations
that were struggling to raise the money and supplies to meet these unprecedented demands urged Ben-Gurion to place limits on the numbers
of immigrants admitted. This he refused to do. Instead the masses of
veteran Israelis supported the government and bore the sacrifices that
such hardship imposed.

National Water Pipeline

In the crucial years before 1967 the most important accomplishment
of Israel's government was the completion of a national water pipeline.
As early as 1950, Israel had undertaken a hydrological survey of the
Jordan River valley. In September 1953 plans were made to build a diversion canal to tap river water about 12 miles north of the Sea of Galilee,
elevated about 900 feet above that body of water. The government's intention was to allow water to flow by normal gravity to other parts of
the country, producing hydroelectric power at the same time. However,
the diversion canal touched on a demilitarized zone established by the
Israeli-Syrian Armistice Agreement of 1949. Some small-scale military
conflicts broke out. Thus, with the United States pressing Israel to abandon the project, it was necessary to find an alternative to ensure water
supplies.

In 1956 Israel found a better method of obtaining water; a system that
exists today. As the Sea of Galilee, or Yam Kineret, is the largest body
of fresh water entirely within Israel's borders, a pumping station could
be located at the northeastern end of the lake. Since then Israel has gradually created the National Water Carrier, which consists of a network of
pipes, aqueducts, open canals, reservoirs, tunnels, dams, and pumping

stations. All are part of an integrated grid. Where salt springs would pollute water otherwise suitable for human needs, they are carefully diverted. Israel's natural aquifers, or underground water supplies, supplement the waters from the Sea of Galilee. Only in the far south of the Negev has it been necessary to use desalinated sea water, an extremely expensive but necessary resource. Israeli science has done advanced research to discover methods to make maximum use of limited and expensive water supply and even water containing some salt.

In years of plentiful rainfall, the Sea of Galilee's waters are pumped into storage areas as reserves for the needs of drier years. The amount of water allowed to flow south to the Jordan River is monitored carefully to avoid waste.

In Israel's long battle to make the best use of its water resources, it has met one notable, self-inflicted defeat. This involves the decision to dry up the swampy portion of the Jordan Valley, north of the Sea of Galilee, known as Lake Hula. In the early twentieth century the Hula was a breeding ground for insects carrying pestilential diseases. As the nascent State of Israel began its struggle to control all its water resources, a decision was made to dry up all the Hula except for a small area to be preserved as a refuge for migratory birds. Today, however, Israel has discovered that the area is not the agricultural bonanza that its engineers had hoped to create. Persons who are involved in the tourist industry and farmers who enjoy government subsidy are struggling to keep the Hula area dry. However, the government is committed to a compromise that will restore a small lake and a carefully monitored and enlarged refuge for migratory birds.

CHANGES IN NEIGHBORING GOVERNMENTS

In the midst of Israel's struggle to ensure its vital water needs, political changes were taking place in the neighboring Arab countries that would affect Israeli political decisions. The first of these was the assassination of Jordan's king, Abdullah, by agents of al-Hajj Amin al-Huseini on July 20, 1951. The grand mufti of Jerusalem, who had been Zionism's most intractable foe during all the years of the British Mandate, struck down the king because Abdullah was regarded as having seized the Palestinian supremacy that the mufti claimed for himself. Although Abdullah had seized as much of Cis-Jordanian Palestine as his army could conquer, he had always been the one Arab national leader with whom the Israelis could communicate in a civil and confidential manner. At his death, his inheritance seemed in dispute. Abdullah's son and heir, Prince Talal, suffered from severe emotional problems, and a regency quietly arranged for his placement in a European sanatorium. Talal's son Hussein, who was hastily enthroned, had been born on November 14, 1935, and was not yet of age. For the moment, the relatively peaceful neighborhood that King Abdullah had maintained seemed suddenly uncertain. Following a series of terrorist attacks against Israel from Jordanian soil, Israel struck back in October 1953 by attacking the Jordanian village of Qibya, which was said to be a principal fedayeen, or Arab guerrilla, base. Sixty-three civilians were killed, including women and children. The attack on Qibya was condemned both by the United Nations and the United States. However, after Qibya, the new and untried government of young King Hussein did make a determined effort to patrol the border and prevent terrorist infiltration. Thus, the Jordan Valley became much quieter and safer.

The next challenge to Israel's peace arose in Egypt. In the aftermath of Egypt's failure to win more than the Gaza Strip in 1949, Prime Minister Nakroshy was assassinated. Amid increasingly destructive street riots and demonstrations, the army seized control. On the night of July 23–24, 1952, young army officers overthrew King Farouk and forced him into exile. Although Major-General Mohammed Naguib was the titular leader of the officers' revolt, the so-called Free Officers were actually led by Colonel Gamal Abdel Nasser. In February 1954, Nasser emerged as Egypt's virtual dictator. He had an ambitious political program to occupy his attention, but no one knew whether he intended peace or war against Israel.

Another area in which Israel found itself faced by troublesome neighbors was Syria. This involved Syria's constant attempts to disrupt Israel's efforts to complete the union of its water resources.

NEW POLITICAL LEADERSHIP IN ISRAEL

Along with this interaction of untested elements, the Jewish state met an unanticipated political crisis. In 1953, Prime Minister Ben-Gurion resigned his office in the face of hostility within his own Mapai Party. He left the cabinet altogether early in 1954. He was replaced in the prime-ministership by Moshe Sharrett, a peaceful dove who stood in marked contrast to the aggressive and militant Ben-Gurion. Sharrett, one of the few Israeli leaders who had served in the Turkish army in World War I, was convinced that peaceful negotiation with the Arabs was possible.

He immediately entered secret and confidential conversations with Gamal Abdel Nasser, the Egyptian strongman. Sharrett believed that Nasser wanted peace and would cooperate in reaching it, once his own domestic political situation would allow it.

Within the Israeli cabinet, even though Sharrett was prime minister the other principal posts were held by allies of the old warrior, Ben-Gurion. Moshe Dayan was army chief of staff, and Shimon Peres was director of the Defense Ministry. However, Pinchas Lavon, a hostile rival of Dayan and Peres, was minister of defense. Such a chorus of political foes in conflict is often found in parliamentary cabinet systems where natural enemies are thrown together to save party unity. Lavon was regarded as a dove, naturally allied to Prime Minister Sharrett. Herein a mystery emerges. Did Lavon make a complete turnaround and become a warlike hawk without telling Sharrett of his changed position? Even more strange, did Lavon become a disciple of Ben-Gurion without revealing that he had become an ally of Dayan and Peres?

The Lavon Affair

What followed remains veiled to this day. According to the somewhat muddied best evidence, Lavon decided, without involving the other cabinet hawks, that it was hopeless to expect Egypt's Nasser to make peace. Thus, without clearing his actions with anyone else, Lavon launched a series of retaliatory attacks on Egypt in response to all terrorist attacks that had been launched against Israel from the Gaza Strip. This might have been justified and tolerable. However, Lavon used Israeli agents and Egyptian Jews to plant bombs and set fires in Cairo and Alexandria. Among the targets chosen were the libraries of the U.S. Information Service. No lives were threatened, but Lavon's goal seems to have been to alienate Egypt and the United States from each other. The other mysterious figure in this plot was Binyamin Givly, director of military intelligence, who was allegedly interested in terrorizing the British in Egypt so that they would not quit Egypt and would lay the blame for all mischief on Nasser's head. However, the entire plot failed. Nasser captured the agents. Two Israelis were hung. Six agents were sentenced to long prison terms. Two Egyptian Jews were acquitted and released.

In the upshot, Sharrett's peace policy died. The Lavon Affair, as it is known, was examined by a commission of inquiry in January 1955. Lavon lost office, but the truth of the full extent of guilt was never ascertained as Lavon, Peres, and Dayan pointed accusatory fingers at one another. Only Givly escaped unharmed. In the aftermath of the scandal, Sharrett lost office. Ben-Gurion returned to the cabinet as minister of defense just before a new Knesset was elected in 1955. In June 1956 he was once again prime minister. However, he now headed a Mapai Party thoroughly demoralized by the Lavon Affair. Though Sharrett remained in political life until he died in 1965, his short stint as prime minister was his only climb "to the top of the greasy pole."

THE BAGHDAD PACT

On the international stage, what followed was a scenario so fantastic that it defies credibility. However, the facts as recorded here seem irrefutable. In 1954, U.S. Secretary of State John Foster Dulles agreed to arm Iraq, adding it to the tier of allies including Greece, Turkey, and Iran. This solid bloc was intended to serve as a shield for the Middle East, deterring Soviet aggression in that region. The so-called Baghdad Pact frightened both Israel and Egypt, although for different reasons. Israel feared that arming the Iraqis might make that Arab state ready for renewed war with Israel; after all, Iraq had never signed an armistice with Israel. Egypt feared that Jordan, Iraq's immediate neighbor, might join the Baghdad Pact, thereby making Iraq rather than Egypt the dominant Arab power. As it turned out Jordan did not join the Pact and instead turned cool to its British advisors, firing even General John Bagot Glubb, who had organized and trained the Arab Legion. Thus ended thirty-four years in which Britain had dominated the Hashemite kings at Amman.

Nasser of Egypt soon realized that there was no danger that Jordan or Syria would join the Baghdad Pact. However, he had already begun to use Egyptian radio to broadcast tirades against European and Christian rule. That double-headed message was effective with Arab Moslems who had been captivated by Nasser's Arab nationalism.

EGYPT ENTERS THE SOVIET BLOC

On September 27, 1955, Nasser announced an arms deal with Czechoslovakia acting as an agent of the Soviet Union. Thus, the Baghdad Pact became self-defeating for President Eisenhower and Secretary Dulles, because it opened the Arab Mediterranean as a base for Soviet expansionism. For the Israelis, also, the sudden intrusion of three hundred tanks and two hundred MiG-15 jet fighters represented a frightening shift against Israel in the regional balance of power.

Quite unpredictably, Britain found itself suddenly prepared to work closely with Israel against their common enemy. Nasser's appeals to the Egyptian masses against Britain and France had made them potential Israeli allies. In this light Britain presented its most persuasive arguments to press the United States to join in opposing a World Bank loan to finance the construction of Egypt's Aswan High Dam. In an immediate reaction, Nasser announced on July 26, 1956, that he had nationalized the Suez Canal Company. The British prime minister, Sir Anthony Eden, then informed President Eisenhower that Britain would be forced to take military action against Egypt.

ANGLO-FRENCH-ISRAELI ALLIANCE

The Irish diplomat and historian Conor Cruise O'Brien, who knew all the principal actors in this drama, speculates that the British wanted to defeat Nasser without alienating their remaining Arab friends. To do so, the British and French would have to encourage Israel to attack Egypt. In that scenario Britain and France could then intervene, when Nasser was in retreat, but quickly enough for Paris and London to pretend to be defenders of world order. They could then retrieve control of the Suez Canal for themselves while acting as referees who had come to separate the Egyptian and Israeli combatants. In other words, Israel was to consent to play the role of the villain while Britain and France assumed heroic stature. Prime Minister Ben-Gurion made the decision to accept such embarrassment in order to end the losses inflicted by fedayeen terrorists and to force the opening of the Red Sea to ships trading with Israel. In return, France would supply Israel with heavy weaponry and aircraft to match the armaments being sent to Egypt by the USSR. To conclude these agreements, Moshe Dayan, Israel's army chief of staff, and Shimon Peres, director-general of the Defense Ministry, as well as Ben-Gurion himself, made very quiet visits to France. Golda Meir made her entry to the front of the diplomatic stage by accepting office as minister of foreign affairs.

With all preparations made, on October 29, 1956, Israel began a surprise attack on Egypt by dropping paratroopers over the Sinai Desert. Within eight days Israel held all of the Sinai, incidentally eliminating all the fedayeen terrorist bases. Here ensued a tragedy of errors.

Israel moved so quickly and its success was so complete that it was hard for Britain and France to make a claim that they were merely buffers striving to separate the Israeli and Egyptian foes. Somewhat belatedly Britain and France sent their own paratroopers to the Suez Canal to separate the Israeli and Egyptian armies. They reached there much too late to be convincing, landing on November 6. President Eisenhower and Secretary of State Dulles took personal affront at having been excluded from what was obviously an Anglo-French-Israeli plot. The United States feared that the Suez Canal campaign might bring the USSR into military action.

The United States Supports the USSR

Thus, the United States brought a resolution before the Security Council of the United Nations ordering a cease-fire and requiring Israel to return to its own border. Britain and France then vetoed the American resolution. November 1956 witnessed the United States and the Soviet Union united in opposition to America's most important allies. As the USSR at that moment was busy crushing rebellion in Hungary and protests in Poland, America's surprising and unexpected support for Soviet goals in Egypt made it easier for Moscow to maintain its empire in Europe.

In retrospect, President Eisenhower and Secretary Dulles may have unwittingly prolonged the life of the Soviet Union and dealt a death blow to the imperial plans of Britain and France. It was, however, Israel that felt the wrath of the world. Even Britain and France joined the majority of the United Nations General Assembly when on November 7, by a vote of 65 to 1, Israel was ordered to make immediate withdrawal from the Sinai. Israel, of course, supplied the one dissenting vote.

ISRAEL GAINS SECURITY

However, what seemed to be an unmitigated defeat was turned into an Israeli victory by the skill of Foreign Minister Golda Meir and Israel's delegate to the United Nations, Abba Eban. Israel consented to withdraw from the Sinai provided that an acceptable international peacekeeping force would guarantee that fedayeen terrorist raids by Egypt would cease, and the Straits of Tiran would be left open for Israeli shipping. It was the latter that would make Eilat, Israel's Red Sea port city, a vital and direct link to Africa and Asia, releasing Israel from its dependence on the Suez Canal, which was closed to its ships.

By March 1957, when the negotiations for withdrawal were completed, Israel had once again achieved reasonably good relations with the United

States. Israeli foreign minister Meir was able to obtain clearance from Secretary Dulles for a speech she delivered to the United Nations, in which she said, "Interference by armed force, with ships of Israeli flag, exercising free and innocent passage in the Gulf of Aqaba and through the Straits of Tiran will be regarded by Israel as an attack entitling it to exercise its inherent right of self-defense." Henry Cabot Lodge, the U.S. representative at the United Nations, had helped to compose Meir's speech, and he gave it full public support. That lent it a solid legal foundation ten years later, in the Six-Day War, when Egypt once again challenged Israel's maritime traffic in the Red Sea. In any event, the settlement of March 1957 gave Israel ten years of relative peace with Egypt.

Growing Immigration and Trade

Israel's greater security during the period 1957–1967 witnessed an upsurge of immigration, mostly Jews from North Africa as well as portions of eastern Europe not under complete Soviet control. In 1954 the Jewish population of Israel was 1,526,000, or 88.8 percent of a population of 1,718,000. By 1967 the Jewish population had risen to 2,384,000 or 85.8 percent of a total population of 2,777,000. The considerable growth in Arab population was accounted for by a high birth rate and Israeli willingness to allow Arab refugees, with close family ties to Israeli Arabs, to return. At certain points the Israelis, for the first time, assigned quotas because they felt that they could not absorb unlimited immigration.

Israel's exports doubled, and the gross national product increased 10 percent annually. The most rapid growth took place in metals, machinery, electronics, and chemicals. Israel became self-supporting in food production, though rising prosperity led to increases in such imports as red meat and luxury fish products. The Israelis continued to suffer an unfavorable balance of trade largely because of the burden of maintaining heavy armaments.

Diplomatic Successes

The numbers of nations in Latin America, Asia, and Africa opening diplomatic relations with Israel steadily increased. Foreign Minister Meir took special interest in bringing Africans to Israel for technical training in fields as varied as agriculture, water management, and medicine. Israeli engineers and other technical experts also became prominent as advisors, especially in Africa.

A particularly touchy subject involved Israel's relations with the new West German Federal Republic. The task was made easier by the fact that such German leaders as Conrad Adenauer and Willy Brandt were free of the Nazi taint, having consistently opposed Hitler. However, Israelis such as Menachem Begin, the former commander of the IZL, campaigned strongly against accepting reparations from the Germans in 1952. Begin also took the lead in protesting the sale of Israeli-manufactured weapons to the Germans in 1959. Furious and sometimes disorderly street demonstrations accompanied Begin's angry speeches. However, in the long run the Israeli mainstream accepted the normalization of relations with Germany.

Adenauer and Ben-Gurion formed a good working relationship, and German Jews who had fled the Nazis found the reparations payments a tremendous aid in adjusting to their new life. In the decades that followed, as German products filled Israeli shops and German autos filled the streets, it was no longer considered shameful to abandon the old boycott. However, only the boldest musicians would dare to play Wagner for an Israeli audience.

The Eichmann Trial

On May 11, 1960, Adolf Eichmann, a principal architect of the Nazi extermination of six million Jews, was discovered hiding in Argentina. Peter Malkin, chief of operations for Mossad, Israel's Secret Service, and a selected force of Israeli undercover agents kidnapped him and carried him to Israel, without eliciting too vehement a protest by the Argentine government. A public trial in Jerusalem opened in April 1961. Eichmann was found guilty. After his appeal to the Supreme Court failed, he was hanged on May 30, 1962. No other person has ever suffered capital punishment in Israel.

Origins of the PLO

In the relative quiet that Israel enjoyed in the years after the 1956 Sinai campaign, one threatening cloud hung on the political horizon. In May 1964 a band of Arab leaders, residing in Jordanian East Jerusalem, founded the Palestine Liberation Organization. The PLO, as it came to be called, was not an activist terrorist organization at first. It became that as a result of the union of three elements.

The first was the emergence of a Syrian-sponsored fedayeen terrorist organization called Fatah, whose intent was to attack Israel from Lebanese or Jordanian soil. The Syrians would thereby avoid direct Israeli retaliation. The second was the rise to power in Fatah of Yassir Arafat, the nom de guerre of Rahman Rauf Arafat al-Quana al-Husseini. It is not clear whether he was born in Gaza or Cairo, though he always claimed to have been born in Jerusalem. The third was to be the composition of the Palestine National Covenant in 1968. All of this, however, lay ahead.

For the Israelis, until 1966 their survival consisted mostly of building the infrastructure of the state and striking as hard as possible against terrorist raids from Lebanese or Jordanian bases. Syria, which created and orchestrated these attacks, avoided direct confrontation. This has consistently been Syria's over-riding strategy regardless of which strongman has held power at Damascus.

During that relatively peaceful decade Egypt was constrained to adopt quiet behavior by the agreements of 1956–1957, negotiated by the United Nations and the United States. All was about to change, however.

8

The Six-Day War and Heady Self-Confidence, 1967–1973

CHANGES IN ISRAELI GOVERNMENT

Ben-Gurion's Last Ministry

In 1955, in the aftermath of the Lavon Affair, Ben-Gurion returned to power once more. First he assumed the office of the disgraced Lavon as defense minister and then, just before the national elections scheduled for that year, he became prime minister. His last years in high office, 1955–1963, marked a dismal ending to the years of glory in which he had taken the leading role in creating the State of Israel.

A new generation that was not a product of eastern Europe was replacing the veteran pioneers of the Second and Third Aliyoth. In Mapai, Ben-Gurion's Labor Party, there was a growing demand by young newcomers for an attempt to negotiate peace with the Arabs. Ben-Gurion gave the appearance of being militant and overbearing. In 1961 he called a snap election and managed to win the prime-ministership. (As noted elsewhere, Israel, like most parliamentary democracies, has empowered the government to call new elections if the cabinet believes that electoral victory is possible.) However, it was increasingly apparent that he would not dominate his party as he had in the past. When the split within

Mapai became bitter and personal, it was Ben-Gurion who led his followers in secession. He resigned the prime-ministership in 1963. His new
party, Rishimat Poalei Yisrael (the Israel Workers' List), was known by
the acronym RAFI, for the first letters of its Hebrew name. In the election
of 1965 Mapai and a small far-left socialist ally won 45 seats. RAFI won
10 seats, which meant that it was in no position to challenge Mapai. Ben-
Gurion thus ended his career as the giant of Israeli political life.

The Eshkol Ministry

Mapai elevated a relative unknown to the office of prime minister in
1963, when Ben-Gurion broke with the party. Levi Eshkol, who headed
the government from 1963 to 1969, gave the impression of being gentle,
conciliatory, and even weak. His minister of foreign affairs, Abba Eban,
argued strongly for attempts to negotiate peace with the Arabs. It was
not surprising that the new Israeli appearance of passivity encouraged
the Arabs to pursue the path of aggressive hostility.

CHANGES IN THE ARAB STATES

Rise and Fall of the United Arab Republic

In 1958 Syria voluntarily merged its sovereignty with that of Egypt,
creating a short-lived entity called the United Arab Republic (UAR). This
elevated Nasser's prestige in the Arab world in spite of his setback at
Suez in 1956. However, his prestige suffered dramatic ups and downs.
In September 1961 the Syrians quit the short-lived UAR, leaving Nasser
to nurse an empty title. With Damascus publicly sneering at Cairo, the
Iraqi dictator Karim Qassem also sought to make points with his people
by radio polemics directed against both Egypt and Syria.

Nasser and the Arab World

The disunity of Israel's three most powerful neighbors caused Jerusalem to develop a false sense of security. At the same time, the Soviet
Union gave Nasser the opportunity he sought to revive his prestige. On
May 13, 1967, the Soviet ambassador to Egypt informed Nasser that Moscow's intelligence service had learned that Israel planned to attack Syria
on May 17 and that the Israeli army was concentrating in the Galilee for
a surprise attack. The Irish diplomat Conor Cruise O'Brien speculates

that the Soviets knew that Israel had no such plan, but that Moscow hoped that Nasser would attack Israel. That would reunite the USSR's clients, Egypt and Syria, strengthening Moscow without risking military action by the United States.

On May 15 Nasser called up his reserves and began to send combat troops into the Sinai in spite of the pledges to avoid such a confrontation that had been worked out by President Eisenhower in 1957. Levi Eshkol sent word to Nasser through third parties that Israel had no hostile intentions against either Egypt or Syria. Nasser interpreted Eshkol's messages to mean that Israel was intimidated and that Egypt could humiliate Israel without risk of war. For Nasser, perhaps it seemed that he could easily build his own prestige and reclaim the title as leader of the Arab world.

On May 18 the Egyptians informed U Thant, the Burmese secretary-general of the United Nations, that he was "to terminate the existence of the U.N.E.F. (United Nations Expeditionary Force) on the soil of the U.A.R. and in the Gaza Strip."

Nasser may have expected some resistance by U Thant, or at least a delay. Instead the secretary-general gave his immediate acceptance of the Egyptian demand. Although U Thant may have been unable to stop Nasser if he truly wanted war, nevertheless his willingness to cooperate with Egypt pushed Nasser into aggressive actions that he may not have truly intended. Israel, however, suddenly found itself stripped of the evanescent sense of security that the illusions of 1957 had spun like a spider's web.

On May 22 in the rapid evolution of an unplanned war, Nasser informed all neutrals that he had closed the Gulf of Aqaba to ships carrying strategic materiel to Israel. As one cannon placed at Sharm el-Sheikh could prevent ships from entering the narrow waters approaching Eilat, Israel, Nasser thereby established an effective blockade. Under international law, the creation of an enforceable blockade is an act of war. Therefore Israel and Egypt were as surely at war as if cannons had been fired.

Israeli foreign minister Abba Eban urged his government to exhaust every legal expedient before rushing to war. He flew immediately to Paris, London, and Washington to obtain the support of the three democracies. At Paris, Charles de Gaulle informed Eban that France had no obligation to defend the guarantees won by Israel in 1957. This was the first hint that France was about to change its position, ending the role of France as Israel's source of arms. Britain's prime minister, Harold

Wilson, was friendly but gave no commitments. In Washington, President Lyndon Johnson confirmed that the United States stood firmly behind the commitments made by John Foster Dulles, Henry Cabot Lodge, and President Eisenhower to Golda Meir in 1957. However, Secretary of State Dean Rusk, on behalf of President Johnson, made it clear on May 31 that the United States would not take any naval action to open the waters leading to Eilat, except as part of a United Nations expeditionary force. The European nations showed no inclination to risk their ties to the Arab world by using force against Nasser. Thus, the guarantees so solemnly given to Israel in 1957 proved worthless in 1967. It may very well have been that President Johnson, despite his good intentions toward Israel, was forced to keep his attention focused on Vietnam, where either the Russians or the Chinese would have welcomed American distraction in the Middle East.

THE SIX-DAY WAR

Even the peace-seeking Abba Eban saw no hope for American help in breaking Nasser's blockade. On May 31 he informed General Yitzchak Rabin, Israel's chief of staff, that he had no objections to the opening of military action. On June 1 General Moshe Dayan, who had been chief of staff during the 1956 Sinai campaign, became minister of defense in Prime Minister Eshkol's cabinet. On that same day a Government of National Unity was formed, so that Menachem Begin and the Israeli right-wing parties joined their old foes, the Israeli socialist left, in the cabinet.

On the morning of June 5, in a preemptive strike, the Israeli air force surprised the Egyptians and destroyed their air force on the ground, before the surprised pilots could even take to the air. The Israeli army overran the entire Sinai Peninsula, even more rapidly than in 1956. Suddenly the Israelis found themselves in possession of hundreds of Soviet tanks and facing the surrender of so many Egyptian prisoners of war that there were major problems in the organization of their internment. Yet even in the midst of the debacle, Nasser continued to boast of victories. The United Nations, certain that Israel faced defeat, saw no immediate need to order a cease-fire. King Hussein of Jordan, believing Nasser's claims of victory, leaped into the war. Syria joined what it expected to be Israel's destruction.

Because of Israel's small population, the nation's armed forces rest on reservists. Men serve in the army for three years and then continue to give a month of every year to *miluim*, or reserve duty. Women serve for two years before receiving discharge. By use of radio broadcasts announcing codes for military units, reservists learn when their contingents are being called to service. Since the country has only a small professional, career Defense Force, civilian life comes to a halt in the middle of a war.

Now, in 1967, careful staff planning made possible a war in which the full force of the Israeli army could subdue the Egyptians in three days, turn to face the Jordanians while the Egyptian front grew quiet, then turn again with some of the same troops to face the Syrians while the Jordanians were forced beyond the Jordan River. In the last days of the campaign the Israelis climbed the Golan Heights, driving the Syrians out of the artillery emplacements from which they had bombarded civilian farmers in the Galilee for nineteen years.

On June 10 the United Nations, suddenly aware of what had happened, ordered a cease-fire. The Six-Day War came to an end. For the Israelis, victory was so complete, sudden, and unexpected that they were unprepared to take full advantage of it.

AFTERMATH OF THE SIX-DAY WAR

Reaction in Israel

During the nineteen years when Jordan held Judea and Samaria, formerly called the West Bank of the kingdom of Jordan, the Jordanians moved aggressively to erase all evidence of previous Jewish residence there. All Jews were expelled, including those pietists of the Old Yishuv who were strongly anti-Zionist and hostile to the political State of Israel. The entire Jewish Quarter of walled Jerusalem was destroyed, including some thirty-five synagogues, many of which housed historic treasures. Before the Arab terror of 1920–1936 drove many Jews out of the walled Old City, an estimated 30,000–40,000 Jews lived not only in the Jewish Quarter on Mt. Zion but scattered throughout the Moslem, Christian, and Armenian Quarters as well. Even at the last hour of the siege of Jerusalem in 1948, 25,000 Jews held out in the Old City until they were forced to leave. Now, with the sacred shrines of the three great monotheistic religions in Israeli hands, Israel moved with deliberate slowness to restore the Jewish Quarter without trespassing on Moslem, Christian, or Armenian rights.

What emerged was an architectural masterpiece. The new Jewish

Quarter made plans for housing only 2,500 permanent residents in dwellings designed to dovetail with one another while retaining the style and appearance of the Old Quarter destroyed in 1948. Israel made no attempt to take custody of the Temple Mount from the Moslem Waqf, which exercised control of Islam's holy places at Al-Haram and El-Aqsa. The Israelis did, however, create a large plaza before the Kotel, Judaism's holiest shrine, and for the first time allowed Jewish synagogual prayer to take place, featuring separate facilities for men and women. During the years that followed, Israeli archeologists were allowed to open and explore ancient tunnels at the foot of the Temple Mount. Taking advantage of the total destruction of the Jewish Quarter by the Jordanians, archeologists were allowed to examine the substrata of earth before new building was begun. Where historically valuable remains including ancient buildings were found, they were preserved beneath the new buildings under construction. Most notably the Cardo, an entire Roman market street, was excavated; and selected modern shops were licensed to operate there. Portions of the restored Jewish Quarter were set aside for *yeshivot* (rabbinical seminaries), schools, student hostels, and commercial enterprises.

Because the restored Jewish Quarter was deliberately limited to a small population, the government of Levi Eshkol moved speedily to create Jewish residential neighborhoods to the north and south of the Old City, ensuring that Israel's reunited capital could not be easily partitioned by its enemies. In fact, newspapers reported that one of the first riders to board a Number 9 bus when service to Mount Scopus was renewed presented the driver with a ticket that he had bought nineteen years earlier. It was accepted.

In a land housing so many jealous and often hostile religious denominations, Israel took care to honor established traditions. Even repairing the roof of an ancient church or mosque could be taken as evidence of possession, so Israel did not challenge the existent old order. To this day at the most sacred Christian shrine, the Church of the Holy Sepulchre, a Moslem family, by hereditary right through generations of practice, locks the doors from the inside at night, barring rival Christian sects that might claim exclusive ownership. Even having lost political possession of Jerusalem and the Temple Mount, Jordan for many years claimed supervisory rights at Al-Haram and El-Aqsa on the Temple Mount. Until 1988 the English-language news broadcast that is televised from Jordan featured a commentator seated before a photo of holy places in Jerusalem. Even today two men, each claiming to be the rightful grand mufti of Jerusalem, hold forth on the Temple Mount. One represents the king of Jordan. The other represents the chairman of the PLO. Israel stays out of the quarrel.

Still shocked by their defeat, the Arab population raised no objection to Jewish reassertion of rights to holy places such as the tombs of the biblical matriarch Rachel, near Bethlehem, and the construction of a yeshiva at the tomb of the biblical Joseph near Shechem or Nablus.

The most knotty problem lay at Hebron. The burial cave of the biblical patriarchs and matriarchs (Abraham, Sarah, Isaac, Rebeccah, Jacob, and Leah) is covered by an elaborate building whose walls were constructed by King Herod. For Jews, the Caves of Machpelah are second only to the Kotel in Jerusalem as a major shrine. Moslems, during their possession of the building, had made it a mosque because Abraham was also the father of the Arabs. They had barred Jews from entering the building. As noted previously, Jews were allowed to mount only the first seven steps leading to the mosque, where they could pray quietly. The Arab massacre of 1929 in which 133 Palestinian Jews were killed, most of them in Hebron, had ended by 1936 with the complete expulsion of Jews from Hebron. When General Moshe Dayan entered Hebron in 1967 at the close of the Six-Day War, the Arab mayor and town notables appeared before Dayan bearing the keys to the mosque. The general returned the keys and assured the mayor that he had no intention of taking the mosque al-Ibrahimi from the Waqf. All that the Israelis demanded was that Jews also be allowed to enter the building and pray there. Jews seeking to improve the interior electrical lighting system, at their own expense, were refused permission to do so.

Any Moslem fear that they would be expelled in retaliation for the Jewish expulsion of 1929 was soon forgotten. It was when Jews returned to Hebron as residents in 1968 that the major crisis surrounding the city erupted. It remains at the center of the ongoing tension between Arabs and Israelis to this day.

During the years after 1967, Israelis enjoyed full freedom to explore the Sinai Desert. Many of the hundreds of captured tanks that littered the desert were reconditioned and sold to Rumania, which was pursuing a modified break with the USSR's anti-Israel policy. Some of the tanks were kept for the Israelis themselves. In addition, samples of all captured Soviet weapons were given to the United States for study. The Americans found such materiel an easy way to study Soviet military technology.

Israeli geologists found oil at sources previously undiscovered by the Egyptians. Thus, for a few years, Israel enjoyed oil independence. Moreover, Israeli archeologists collected a treasure trove of ancient Egyptian artifacts hidden beneath the desert's sands. Soon thereafter the Israeli tourism industry began constructing hotels and beach resorts along the shores of the Red Sea.

Reactions in the Diaspora

Two human dramas were unforeseen products of Jewish euphoria at the military triumph. American Jews who had never visited Israel had asserted their support for the embattled state as soon as Nasser began his rhetorical threat to its survival. Mass rallies were held that, for the first time, witnessed entire Jewish communities united as never before. Reform Temples and far-right orthodox synagogues that had previously distanced themselves from secular Israeli nationalism now allowed the sale of Israeli bonds on their premises. American Jews volunteered to provide civilian services to the country while the reservist population was in combat. Long before these American volunteers reached Israel, the crisis was over. However, American and British Zionism enjoyed a vitality that had been unknown beforehand. Young Jews felt an assertive pride in their Jewish identity, which their immigrant parents had nursed in silence.

Even more significant, Russian Jewry suddenly came to life. Since the advent of the Russian Revolution, the Communist state had been engaged in closing synagogues and making Jewish religious practice almost impossible. In the USSR the teaching of religion was prohibited to students younger than 18 years of age.

In the fifty years spanning 1917–1967 the Soviet policy had essentially made Jewish religion a "hobby" for retired elderly people no longer having to work for a living. The Hebrew language had become an antique, studied by university language specialists as though it were an ancient dialect. The Soviets had no objection to Jews speaking Yiddish but declared that the Jewish homeland was Birobidjan, a Communist community on the borders of China.

However, in the aftermath of the Six-Day War an intellectual rebellion took place among Russian Jewish youth. The Soviet Union's television, radio, and newspapers had given only the government line about Israel. The official voice of the USSR had portrayed Israel as a western, imperialist aggressor. However, in the autumn of 1967, Russian Jewish youth began to express their Jewish identity for the first time in fifty years. These young Jews knew no Hebrew and were essentially ignorant of

Jewish religious practice. Nevertheless on the eve of the holiday Simchas Torah, when only elderly Jews went into the few remaining synagogues to pray, dozens of young Jews gathered on the streets outside—to sing the few Hebrew songs they had somehow learned, to dance what they thought were Israeli folk dances, and to socialize with one another, opening a league of friendship with other Jews who had previously kept their Jewishness a secret.

In response to this peaceful rebellion the Russian police jailed young people on charges of drunken disorder. However, after 1967 the assemblies on synagogue streets grew. Hebrew study groups began to meet secretly in homes. The real rebellion, however, was yet to come, as hundreds of Russian Jews requested exit visas, lost their jobs, or went to prison. Also yet to come was the coordinated assistance given to Russian "Refusenicks" offering succor and encouragement to those striving to recover their lost heritage and to somehow reach Israel.

The Soviet Union, however, covered its chagrin at Israel's newly acquired sense of security by mounting a war of condemnatory resolutions against Israel in the United Nations. Charles de Gaulle's France abandoned its previous support for Israel and initiated an intensive courtship of the Arabs. The French did, however, avert their eyes long enough to allow some naval missile boats, built in France and paid for by Israel, to "escape" from the French naval shipyards at Cherbourg.

Resolution 242

The United States became Israel's benign patron at the United Nations Security Council. From Israel's perspective nothing could be accomplished at the General Assembly, where the USSR's claque was in command. At the Security Council, however, the United States possessed a veto capable of blocking resolutions. To the surprise of a great many, Prime Minister Harold Wilson of Great Britain showed himself prepared to back American and Israeli resolutions in the Council.

On November 27, 1967, a British proposal known as Resolution 242 passed the Council. It had been accepted quietly in advance by the United States and Israel. The English-language text, which Israel accepted as binding, resolved that there was to be:

1. Withdrawal of Israeli armed forces from territories occupied in the recent conflict.

2. Termination of all states of belligerency, and respect for and acknowledgment of the sovereignty, territorial integrity, and political independence of every State in the area, and their right to live in peace within secure and recognized boundaries.

Israel was able to accept this text because it could be interpreted to imply that the boundaries of Israel could be determined only after the Arabs negotiated peace treaties, complete with definitive maps. Jerusalem made it clear that the old armistice line maps of 1949 were not sacred and immutable.

The French and the Russians, however, held to the French-language version of the resolution, which referred to *"des territoires occupés."* The use of the definite article in French implied that Israel would have to abandon every inch of the territories seized in the Six-Day War. The English version on which Israel, Britain, and the United States had been in agreement merely implied that Israel would have to negotiate new boundaries with the Arabs. Thus, the famous definite article of 242 gives diplomats room to debate, even to this day.

Effect of the War on the PLO

Of more immediate concern to the Israelis was the metamorphosis of the PLO after the Six-Day War. When the organization was founded (in May 1964) in what was still Jordanian-ruled East Jerusalem, it was not much more than an outlet for rhetoric. After all, most of the Arab-inhabited section of old Palestine was in Arab hands. However, the defeat of three Arab states in the war meant that Israel now ruled large Arab populations living in the Sinai Desert, the Gaza District, Judea and Samaria (formerly the Jordanian West Bank), and the Golan Heights. The recognition of Yassir Arafat as leader of the Syrian-backed fedayeen made him the head of the PLO.

In 1968 the revitalized organization, which had not dared to proclaim a Palestinian state when Jordan ruled on the east and west banks of the Jordan River, now discovered an entirely new program. Its goal was to create a Palestine encompassing both the east and west banks of what had once been the British Mandate for Palestine. That program, under Syrian inspiration, was equally threatening to King Hussein's Hashemite kingdom of Jordan and to the State of Israel. In 1968 the PLO published a charter of thirty-three articles known as the Palestine Covenant. The charter was forthright in its claim that only revolutionary war could end the existence of Israel. Thirty of the thirty-three articles call specifically for the destruction of Israel. Article 20 states in part that "Claims of historical religious ties of Jews with Palestine are incompatible with the facts of history." The same article, however, asserts in part that "Judaism being a religion, is not an independent nationality. Nor do the Jews constitute a single nation with an identity of its own." The charter concedes that Jews who lived in Palestine before 1947 may consider themselves to be Palestinians and may continue to live in the new Palestinian state, to be created. Most striking, the PLO charter while speaking of the Arab cause declares that Palestinians are a distinct ethnic nationality. The implication is that Palestinians have a distinct identity, rendering them uniquely different from other Arabs.

Article 33 states that "This Charter shall not be amended save by [vote of] a majority of two thirds of the total membership of the National Congress of the Palestine Liberation Organization [taken] at a special session convened for that purpose." This article sparks the most heated debate concerning the legitimacy of any negotiations between Israel and the PLO.

As head of the PLO, Yassir Arafat constructed an empire of terrorism that for twenty-three years enabled him to move frequently from safehouse to safehouse, always carefully guarded. He was supported by money from Arab rulers who gained safety for themselves by buying exemption from violence. At the simplest level, PLO terrorism involved sending infiltrators to Israel to seize a random Jewish school, a bus, or a hotel, and murder civilians. PLO demands for the release of their fellows in Israeli prisons usually were ineffective. Meanwhile Israel began to train an elite corps of commandos to destroy terrorist cells. Although the PLO continued to recruit young men and women who were ready to commit suicide for their cause, the Israelis usually refused to bargain with them. Moreover, that method was proving sterile.

Much more dramatic, though not much more profitable, was a long series of airplane hijackings. In its boldness, however, the PLO overreached itself. In a gesture of contempt for King Hussein of Jordan, PLO gunmen virtually took over the streets of Amman, capital of Jordan, in the summer of 1970. During those painful months, three aircraft were hijacked and forced to land at the Amman airport or at the unused airfield at Zarka, where the owners of the planes were obliged to negotiate terms with the hijackers or to stand idly by while their planes were destroyed.

The king realized that his throne and the independence of his country were in danger. In September 1970 during three bloody days the Jordanian army, loyal to the king, smashed the PLO in Jordan. An estimated three thousand terrorist gunmen died. The bulk of their forces fled, most of them to the Republic of Lebanon. Until then, Lebanon had been a refuge from the battles of its neighbors. In a carefully designed balance, the principal government offices were divided between Maronite Roman Catholic Christians, Sunni Moslems, Shi'ite Moslems, and Druse clansmen. Beirut was considered the Paris of the East, as sophisticated French-speaking Lebanese businessmen, regardless of religion, ensured the country's peace and prosperity.

For Lebanon, the sudden arrival of the PLO members and their families, expelled from Jordan, marked the end of peace and prosperity. These intruders settled in the villages of south Lebanon and established what came to be called Fatahland, the center for intensified raids on Israel.

Reaction of Syria

For the Syrians, "Black September" was a blunt challenge. They mobilized their army, and for a moment it looked as though they might avenge the humiliation of their PLO clients. An invasion of Jordan seemed imminent. However, the Israelis called up their reserves, and the U.S. Sixth Fleet gathered in the eastern Mediterranean where its air power could be persuasive. The Syrians drew the conclusion that they could not easily annex Jordan. They ultimately found Lebanon to be an easier victim.

In 1966, after one of Syria's many violent transmissions of power, a young army officer by the name of Hafez el-Assad became minister of defense. In 1970 he became the all-powerful dictator of the country. As a member of the Alawite Moslem minority in Syria, he was hated and feared by the Sunni Moslem majority. He would spend most of his career building an autocracy resting on an army directed by his fellow Alawites. He was to prove that he would not hesitate to slaughter Sunni leaders who challenged him. He also became the builder of a "Greater Syria."

Improved Relations between Israel and Jordan

In Israel, Moshe Dayan, as a dominant cabinet member, persuaded his colleagues to venture a risky but, as it proved, successful plan. It was Dayan who entered secret negotiations with the Jordanian government.

What emerged, without a formal treaty, was an Israeli-Jordanian under-standing to open traffic across the Jordan River in 1971. The Arab in-habitants of Judea and Samaria who held Jordanian citizenship continued to hold it, and passports and other legal documents were is-sued at Amman. Jordan still controlled the curricula of schools, paid the teachers, and named religious officials. Arab farmers living in Judea and Samaria could ship their farm produce into Jordan in unmarked crates. Tourists and businessmen were admitted to Israel from Jordan, it being understood that Israeli customs would not stamp passports, sparing for-eign Arabs the embarrassment of having to admit, in their home country, that they had set foot in Israel. Many foreign Christian tourists soon discovered that they could fly to Amman aboard Alia, the Jordanian national airline, at a much lower fare than any other airline offered. From Amman they could go by bus into Israel and complete a tour of the Holy Land without having their passports marked with any kind of evidence that they had visited Israel.

For the Israelis, those golden days gave them the illusion that peace was imminent. Arab merchants greeted the tourist buses with bottles of cold Coca-Cola. Arab workers made a prosperous living in the towns of Israel. Gradually indoor plumbing and solar heating became common in Arab villages. Colleges that ultimately became universities were estab-lished, though none had existed under Jordanian rule. Driving across Samaria, Israeli travelers could stop for ice cream in an Arab café without sensing hostility. If Arab and Jew did not love one another, they seemed reconciled to living peacefully under one flag.

In the aftermath of the Six-Day War, Israel offered peace to the Arabs. The usual position of the Israeli government was that all the conquered lands were negotiable except for Jerusalem, Sharm el-Sheikh, and the Golan Heights. The Arab reply was expressed very clearly at the Arab summit conference at Khartoum in August 1967. The famous "three no's" asserted "no peace with Israel, no recognition of Israel, no nego-tiations with Israel." Israel still sought legitimacy in vain.

9

The Yom Kippur War and Reappraisal, 1973–1977

THE WAR OF ATTRITION

Immediately after Egypt's defeat and expulsion from the Sinai Desert in 1967, Nasser was determined to force the Israelis to retreat without making any political concession to them. In March 1969 Egypt launched a "War of Attrition," exposing Israelis camped along the Suez Canal to constant bombardment. This bloody and undeclared war brought Israeli retaliation that soon cost Egypt more than it could afford, as the Israeli air force struck deep into Egypt. Face-to-face with another defeat, Nasser sought and obtained advanced Soviet weapons, including missiles, in February 1970. This forced the Israelis to seek and to obtain U.S. weaponry to match that of the Soviets. As a result, the War of Attrition was moving rapidly toward the level of a major conflict.

The Rogers Plan

In January 1969, Richard M. Nixon assumed the presidency of the United States. Golda Meir became prime minister of Israel following the death of Levi Eshkol in February 1969. Mrs. Meir formed a warm and confidential relationship with President Nixon. However, William Rogers, Nixon's secretary of state, worked to persuade the president that the most direct path to an end to the War of Attrition would be to press the Israelis to pledge to make a complete withdrawal from all land taken in the Six-Day War. The so-called Rogers Plan, although revised several times, was so extreme that it offended the most dovish and conciliatory Israelis. Rogers told Israeli foreign minister Abba Eban that he did not demand that Jerusalem be divided, as it had been before 1967, but that Jordan ought to share the city's administration with Israel. That approach brought a united Israeli opposition to the Rogers Plan.

In April 1969, Rogers attempted to bring pressure on the Israelis through consultations with Britain, France, and the Soviet Union. Not even the Big Four, however, could move Israel to accept a complete retreat to the old boundary that predated the Six-Day War. Israelis well remembered having trusted the guarantees of the Great Powers when they had surrendered the Sinai to Egypt in 1957, only to find themselves deserted when Nasser imposed a blockade in 1967.

Rogers's next approach was to threaten to cut off the supply of new weapons to Israel. Even in the face of that threat, while the War of Attrition still raged, the Israelis refused assent to a full retreat to the boundary of June 1967. In the end, although the Nixon administration continued to support the Rogers Plan as long as Nixon remained in office, all sides found a means of diplomatic retreat without losing face. The Israelis agreed to reaffirm Resolution 242, knowing full well that no Arab state would accept their definition of that United Nations act. In return for Israel's reaffirmation of the Resolution, which Israel itself had helped to design in 1967, the United States agreed to resume arms shipments. The one positive result of this diplomatic minuet was that Israel and Egypt agreed to a three-month cease-fire in June 1970. The War of Attrition came to an end and was not resumed.

THE ARAB WORLD AFTER THE DEATH OF NASSER

Black September and the expulsion of the PLO from Jordan in 1970 forced all the Arab states to reevaluate their anti-Israel policies. Nasser of Egypt called an all-Arab conference at Cairo. On September 27, 1970, King Hussein and Yassir Arafat signed a cease-fire. For appearance's sake, at least, Arab unity was restored. On the next day Nasser died suddenly. Shortly thereafter a new and untried leader, Mohammed Anwar Sadat, became Egypt's president.

From 1971 to 1973 the Arab world, far from attaining unity seemed torn by centrifugal forces. Splinter groups, increasingly extreme, broke off from parent groups of terrorists, engaging in power struggles totally foreign to the war against Israel. Dr. George Habash, a physician and a Christian, led the Popular Front for the Liberation of Palestine (PFLP) in a secession from the PLO. Nazif Hawatmeh broke with the PFLP to found the Popular Democratic Front for the Liberation of Palestine (PDFLP). With Syria giving most of the help to the PLO and some of its subsidiary secessionist groups, Iraq chose to advance its own goals and support the PFLP. Fatah, although a pure PLO organization under Arafat, chose to call itself "Black September" to pursue terrorist goals. In 1971 Black September murdered Wasfi al-Tal, the Jordanian prime minister. It was also Black September that engineered the murder of Israeli athletes at the 1972 Munich Olympics. On March 1, 1973, Black September murdered three guests of the Saudi Arabian ambassador to the Sudan.

ISRAEL'S VELVET GLOVE IN THE TERRITORIES

In the face of terrorism, Israel pursued a double-edged policy. Within Judea and Samaria, Israel extended a maximum degree of self-government to Arab inhabitants, most of whom held Jordanian citizenship. Freedom of movement to seek and obtain jobs within the borders of Israel also improved the economy of the territories. In March and May 1972 the larger Arab towns were allowed free municipal elections. Overwhelmingly, the mayors and other elected officials were loyal to King Hussein. Israel, at that hour, still believed that it was only a matter of time before the Arab states would agree to make peace by recognizing the legitimacy of the State of Israel.

Israel was fully prepared to give the Arab-inhabited parts of Judea and Samaria to the kingdom of Jordan. King Hussein, too, emphasized his willingness to pursue that goal. However, in spite of the fact that Jordan had worked out a de facto peace agreement with Minister of Defense Moshe Dayan, King Hussein avoided a formal peace treaty. Evidently he feared giving offense to the other Arab states, which still resisted giving recognition to Israel. However, Israel's foreign minister, Yigal Allon, won the consent of the cabinet to prepare a specific new map, which remained the Labor Party's peace proposal until 1993.

The Allon Plan

Briefly, the Allon Plan proposed that Israel keep control of the sparsely inhabited lowlands of the Jordan Valley to deter invasion from the east. The mountains would be ceded to the Jordanians, who would be allowed to possess Jericho and a road connecting Jordan to the highlands in Judea and Samaria. Allon also proposed that Israel annex lands to the south of Jerusalem regarded to be essential to the defense of the capital. At least some Laborites favored keeping Israeli control of Hebron as part of that southern line of defense.

ISRAEL'S IRON FIST IN GAZA

However, in areas such as the Gaza Strip there was no Arab leadership willing or able to cooperate with the Israeli authorities. There Israel showed an iron fist rather than a velvet glove. The Gazans had been ruled by Egypt from 1948 to 1967 and were essentially stateless persons because they had never received Egyptian citizenship. The Gazans particularly infuriated the Israeli military governors by refusing to allow the incorporation of the sewage and electric systems of the Arab refugee camps into the facilities serving the Gaza Strip's urban population. The Gazans insisted that to offer the homeless refugees an improvement in the quality of their life would imply that they were permanent residents rather than refugees who would eventually return to the homes from which they had fled in 1948. When they gave overt support to the various terrorist groups, General Ariel Sharon, who was at the head of Israel's Southern Military Command, broke the back of opposition through rigid curfews, arrests, expulsions, and the relocation of large masses of Arab civilians. He was successful in quieting Gaza but probably stirred the hatred that ultimately made Gaza a terrorists' nest. However, whether by gentle or harsh methods, Israel governed its Arab-inhabited lands without serious trouble from 1967 to 1973.

ANWAR SADAT AND THE YOM KIPPUR WAR

In 1973 disaster struck. In the three years since Anwar Sadat became Egypt's president, the Israelis had dismissed him as a braggart who offered no serious threat. Popular wisdom assumed that Egypt could not conquer the Sinai Desert. Sadat's ferocious speeches regularly promised exactly that, but few took him seriously. Indeed, in July 1972 Sadat dismissed his Soviet military advisors, a move interpreted as pacific.

In the spring of 1973 a partial mobilization of the Egyptian army took place. Fully aware of it, Israel countered with a partial mobilization of its own. In Israel, where almost all adult men were in the reserves at that time, even a partial mobilization could bring civilian economic life to a halt. When the Egyptians finished their military maneuvers, their army went home. Israel also demobilized its reserves. The experience was disruptive and expensive for Israel. Therefore, when in October 1973 Israel became aware that the Egyptians were beginning to mobilize again, Jerusalem did not respond. More ominous, the Syrians also mobilized in October. Ironically, Prime Minister Golda Meir failed to see the danger. Israeli intelligence services also failed to recognize the seriousness of the threat. Indeed, close observers of Egyptian behavior concluded that no attack was likely.

October 6 was the most solemn of Jewish fast days: Yom Kippur. Even irreligious Israelis avoid work and their normal routine on that day. The streets are empty. In the morning, Israeli soldiers stationed at the Suez Canal could see Egyptian soldiers on the opposite bank lying bare-chested there, sunning themselves.

The Israelis had fortifications on the east bank of the canal, separated by 7 or 8 miles each. Named the Bar-Lev Line for the Israeli chief of staff, General Chaim Bar-Lev, the scattered fortresses were intended to prevent attacking Egyptians from creating a unified front. That theory was to prove untenable.

On that afternoon the Egyptian artillery and air force opened a heavy and coordinated attack on the Israeli fortifications. In the gaps between the Bar-Lev fortresses, Egyptian infantry constructed pontoon bridges and crossed the canal, bypassing the fortresses. Hafez el-Assad's Syrians launched a carefully coordinated attack on the Golan Heights. Because of the critical importance of the Golan to Israel, the Israelis made sure that the Syrians never reached Israel proper.

The Jordanians profited from their disastrous experience of 1967 by remaining aloof. Some units of the Jordanian army were sent northward to support the Syrians, but their role was symbolic. Peaceful traffic across the Jordan River continued. King Hussein did not become involved with his old enemies the Syrians and the often hostile Egyptians.

Israel's system of calling up its reserves by radio signal worked well, and the army reported for duty promptly. Nevertheless for several days Israel's survival was in doubt. Minister of Defense Moshe Dayan was briefly gripped by panic and informed senior air force officers that the Third Temple—meaning the State of Israel—was in danger.

However, the United States, after a relatively brief hesitation, began to send essential supplies to Israel. The tide turned immediately, as the Israeli reserves responded effectively. In a brilliant though risky strike, General Ariel Sharon punched through the Egyptian lines, crossed the

Suez Canal, then circled and trapped the Egyptian Third Army. The Israelis found themselves only 50 miles from Cairo as the Third Army was faced with surrender. In the north, the Israelis quickly recovered lost ground and went beyond the Golan Heights until they were only 19 miles from Damascus. The Syrian attack was broken in only three days of fighting. In the Sinai, Egyptian defeat was manifest by October 14. By October 24 all fighting stopped with a total military victory for Israel. The United Nations' call for a cease-fire on October 23 saved Egypt and Syria from further humiliation.

Nevertheless the war had disastrous effects on Israeli morale. The casualty rates were demoralizingly high. Since 1967 the nation had been borne aloft on a euphoria that was now shattered by the sudden realization that Israel was vulnerable. Ordinary Israelis blamed Golda Meir, Moshe Dayan, and the intelligence services for having failed to foresee the Egyptian-Syrian attack.

In 1974 the Knesset authorized the creation of the Agranat Commission, which was charged with assigning blame for the shortcomings of the politicians and the soldiers. Thereafter, although Golda Meir retained the prime-ministership in the national election of December 1973, the Labor Party lost 10 percent of the votes it had won in the 1969 election. Mrs. Meir was led to resign in April 1974 as head of the government and was replaced by General Yitzchak Rabin, who had been chief of staff during the Six-Day War and had served as Israel's ambassador to the United States during the relatively tranquil years that followed. As minister of defense the temporarily disgraced Dayan was replaced by Shimon Peres, at that time considered a conservative Laborite disciple of the late Ben-Gurion. Peres had strongly opposed Rabin for the prime-ministership and, having failed to win it, was serving in the Defense post. (It is interesting to note that Peres and Rabin spent the rest of Rabin's life struggling for that office. Ironically, Peres achieved it only after Rabin was assassinated in 1995. He never succeeded in winning the prime-ministership by popular election.)

AFTERMATH OF THE YOM KIPPUR WAR

Immediately on the outbreak of the war, Arab members of the Organization of Petroleum Exporting Countries (OPEC) declared a ban on petroleum exports to the United States and the Netherlands, which were considered to be pro-Israel. U.S. imports of Arab oil dropped from 1.2 million barrels a day in September 1973, to fewer than 20,000 barrels a day in January 1974. Long lines of cars formed at gas stations and limited amounts were allowed to customers. The crisis did not last long, and the only permanent result was a steadily rising price of gasoline, artificially pressed upward by OPEC. However, in a political sense the United States began to press Israel to make concessions to the Arabs, without reciprocation.

Kissinger's Diplomacy

Dr. Henry Kissinger, President Nixon's secretary of state, was also his national security advisor. All that we can say with certainty, now, is that Kissinger believed that it was more likely that a peaceful resolution of the conflict could be reached if Egypt and Syria obtained some of the fruits of victory, through American mediation, even if they had not been won on the battlefield. It is certain that Kissinger saved the Egyptians from the humiliation of having to concede the surrender of their Third Army, encircled by General Sharon's Israelis. It is, however, equally certain that it was Nixon who threw the full weight of his presidential influence into ensuring that Israel received essential military supplies in the first days of the war when it appeared that defeat was possible.

There is little doubt that Kissinger's "shuttle diplomacy" meant that the secretary of state played a more personal role in formulating a peace settlement than any secretary of state before him. He bypassed the normal service of ambassadors and flew between Jerusalem, Cairo, and Damascus to press everyone to accept the settlement he had designed. He pressured the reluctant Israelis to give the Syrians a slice of the Golan Heights, centered at the town of Kuneitra, although Israel received nothing in return. In face-to-face meetings between Israeli and Egyptian army commanders, Kissinger managed to force an Israeli retreat from the Suez Canal, creating parallel thin zones held by lightly armed Egyptian and Israeli troops. Thus, the entire canal was once again in Egyptian hands. All of Kissinger's energy, however, did not induce any of Israel's neighbors to sign a peace treaty recognizing Israel's legitimacy. In a second disengagement of 1975, Sadat did agree to open the Suez Canal to non-military cargoes going to or from Israel. In retrospect, Sadat's ultimate decision to make peace in 1977 may have had its origins in the shuttle diplomacy of 1973–1975.

The Triumphant PLO

Perhaps more significant, the aftermath of the Yom Kippur War featured a dramatic resurrection of the PLO. It had been counted as lost after the expulsion from Jordan in 1970 and its patronage of terrorism thereafter. Even Arab states that privately detested or feared the PLO's terrorism found it useful to adopt Yassir Arafat and his followers after the Yom Kippur War. In fact, in November 1973 an Arab summit conference in Algiers declared that the PLO was the "sole legitimate representative of the Palestinian People." Even the Jordanian government swallowed its chagrin at that usurpation of its claims, although the greatest portion of Palestinian Arabs held Jordanian citizenship and still considered themselves to be subjects of King Hussein. Indeed, the Jordanians continued to support the schools and pay the salaries of Arab teachers, religious authorities, and municipal authorities exactly as they had when Jordan ruled what was then called the West Bank. A summit meeting of the Islamic Conference Organization in February 1974 likewise declared the PLO to be "the sole legitimate representative of the Palestinian people and its struggle." By October 1974 at another Arab summit in Rabat, Morocco, Jordan joined in voting for the resolution that consented to replace itself with the PLO.

The PLO was also gaining recognition at the United Nations. On November 13, 1974, Yassir Arafat was invited to address the UN General Assembly. The UN then granted the PLO "observer status" and passed a resolution recognizing the "inalienable rights" of the Palestinian people, including "the right to national independence and sovereignty." [In the summer of 1975 the UN came close to expelling Israel. In November 1975 the UN declared Zionism to be "a form of racial discrimination."] This exercise was remarkable coming from 23 Arab states, most of whom did not allow Jews and some of whom did not allow Christians or Jews to reside in their territory. In November 1975 the UN also established a Committee on the Exercise of the Inalienable Rights of the Palestinian People. Thus, a small segment of the world's Arab population was declared officially to be a separate and distinct ethnic minority, even though they are essentially no different in language or other important cultural features from Arabs living outside historic Palestine. In 1976 the UN declared that "no solution in the Middle East can be envisaged which does not fully take into account the aspirations of the Palestinian people." As understood by the PLO and expressed in its charter, those aspirations called for the elimination of the State of Israel.

Lebanon's Agony

Israel's victory of 1973 had been transformed into a defeat by the world, and indeed by the Israelis themselves. Three changes grew directly out of that change in attitude. The first involved the transformation of Lebanon. That republic had been created by the French after World War I. Within its arbitrarily drawn borders Paris designed a mandate in which a bare majority were Roman Catholic Maronites. Although Arabic was the vernacular tongue of the Maronites, intensive French efforts created a school system that emphasized French language and culture. A French-speaking elite made Lebanon more European than any other Arab nation. The French unwittingly erred, however, in enlarging Lebanon through the inclusion of large minorities of Shi'ite and Sunni Moslems, as well as Druse clansmen. Until 1973 a pious pretense was maintained that Lebanon was a Christian country with a Maronite majority.

The sudden arrival of the bulk of the PLO with their families and dependents upset the balance in 1970. Although the old, polite, carefully balanced division of offices between the major religious minorities continued, a battle now ensued to test whether the conservative Maronites and their allies, or the radical PLO and its allies, could take control of the old system. There was nothing new about battles between Lebanese religious factions. What was new was that foreign political forces were ready to exploit the old jealousies for causes unrelated to Lebanese interests. In 1975–1976, in a bloody war, Syria saw the opportunity to intervene. Hafez el-Assad was able to pose as an altruistic peacemaker. Depending on how it suited the Syrians at any moment, they regarded the PLO as an ally or an enemy. Damascus could also support some factions of the PLO and oppose others, as the demands of the moment might indicate.

When the shooting stopped in 1976, Yassir Arafat and the principal factions supporting him became, temporarily, Syria's allies in Lebanon. The PLO, now firmly entrenched in southern Lebanon, began to launch terrorist raids against Israel. Israel therefore established its own security zone in Lebanon, creating a Lebanese militia made up mostly of Maronites, to repel PLO attacks on Israel.

Changing Arab Attitudes within Israel

A second startling change in the wake of the October War involved the Arabs of Judea and Samaria, who were formerly subjects of King Hussein residing on the West Bank of Jordan. In 1972 Israel had allowed these Palestinian Arabs to elect their own municipal officials. Overwhelmingly they had swept conservative, pro-Jordanian leaders into office. In 1976, however, the elections marked a triumph for the PLO.

Younger, better-educated merchants and professionals, such as doctors, lawyers, and teachers, replaced the old land-owning aristocracy in power. Israel did not realize that the events transpiring in the greater outside world were transforming the self-concept of the provincial notables. Thus, 1976 marked a clash between Israel and the Arab leadership in Judea and Samaria that was quite new.

The Arab citizens of Israel were also undergoing transformation. Prior to 1967, Israeli Arabs tended to press for their own political interests within the general Israeli political party structure, usually in left-wing Socialist or Communist parties led by Israeli Jews. Increasingly after 1969 they tended to support left-wing Arab political parties in the Knesset, which were increasingly bold in defense of PLO policies. Of course, they did not identify themselves as PLO, because that party was regarded as illegal and subversive. However, they were becoming increasingly skillful in grasping all the benefits that participation in Israeli democracy offered them, while at the same time expressing public disdain for Zionist ideology.

The Gush Emunim

The third startling change was the birth of the Gush Emunim, or "Bloc of the Faithful," in 1974. The Jerusalem yeshiva, Merkaz Harav—deriving its ideology from the religious Zionist philosophy of the first Ashkenazic chief rabbi, A. I. Kook, and his son Rabbi Zvi Yehudah Kook—taught that it is a religious duty for Jews to settle all of the Land of Israel, including Judea and Samaria. Prior to 1974 settlement in Judea, Samaria, Gaza, and the Golan had already begun. Settlement in the Golan Heights started in 1967. A principal goal was the reestablishment of towns that the Arabs had destroyed and depopulated during the War of 1948–1949. K'far Etzion, just south of Jerusalem, was rebuilt in 1967, and Allon Shvut was reestablished in 1970. In 1968 Rabbi Moshe Levinger led a group of Jews to Hebron, where they resided at first in a hotel and then in a police station, and shortly thereafter founded Kiryat Arba, a short distance from the tombs of the biblical patriarchs. They have also moved into Hebron proper, occupying houses and other property that were Jewish-owned prior to the Arab massacres of 1929.

Secularist Socialism and Settlement in the Territories

There are careless observers who categorize all those Jewish settlers who have built homes in the new territories as religious. In fact, it was a succession of Labor governments that encouraged the building of Jewish communities in the Jordan Valley and in the Golan Heights. Labor governments built the road named Derech Allon, or "Allon's Way," in honor of Foreign Minister Yigal Allon (who, as noted previously, had drawn a map proposing that Israel retain the Jordan Valley but cede the mountains to Jordan). Derech Allon runs through the eastern valley connecting the north to Jerusalem but bypassing the large Arab towns such as Ramallah. Most of those settlers are secularist. A majority of the pioneers who established towns in the mountains are religiously motivated, striving to ensure that all the Land of Israel remains Israeli. However, even in the towns that are not protected on Yigal Allon's map, substantial numbers of pioneers are secularist. Perhaps their motivation is nationalist, or perhaps they seek affordable housing within commuting distance from Israel's big cities. For example, 40 percent of the residents of Kiryat Arba are secular, and a large part of Kiryat Arba's population commutes to jobs in Jerusalem every day. The growing city of Ariel is overwhelmingly secularist. To this day, the majority of Jews on the Golan are secularist. Considering what was to transpire later, it is important to note that at one time even Shimon Peres was an enthusiastic supporter of settlement in Judea and Samaria.

THE ENTEBBE TRIUMPH

The years 1976–1977 marked an end to the long era of dominance by the Labor Party. Scandals marred the Israeli political scene, even as the country entered a crucial election campaign. Ironically, one of Israel's most memorable moments created contrast between the heroic and the sordid. In July 1976 a band of PLO terrorists hijacked a French airliner and forced it to land in Entebbe, Uganda. The air pirates then made a point of holding Jews or Israelis while releasing other passengers. The pilot, however, refused to accept release as long as any of his passengers were held. Idi Amin, the dictator of Uganda, cooperated fully with the air pirates while they addressed demands to Israel. They apparently believed that they were beyond the reach of any military action by Israel.

In the face of the crisis, all the major parties in the Knesset united in support for the government. A brilliant rescue was carried out, with the cooperation of the government of Kenya. The Israelis managed to deliver all the captives safely—with the exception of Dora Bloch, who had fallen ill and been taken to a Ugandan hospital, where she died under mysterious circumstances. The Israeli commander of the expedition, Yonathan Netanyahu, died in the action, the only casualty in the rescue. (His brother Benyamin was to become prime minister of Israel twenty years later.) On July 4, 1976, all Israel erupted in joyous celebration of the completion of what had been thought to be an impossible rescue.

Overall, the years 1973–1977 were a peculiar mixture of depression or uncertainty, and an ebullient confidence that a secure State of Israel could be built.

10

The Likud Revolution, 1977–1983

THE ELECTION OF 1977

Originally, Israel's national election was scheduled for the autumn of 1977. However, Israel is a parliamentary democracy whose government enjoys the privilege of calling a snap election if the prime minister perceives that his or her popularity is at its height and that an early election would enhance his or her party's chances of victory. Therefore the vote in 1977 was moved up to May. Yitzchak Rabin, who had been prime minister since June 1974, was able to claim an impressive record for having built Israeli military strength through a steady flow of the most advanced American military aid. It is therefore ironic that the very search for military strength helped lead to his defeat.

Attempting to highlight the growth of the Israeli air force, the Rabin government committed the social and political blunder of scheduling the arrival of a flight of F15 fighter planes as the sabbath began on a Friday afternoon. Religious Israelis regarded this as a gesture of contempt for them. As a result, the religious parties in the Knesset brought a no-confidence measure against the government. The National Religious Party, which belonged to Rabin's cabinet coalition, abstained from the vote, but the other religious members voted against the government.

Rabin then resigned. In accordance with parliamentary tradition, however, he would remain the acting prime minister until the May 17 election. He was confident that he would then receive a new mandate and hold office firmly. However, a series of political disasters struck Rabin and brought Likud to power.

First, at this moment of vulnerability, Rabin's old personal rival and foe, Shimon Peres, announced his candidacy for the prime-ministership. That challenge was averted when, on February 22, a convention of the delegates of the Labor Party gave its support to Rabin (although by an embarrassingly narrow margin). The Labor family squabble worked to the advantage of Likud.

Then other blows struck Rabin during that unlucky winter. A member of his cabinet committed suicide after being accused of misuse of funds belonging to the Histadrut, Israel's largest labor union. The governor of the Bank of Israel, also a Rabin nominee, was jailed for five years for taking bribes and evading taxes. It was revealed that Leah Rabin, the prime minister's wife, had broken Israeli law by maintaining two bank accounts in the United States. Rabin had claimed only one bank account of $2,000, but the Rabins were found to have accounts totaling $23,000. The accusation of having lied hit Rabin hard when it was revealed by the newspapers on March 15, 1977.

Concurrent with these embarrassments, Rabin had hoped to gain some political credit by paying a courtesy call on Jimmy Carter, president of the United States. To Rabin's distress, President Carter took the occasion of Rabin's visit on March 8 to state publicly that he expected Israel to withdraw to its 1967 borders. Ten days later Carter urged the need for a Palestinian homeland. This is all the more peculiar because Jimmy Carter confessed that he had never met an Arab head of state who had wanted to see another state created west of the Jordan. If he meant to say that he supported the Allon Plan and hoped that lands vacated by Israel would be annexed by Jordan, that is not what he seemed to be saying. Support for the Allon Plan would have been Labor Party policy. What President Carter and his Secretary of State, Cyrus Vance, did in fact say, amounted to a reassessment of American policy toward Israel. It was another blow to Rabin's chances in the election.

The Nature of a Likud Government

The Likud victory of May 17, 1977, was not a surprise. Rabin personally, and the Labor Party in general, were the victims of a legion of disasters that hit them hard. Nevertheless it required some emotional adjustment to accept the fact that for the first time in the twenty-nine years of Israel's independence, the government was headed by persons who had always been in opposition to the party of David Ben-Gurion, Golda Meir, Yitzchak Rabin, and Shimon Peres by more than standard electoral battles. Menachem Begin was an austere, sincerely religious, scrupulously honest, but unyielding idealist. In the tradition of Ze'ev Jabotinsky, he had no intention of yielding one inch of the Land of Israel to the Arabs. Indeed, he had bought a retirement home for himself at Yamit in the Sinai Desert. He also had been commander of the Irgun Zvai Leumi (IZL) during the 1948 battle for independence.

Likud stood in contrast to the Laborite socialists because a large segment of the party was committed to capitalism and a free-market economy. This implied a determination to sell government-owned enterprises to private capitalists and to reduce the size of Israel's bloated bureaucracy. Such goals were easier to propose than to realize—especially because the Histadrut, Israel's giant labor union, was also dominant in the management of many industries.

Creating a Coalition

The election results presented Likud with 43 seats in the Knesset, making it relatively easy to create a solid coalition well beyond the required 61 supporters. Certainly the religious and nationalist parties found it easy to support Menachem Begin, a man whose personal lifestyle was much more compatible with their philosophy than that of the Laborite politicians had been. Defeated Labor won only 32 seats. Begin strengthened himself further by making the Laborite Moshe Dayan his minister for foreign affairs. Ezer Weizman, his minister of defense, was a nephew of Israel's first president, the late Dr. Chaim Weizmann. As one of the creators of the Israeli air force and a war hero, he made special contributions to Begin's strength. Ezer Weizman had also managed Begin's election campaign.

Brzezinski and the Comprehensivists

The great challenge for Begin, however, lay not in Jerusalem but in Washington. The principal advisor of President Jimmy Carter and Secretary of State Cyrus Vance was Zbigniew Brzezinski, their national security advisor. He stood in marked contrast to Henry Kissinger, a pragmatist who was prepared to solve one problem at a time. Brzezinski may be called a "Comprehensivist" who believed that it would be possible to resolve all the conflicts of the Middle East as part of a seamless garment: all or nothing. Brzezinski was co-author of the *Brookings Institution Report* of 1975, in which that prestigious think-tank set forth the essence of "comprehensivism." Very simply, as it would have been seen by Menachem Begin, the *Report* called for:

1. Israel to abandon all lands captured in 1967, returning to the pre–Six-Day War boundary. The UN was to supply troops to guard those borders.

2. The Palestinian Arabs were to be self-governing, either through the creation of an independent state or through federation with Jordan.

The *Report* did not specify what was to become of Jerusalem but required that each faith control its own holy places and that each national group exercise a great deal of autonomy in its own neighborhoods within the city. The *Report* was unclear on other issues such as the award of authority to Jews or Moslems contending for control of the same religious shrine; it did not discuss battles between Christians of various denominations or Moslems of various political loyalties seeking control of their shrines. Moreover, by 1977 the building of new Jewish neighborhoods in what was to become an enlarged Jerusalem could not be dealt with as though nothing had changed since 1967.

The Comprehensivists also lumped together all of Israel's Arab neighbors although they did not have the same priorities. In a move of unofficial diplomacy President Carter's wife, Rosalynn, was sent to talk to Yassir Arafat in order to try to persuade him to concede the right of Israel to exist. Both Rabin and later Begin were saved considerable embarrassment when Arafat was not prepared to accept U.N. Resolution 242. However, all of this unofficial diplomacy seemed to indicate that the Carter-Vance-Brzezinski diplomacy did not recognize that Arafat was controlled by Hafez el-Assad of Syria, that Syria dominated Lebanon, and that the USSR regarded itself as the patron of all. Assad, the Syrian strongman, did not want to see a separate Palestinian state. He had visions of incorporating those territories into his own intended "Greater Syria." Therefore, Assad was happy to talk to Carter at great length, but his goal was Syrian domination of Lebanon, as much of Palestine as he could seize, and Jordan as a bloc opposing rival Egypt.

Begin's Unexpected Flexibility

Menachem Begin, forming his government in June 1977, was fully aware that in the Carter administration he was faced with potential hostility. Therefore, this disciple of Ze'ev Jabotinsky revealed an unexpected flexibility. His public statements volunteered a willingness to enter negotiations about the Sinai Desert and the Golan Heights. He showed no intention of yielding control of Judea and Samaria, either to Jordan or to the PLO.

THE THREAT OF A GENEVA CONFERENCE

In their personal meetings Carter and Begin managed to get along well, but Carter was disturbed by Begin's absolute refusal to consider returning to the boundaries of 1967. Begin made it clear that he intended to settle Jews in all the disputed territories. Subsequently Carter shocked the Israelis when he announced his intention of convening an international conference at Geneva, including the Russians and a delegation of Palestinians. The proposed conference would involve all of the major powers. It was apparent that the United States proposed to settle all aspects of the Arab-Israeli conflict in one great movement. It was not immediately clear which Palestinians were to be involved, especially because Israel still held to the security of Kissinger's assurance that the United States would not deal with the PLO as long as it refused to accept UN Resolution 242. Then, on September 12, 1977, the State Department issued a statement that:

> The status of the Palestinians must be settled in a comprehensive Arab-Israeli agreement. The issue cannot be ignored if the others are to be solved. Moreover, to be lasting, a peace agreement must be positively supported by all of the parties to the conflict, including the Palestinians. This means that the Palestinians must be involved in the peace-making process. Their representatives will have to be at Geneva for the Palestinian question to be solved.

Begin felt that Israel's needs had been ignored. However, the American Comprehensivists proceeded with their plans. The Americans and Russians prepared a joint statement to be released on October 1. They made it clear that the Geneva Conference would seek a settlement of all problems including the Palestinians, the West Bank, and Jerusalem. The Americans did not show the document to Israeli foreign minister Dayan until a day before it was to be publicized.

Dayan was spared the necessity of standing alone in protest. A good number of American policymakers were distressed that Carter, Vance, and Brzezinski were about to bring the USSR into a matter from which they felt it ought to have been excluded. Senator Henry Jackson, always supportive of Israel, said, "The fox is back in the chicken coop. Why bring the Russians in at a time when the Egyptians have been throwing them out?" In the face of the outcry, President Carter and Secretary of State Vance renewed the promise to Foreign Minister Dayan that the PLO would not be invited to Geneva. Indeed, the Geneva Conference was fated never to meet.

Sadat Fears a Geneva Conference

In September 1977, when comprehensivism was most aggressive, Moshe Dayan visited Morocco. King Hassan II of Morocco is the only Arab leader who has allowed an ancient Jewish community to live securely within his realm. Thus, although Israel and Morocco had no diplomatic relations, Israeli political leaders as well as ordinary Jewish tourists have always visited the country. It was during his sojourn in Morocco that Dayan hinted broadly that Menachem Begin would be willing to concede land outside Israel proper in exchange for peace. At the same moment, the Rumanian dictator Nicolae Ceausescu was informing Egypt's Anwar Sadat of the same message. Ceausescu, though a Communist, was independent of the USSR. He had long been in a lively and profitable trade relationship with Israel. He allowed Jews to practice their religion at home in Rumania or to migrate to Israel, provided that Israel paid well for such favors. There was every reason to believe that he was a reliable informant on Israeli policy.

On the basis of these testimonies that Menachem Begin would strike a deal concerning the Sinai, Anwar Sadat took a leap of faith. After all, he was almost as concerned as the Israelis at the possibility that the Soviets would be present as sponsors of a Geneva Conference. Sadat realized that the principal beneficiary of Soviet patronage would be Syria, his enemy.

Sadat Travels to Jerusalem

On November 9, 1977, Sadat addressed the Egyptian parliament, surprising his audience by offering to go anywhere to make peace with Israel—even to the Knesset itself. Begin did not miss his cue. On November 14 the Israeli prime minister told some visiting French notables that he was extending an invitation to Sadat to come to Jerusalem and make peace. In fact, American diplomats had already delivered Israel's invitation to Sadat. With breathtaking speed Sadat accepted the invitation, arriving at Ben-Gurion Airport in Israel on the night of Saturday, November 19, 1977, some hours after the close of the Jewish sabbath.

Menachem Begin made the occasion a celebration of Israeli unity, as all the leaders of the Labor Party were at the state dinner, side-by-side with Begin's Likud. If peace was to be made with Egypt, perhaps it was of even more importance that left-wing and right-wing Israelis have a chance to bury old hatreds. The ghosts of Arlosoroff, the Season, and the *Altalena* seemed at last to be exorcised.

The formal addresses to the Knesset were, of course, the high point of Sadat's visit. All the Israeli notables had a chance to speak. However, the world listened closely to the words of Sadat and Begin.

Sadat's Diplomacy

Sadat did not offer a single concession to the Israelis. He demanded that Israel yield every inch of the land lost by the Arabs in the Six-Day War. He demanded a Palestinian state. He pressed the theme that the Arab areas of east Jerusalem would have to be part of the Palestinian state.

In an impressive feat, Sadat managed to please the Carter-Vance-Brzezinski Comprehensivists by pretending to favor the Geneva Conference approach. What he actually wanted, and eventually got, was the return of the entire Egyptian Sinai. Begin also performed a feat. While repeating the traditional Likud claim to an enlarged Israel, he avoided blunt confrontations with Sadat. It seemed to observers as though the two leaders had already reached a private understanding. Long before the Comprehensivists awakened to what had actually happened, Hafez el-Assad of Syria realized that he and his allies would get nothing and that the Soviet Union and the much-touted Geneva Conference had been circumvented.

Following Sadat's return to Cairo, a joint Israeli-Egyptian political committee began to lay out a peace agreement. However, both parties were busy "grandstanding" to their separate audiences. Israel and Egypt leaked their most extreme positions to the press, a move that usually undermines successful diplomacy. As the months dragged by, it began to appear that the cordial relations that showed so much promise during Sadat's visit to Jerusalem would become yet another disappointment.

THE CAMP DAVID SUMMIT

The deadlock was broken when Foreign Minister Dayan visited Washington, D.C., on April 26–28. He made proposals that would permit Secretary of State Vance to abandon comprehensivism while appearing to advance it. The mutually satisfactory pretense was maintained that the ultimate goal of negotiations would be a settlement of all disputes in the Near East. However, Dayan confined his promises to an assurance that Israel would consider granting self-government to the Arab population of Judea, Samaria, and Gaza. No promise was made concerning an eventual Palestinian state. Israel yielded nothing in terms of a promise to cease settling Jews in the disputed territories. Thus, Menachem Begin revealed his willingness to give the Sinai Desert to Egypt while making no concessions on the right of Jews to reside in "the Land of Israel." Everyone had saved face, and the road had been cleared for American intervention in the talks that interested Sadat—namely, the cession of the Sinai to Egypt.

At the end of July 1978, Carter sent Vance to visit Sadat and Begin to invite them to Camp David, Maryland, where they could confer without having to speak to the press. Acceptance was immediate. Top-level talks among Begin, Sadat, and Carter were held during the period September 5–18. At first the atmosphere was not good. Both parties persisted in recalling every hostile act taken by the other over the last thirty years. Two men in particular worked effectively to achieve success. One, Defense Minister Ezer Weizman, was one of the few top-level Israelis who spoke a fluent colloquial Arabic. Weizman and Sadat established a warm and confidential personal relationship that lasted as long as Sadat lived. President Carter failed to charm his companions, but he managed to show the world that a president of the United States who is determined to achieve success can usually do so if he drops all other business and devotes himself to thirteen days of persistent, personal negotiations.

For Begin, the greatest problem was to agree that all Israelis would have to evacuate the Sinai if the land was transferred to Egypt. Begin regarded it as a personal humiliation that all Jewish residents of that territory would have to leave. It reminded him of his own youth in Poland when Hitler had attempted to make the world *Judenrein*, or "free of Jews." In the end, however, under presidential pressure Begin surrendered.

The Camp David treaty that ultimately emerged covered two areas. The first concerned the cession of all of the Sinai to Egypt and its evacuation by all Israelis. This was clear-cut and manageable. It provided that Israel was to carry out a phased withdrawal from the Sinai within three years, beginning no later than nine months after the signing of the treaty. United Nations personnel were to be stationed in the territory, and they were not to be removed without the consent of both Israel and Egypt. (This was a reference to the speed with which U Thant had pulled out his UN peacekeeping forces when ordered by Nasser to do so in 1967.) Within nine months of the signing of the treaty Israel and Egypt were required to exchange ambassadors, completely normalize relations, and permit free movement across borders. Israel was to enjoy the same right of free navigation through the Suez Canal as all other nations. Israel was to surrender all oil wells that had been discovered and exploited by Israelis in the Sinai, but Egypt undertook to sell oil to Israel under normal commercial terms. Though it was not clearly defined in 1978, Israel ultimately agreed to interpret the treaty so that all ancient artifacts found by Israeli archeologists in the Sinai, and taken to Israel, would be given to the Egyptians. It was agreed that small parcels of land at the border, whose ownership was uncertain, would be awarded by mutually acceptable international inquiry commissions. The most celebrated of these was an Israeli luxury hotel at Taba, close to Eilat, which became an Egyptian hotel.

The other part of the treaty, referring to Palestinian self-rule, was much harder to implement. This was the fruit of the Carter-Vance-Brzezinski Comprehensivist proposals. At Camp David, only President Carter truly served as the Palestinians' advocate. They were anathema to Begin. They were important to Sadat only as a means of maintaining his role as a leader of all Arabs. Privately, he saw no advantage to Egypt in creating a Palestinian state that could be of value only to the USSR, the PLO, and Syria, or to King Hussein of Jordan. Nevertheless, Sadat went through all the motions in demanding Palestinian rights. To bridge the abyss between the Israeli and Egyptian claims in Judea and Samaria, the treaty signatories finessed their differences.

Explanatory Letters Bridge Abysses

Where there was a major difference in interpretation, Sadat and Begin each presented an explanatory official letter to Carter, which he was to forward to the other signatory. The texts of the following letters—all published immediately by the *New York Times*, the *Baltimore Sun*, the *Washington Post*, and other papers—are good examples of the escape clause that allows evasion of problems that cannot be easily settled.

To President Carter from President Sadat:
I am writing you to reaffirm the position of the Arab Republic of Egypt with respect to Jerusalem.

1. Arab Jerusalem is an integral part of the West Bank. Legal and historical Arab rights in the City must be respected and restored.

2. Arab Jerusalem should be under Arab sovereignty.

3. The Palestinian inhabitants of Arab Jerusalem are entitled to exercise their legitimate national rights, being part of the Palestinian People in the West Bank.

4. Relevant Security Council Resolutions, particularly Resolutions 242 and 267, must be applied with regard to Jerusalem. All measures taken by Israel to alter the status of the City are null and void and should be rescinded.

5. All peoples must have free access to the City and enjoy the free exercises of worship and the right to visit and transit to the holy places without distinction or discrimination.

6. The holy places of each faith may be placed under the administration and control of their representatives.

7. Essential functions in the City should be undivided and a joint municipal council composed of an equal number of Arab and Israeli members can supervise the carrying out of these functions. In this way, the City shall be undivided.

To President Carter from Prime Minister Begin:
I have the honor to inform you, Mr. President, that on 28 June 1967—Israel's Parliament promulgated and adopted a law to the effect: "The Government is empowered by a decree to apply the law, the jurisdiction and administration of the State to any part of the Eretz Israel [Land of Israel], as stated in that decree." On the basis of this law, the Government of Israel decreed in July, 1967, that Jerusalem is one city indivisible, the Capital of the State of Israel.

To President Sadat from President Carter:
I have received your letter of September 17, 1978, setting forth the Egyptian position on Jerusalem. I am transmitting a copy of that letter to Prime Minister Begin for his information.

The position of the United States on Jerusalem remains as stated by Ambassador [Arthur J.] Goldberg in the United Nations General Assembly on July 14, 1967, and subsequently by Ambassador [Charles W.] Yost in the United Nations Security Council on July 1, 1969.

To Prime Minister Begin from President Carter:
I hereby acknowledge that you have informed me as follows:

> A. In each paragraph of the Agreed Framework Document the expressions "Palestinians" or "Palestinian People" are being and will be construed by you as "Palestinian Arabs."

> B. In each paragraph in which the expression "West Bank" appears, it is being and will be, understood by the Government of Israel as Judea and Samaria.

THE ISRAELI-EGYPTIAN PEACE TREATY

The treaty of peace between the two formerly irreconcilable enemies was signed at the White House on March 26, 1979. Israel began the process of evacuating the Sinai immediately. On April 30, Israelis could sit before their television sets and watch the first ship flying the Israeli flag going through the Suez Canal. The ultimate evacuation of all the Sinai was accomplished without violence, although some residents of abandoned Yamit had to be carried physically to the evacuation trucks by Israeli soldiers. The town that Begin had once planned to retire in was abandoned to the desert. The government of Israel paid compensation to those who lost their property and helped them find homes elsewhere. A few simply left the country altogether.

Anwar Sadat managed to persuade the Israelis to accept extremely unpalatable conditions while convincing themselves that they had achieved real peace with an Arab neighbor. As soon as normal bus, air, and sea connections opened between Israel and Egypt, thousands of Israelis crowded across the border to visit the pyramids and the other wonders of ancient Egypt. At first it was not so obvious that only a few score Egyptians, mostly scholars, made the return trip. While Anwar Sadat lived, the controlled Egyptian press curtailed or eliminated the open attacks on Jews that had been the hallmark of unrelenting cartoons before the talks of Camp David. Jehan Sadat, the Egyptian president's wife, continues to travel untiringly to construct a bridge of friendship to Jews around the world.

Building Jewish Residence in Judea and Samaria

After the talks at Camp David, Menachem Begin heightened his devotion to Jewish settlement in Judea and Samaria. Dozens of new Jewish towns were established on hilltops in the desolate mountain country. Accompanying all that building was the necessity of designing roads, creating bus service, establishing military camps, and making provision for water, electricity, and telephone service. Begin regarded the permanence of Jewish residence in all parts of Eretz Israel (the Land of Israel) as Israel's compensation for the sacrifice of the Sinai. But President Carter became increasingly critical of Israeli settlement in the territories, regarding it as an obstacle to peace. The nations of the Common Market (the European Economic Community), dependent on Arab oil and trade, became even more overtly anti-Israel. Israel's final evacuation of the Sinai was to be completed by April 1982.

As the date of Israel's final retreat from the Sinai approached, Israelis who had applauded the Camp David talks began to feel pangs of regret. The feeling of security they had felt when the Sinai and Red Sea were securely in Israel's hands began to wane as other clouds appeared on the horizon. A war in Lebanon heightened that sense of malaise. To make things worse, Egypt, certain of the repossession of the Sinai, joined in damning Israel's settlement policy in Judea and Samaria.

BEGIN'S ELECTORAL CHANCES

Israel was scheduled to have an election on June 30, 1981. Begin was losing popularity rapidly. The economy was in a critical state as inflation climbed to 130 percent. Black-market money-changers operated openly in the streets. The long-established Israeli financial practice of quoting loans or mortgages in dollars, rather than Israeli shekels, now became routine. Indeed, the state of the economy was so bad that Moshe Dayan and Ezer Weizman, the two Laborites who had served as cabinet ministers in the Likud government, joined their old Labor comrades in voting "no confidence" in November 1980. The government did not fall, but its chances of an electoral victory seemed slight.

Operation Babylon

However, a number of events saved Begin and Likud. The most important was Israel's destruction of Iraq's nuclear reactor at Osirak, close to Baghdad. Israel's intelligence services had persuaded Begin that Iraq was preparing atomic weaponry. The USSR had built the plant. France had agreed to provide scientific staff to develop it in exchange for a sure supply of Iraqi oil. Iraq denied that it had any intention of producing atomic weaponry. (However, considering its prolonged war against neighboring Iran, and its aggression against neighboring Kuwait nine years later, its motives might be suspect.)

Operation Babylon, as Israel named the strike at Osirak, was a model of textbook efficiency. Just before sunset on June 7, 1981, when the work force had gone home, eight Israeli fighter bombers swept down on Osirak, dropped their bombs, and utterly destroyed the nuclear plant within two minutes. For Israel, the destruction of Osirak was a victory against a clear and present danger.

Perhaps the rest of the world privately applauded the elimination of an atomic threat, but the delegates in the United Nations chose to condemn Israel. Nonetheless, whatever the UN may have thought, the destruction of the atomic plant served as a great boost for Begin's election campaign. It was also his good fortune that the two leaders of the Laborite opposition, Yitzchak Rabin and Shimon Peres, were bitterly and personally hostile to each other. Laborite openly criticizing Laborite gave Likud an unexpected advantage. Finally, Labor was perceived as the party of Ashkenazic Jews of European ancestry. Likud, though led by Ashkenazim, had the reputation of having always championed the Sephardim, the Near Eastern and North African Jews. This ethnic jealousy between the two Jewish camps also worked to the advantage of Likud.

Results of the 1981 Election

The election of 1981 was not the Likud landslide that the election of 1977 had been. Nevertheless, Begin was able to obtain the necessary minimum of sixty-one Knesset votes by forming a coalition among Likud, two religious parties, and an oriental Jewish ethnic party. In what may have been a mixed blessing, the government strengthened its hand by naming General Ariel Sharon as minister of defense. The general was a courageous and effective field commander who had become a national hero through his battlefield victories in 1956, 1967, and 1973. In 1973 by entrapping the Third Egyptian Army he had turned defeat into victory. However, the new minister's supreme self-confidence did not lend itself to seeking the opinion of others.

It was Begin's hope that he could advance Israeli settlement in Judea and Samaria while offering the Arabs greater autonomy in their own areas. However, he was stymied from the beginning when Jewish terrorists attempted to murder Arab mayors, succeeding only in injuring them severely and causing them to become heroic martyrs. In addition, the ultra-conservative Saudi government threw its considerable weight behind the PLO. Finally King Hussein, cautious as always, moved toward the PLO even though Jordan had been hostile to Yassir Arafat since Black September of 1970.

As a final disappointment to Begin's hopes to pacify Judea and Samaria, the Arab universities became centers for violent hostility. Those institutions had come into being only after Israel took over the territories in 1967 and encouraged their establishment. However, native and foreign academics adopted the PLO with enthusiasm and made it a cause through which student protest could thrive. Thus began a long process in which Israel closed and reopened universities, giving the PLO generous opportunities to propagandize against Israel.

THE ASSASSINATION OF SADAT

Then, on October 6, 1981, Moslem fundamentalists assassinated Anwar Sadat. The president who had conceived peace for Egypt was widely condemned in the Arab world for having dealt with Israel at all. His successor, Hosni Mubarak, while maintaining diplomatic ties with Israel, became openly hostile. Although he gave prompt and courteous attention to the official demarches, or diplomatic moves, of the Israeli ambassador, his public demeanor was glacial. The Egyptian press, taking its direction from the government, resumed the familiar anti-Jewish drum beat, offering a diet of cartoons picturing Israelis as Hitler's press had always portrayed Jews. In this roll call of Israeli misfortunes, one more struck Jerusalem hard.

President Ronald Reagan, having just defeated Jimmy Carter, was regarded as a strong friend of Israel. However, the new Reagan administration was preoccupied with saving Saudi Arabia from the revolutionary fate of Iran, in which Moslem fundamentalists had overthrown the shah in 1979. As a gesture in that direction, Reagan fought hard and successfully to obtain the Senate's consent to sell American

AWACS surveillance planes and equipment to the Saudis. Although the Saudis themselves were not a threat to Israel, their ability to track all Israeli military movements in most of the country implied danger, especially as the Saudis had moved close to the PLO. Saudi king Fahd had assumed a newly aggressive role, urging the creation of an independent Palestinian state. His new closeness to Yassir Arafat seemed to indicate that the PLO would inherit any state thus created. Of course, any such state would spell death for Begin's concept of Arab autonomy in Judea and Samaria.

PLANNING "PEACE IN GALILEE"

Against the background of these events Israel decided to strike the PLO and its bases in Lebanon. Yassir Arafat had assembled an army in southern Lebanon, equipped with standard infantry weapons and an arsenal of short-range missiles capable of striking a large part of the Galilee. These forces were able to terrorize northern Israel and were encamped in the midst of civilians. Israeli attempts to retaliate against PLO missile strikes inevitably would mean hitting innocent non-combatants as well.

For the Israelis, the great challenge was how to crush the PLO without precipitating full-scale and open war with Syria. It must be remembered that since 1976 Syria had occupied Lebanon's Bekaa Valley. Hafez el-Assad was well on his way to creating "Greater Syria," though he had not yet dared to snuff out the independence of Lebanon completely.

Menachem Begin tested the wind carefully. In December 1981 the Knesset extended Israeli law to the Golan Heights. This gesture stopped short of annexing the territory taken from Syria in 1967. Theoretically it merely applied the authority of civilian Israeli law courts to what had been the province of Israeli military law. Nevertheless it was a challenge to Syria that assertively claimed the lost territory. Syria, on that occasion, showed no intention of making the Golan an issue that would precipitate war.

When, on October 6, 1981, Egypt's Anwar Sadat was assassinated by Moslem fundamentalists, Israel watched closely to see how Syria would react to the fundamentalist threat. After all, Hafez el-Assad and a great number of Syria's army officers were members of the Alawite Moslem minority sect, and they were likely to feel threatened by the growth of fundamentalism in the Sunni Moslem majority. The Syrian dictator gave his answer in February 1982 when the Syrian army attacked Hama, a center for Sunni opposition to the Alawites. After taking the city, Assad's troops slaughtered an estimated 25,000 civilians. Israeli intelligence concluded that Syria would hold aloof from interference if Israel smashed the PLO in Lebanon, provided that Syria was not interfered with in any way. The Israelis then withdrew from the country. In other words, Assad would have no objections to the destruction of the PLO provided that Syrian hegemony was advanced. He evidently did not want war with Israel.

Israeli Goals in Lebanon: The Peace in Galilee Campaign

The new U.S. secretary of state, Alexander Haig, was friendly to Israel. Perhaps expecting that U.S. support was likely, Israeli policymakers considered the idea that Israel might invade Lebanon, crush and expel the PLO, then install a Lebanese government that would be prepared to enter an alliance with Israel. In retrospect, perhaps Israel was unrealistic in imagining that Lebanon could be converted into an ally of Israel without infuriating Syria and antagonizing the USSR.

There is no doubt that Prime Minister Begin favored a quick and thorough strike that would carry the Israeli army 40 kilometers into Lebanon, thereby pushing PLO missiles out of range for strikes at Israel. It is less clear how much the plans of Minister of Defense Ariel Sharon exceeded those that had been approved by the prime minister. Some witnesses affirm that Begin knew that Sharon planned to go all the way to Beirut. Others claim that the prime minister was surprised by the extent of Sharon's plans.

Menachem Begin ordered the army to invade Lebanon at 11:00 A.M. on June 6, 1982, naming the campaign Peace for Galilee. He gave public assurance that Israel would not attack the Syrian army in Lebanon if it did not attack the Israelis. The first week of the invasion witnessed an easy Israeli victory that eliminated the surface-to-air missile systems of Soviet origin, gained control of the skies, and went well beyond the 40 kilometers to the outskirts of Beirut. The Israeli navy closed off all the sea approaches to Beirut. The army overran all the PLO positions and seized its huge weapons supply. There, however, the victorious march faltered.

Israel had counted on the active support of Lebanon's Maronite Christians, who had been pushed out of their historic position of dominance by the PLO. That hope was disappointed badly, however. The Maronite leader, Bashir Gemayel, had pinned his hopes on an Israeli victory that would permit him to be elected president of Lebanon without exposing his own followers to risk. Failing to receive the anticipated Maronite support and unwilling to endure heavy Israeli casualties in a block-by-block conquest of the PLO in Beirut, Israel sought to obtain a negotiated PLO retreat, which would be arranged by Philip Habib, the U.S. ambassador-at-large. Habib, however, was unsuccessful, and the victory that had seemed within Israel's grasp in June withered in a bloody, nine-week siege of Beirut.

However, not a single Arab power intervened to save the PLO, and by August the battle seemed over. Evacuating Beirut, Yassir Arafat and thousands of his minions were carried to distant Tunisia. It seemed as though Menachem Begin could indeed claim the security of Peace for Galilee.

American Interference

President Reagan launched his own peace initiative on September 1, 1982. The president informed Israel of the substance of the plan only one day before he presented it to the world on television. In effect, it supported a Palestinian state and denied the right of Jewish residence in Judea and Samaria. As it denied the central doctrines of Likud and Prime Minister Begin's basic philosophy, Begin would not consider it. Precisely because the Reagan initiative embarrassed Begin, it was applauded by the Arab states and drew friendly comments from the PLO. However, like all public diplomacy announced on television, it was stillborn.

The End of Israel's Lebanese Illusions

At the same time, Israel's illusions died. On August 23 Bashir Gemayel, who had done nothing to advance the defeat of the PLO, was elected president of Lebanon. However, on September 14 a bomb detonated in East Beirut, killing the newly elected president and twenty-six other people. Evidence pointed responsibility for the blast at Hafez el-Assad of Syria. Damascus had warned Israel that it would tolerate the expulsion of the PLO, but not the diminution of Syria's control of Lebanon.

Amin Gemayel, who replaced his brother as president of Lebanon, signed a peace treaty with Israel in May 1983, but it became meaningless almost before the ink could dry. The true ruin of Israel's efforts to pacify

Lebanon came quite unpredictably. On the night of September 14, 1982, the Israeli chief of staff, Rafael Eitan, under the direct orders of Minister of Defense Ariel Sharon, allowed hundreds of armed Maronites to enter Palestinian refugee camps at Sabra and Chatila. Reputedly the Maronites were only charged with eliminating pockets of PLO armed terrorists who had found shelter in the midst of civilians. What actually happened was that an unrestricted slaughter of more than seven hundred unarmed men, women, and children began. The carnage continued for almost two days before the Israelis intervened to stop the bloodshed. The news of that atrocity electrified Israel.

Sabra, Chatila, and Israeli Demoralization

On September 25, 1982, a massive protest rally involving several hundred thousand Israelis filled the streets of Tel Aviv. Israel was shocked that what had been considered a justified act of war against PLO strongholds in June had become a shameful betrayal of all those virtues in which Israelis had always taken pride. After several days spent in denying what witnesses said had happened, the cabinet was forced by popular demand to convene a commission whose chairman was the president of Israel's Supreme Court. Known from his name as the Kahan Commission, the hundreds of pages of testimony spared no one. Sharon was forced to surrender the Ministry of Defense, but he was not forced to leave the cabinet.

In the aftermath of the findings of the Kahan Commission, Menachem Begin went into seclusion. He retired on September 15, 1983. The man whose life had always been marked by courage, unostentatious religious faith, and personal dignity felt himself stained by the horrors at Sabra and Chatila.

An international armed expedition replaced the Israelis as they retreated from Beirut. No one won any victories. Hundreds of U.S. Marines died when their barracks in Beirut were blown up by Lebanese Shi'ite suicide bombers. In the end, television showed the mightiest warships in the U.S. navy firing artillery rounds at the mountainous Lebanese coast as President Reagan called his forces home in February 1984. More than four hundred Israeli soldiers had died in attaining Peace for Galilee. Although Yassir Arafat was now in distant Tunisia, how long would he stay there?

11

The Uncertain Direction, 1983–1992

A TIME OF TRANSITION

The Lebanese Cauldron

The retirement of Menachem Begin did not cause the uncertainty that beset Israel, but symbolized it. Even after the retreat of the Israeli army from Beirut, the Israelis remained camped in southern Lebanon to provide a protective screen for Israel proper. Over time they enlisted a native southern Lebanese military contingent, made up mostly of Maronite volunteers, in that effort. Israel's efforts to win large-scale new alliances with the Lebanese exacerbated that troubled situation. It was evident that Israel could not maintain an alliance with the Druse while upholding the old alliance with the Maronites. Israel found itself drawn into the maelstrom setting Druse, Maronites, and Sunni and Shi'ite Moslems against one another. (It is interesting to note that Israeli archives contain an unsigned twenty-eight page document, written in 1860 by a Prussian secret agent, describing the Lebanese civil war of that era. The similarity of leaders, places, and events was striking. Even the names of the clan chiefs were the same, although separated by many generations.)

By 1984 Israel had lost six hundred soldiers in a war that was gaining little for Israeli security. The nation was becoming increasingly divided between those who regarded a military presence in Lebanon as necessary, and those who urged retreat even if it meant the return of the PLO. Israeli groups such as Shalom Achshav ("Peace Now") made headlines with dramatic pleas to force the government to quit Lebanon. Defenders of the government dismissed Shalom Achshav as Shalom Achzav ("Deluded Peace"). Still other small groups urged Israeli soldiers to refuse to serve in Lebanon. A few urged insubordination on soldiers stationed in Judea or Samaria. These voices, though small in number, were distressing because throughout most of Israel's short history both the political left and right had accepted Golda Meir's view that *ain brera* ("no choice") was the reality for Israelis facing the Arab determination to destroy the state.

Prime Minister Yitzchak Shamir

Following the departure of Begin, the prime-ministership passed to Yitzchak Shamir, who had been the commander of LEHI during the War of Independence. His tenure of power was very short because the Labor Party was able to exploit economic problems to force early elections. The war and its consequences had required austerity, which delayed national economic growth. Foreign currency reserves were below $3 billion. Inflation was eating up the savings of the poor. All this, coupled with the discouraging news from Lebanon, brought on a "no confidence" parliamentary vote. New elections, nearly a year early, were forced on Yitzchak Shamir on July 23, 1984.

The National Election of 1984

One unique feature of the newly elected eleventh Knesset was that twenty-six parties ran for seats. Since it was highly unlikely that all of them could win enough votes to win even one seat, the final result would be a cacophony of small claques, each concerned with single causes. The final result would inevitably force the prime minister, heading the largest party, to sign complex agreements with small parties in order to construct a shaky coalition giving him the required minimum of sixty-one Knesset votes. On both the right and left, tiny and fragmented one-cause parties would be very difficult for a prime minister to appease.

To the right, Kach, with only one member of parliament (Rabbi Meir Kahane, its founder), proposed to induce, persuade, or force all Arabs to leave the country. Four parties were closely tied to the Gush Emunim

("Bloc of the Faithful"), which was almost exclusively concerned with building Jewish residence in Judea and Samaria. To the left, the Citizens' Rights Movement held three seats and was closely identified with Peace Now. The Jewish-Arab Progressive List for Peace, a Communist Front Party, won two seats. Still other tiny parties contributed to the electoral chaos. It was apparent that neither Labor nor Likud could form a government devoted to Zionist principles that could count on sixty-one votes.

A Government of "National Unity"

Two months of desperate attempts failed to patch together a government composed of either Likud or Labor with a coalition of small parties. None of the small factions had more than five members in the Knesset. In desperation, Likud proposed a government of national unity in partnership with Labor. In September 1984 the two largest parties joined with four religious parties and a patchwork of small factions. Although the fringe parties, plus Likud and Labor, created a coalition of ninety-seven votes, some of them were so ideologically opposed to one another that effective government would be difficult to achieve unless everyone walked a precarious tightrope of compromise.

Peres, Rabin, and Shamir as Partners

This strange and easily threatened government created an unprecedented division of power. Shimon Peres of Labor, who had never before served as prime minister, was to receive that office for twenty-five months. Yitzchak Shamir of Likud would then hold the prime-ministership for the next twenty-five months. The two men, when not prime minister, would be foreign minister. Throughout the entire fifty-month period Yitzchak Rabin would serve as minister of defense.

In the course of the years of uncertainty typified by the National Unity Government, two extraordinary reinforcements reached Israel. They were the Jews of the Soviet Union and the Beta Yisrael, or Black Jews, of Ethiopia.

IMMIGRATION OF SOVIET JEWS

Perhaps the most dramatic development of the years following the Camp David accords was the emergence of Russian Jewish immigration. As described previously, the rebirth of Soviet Jewish ethnic consciousness can be dated to 1967. At first it was almost entirely dominated by young people and lacked direction. However, by 1970 foreign Jews—chiefly in the United States—began a multifaceted campaign. On one level this consisted of smuggling prayerbooks, Hebrew grammars, Jewish calendars, and Jewish ceremonial objects past the Soviet customs officials who were searching the luggage of Jewish tourists. Because Soviet Jews found it extremely difficult to entertain foreign guests, as all tourists were under the watchful supervision of government agents, foreigners usually visited a synagogue where they could "accidentally" leave their gifts on a bench, hoping that the gifts would be taken home by a serious worshipper rather than one of the ubiquitous agents planted by the government in the few remaining Jewish institutions. At the same time, Hebrew language and religious study groups began to form in private homes.

Paralleling this, a small but growing group of Jewish dissidents began to seek visas to immigrate to Israel. Jews seeking such visas had to present a letter from a close relative in Israel. After 1967 there was no Israeli embassy in Moscow. Therefore, the Embassy of the Netherlands acted on behalf of Israel in processing visas issued by the USSR. The usual result for a would-be immigrant was either the loss of employment or intolerable harassment. Persons who had received an advanced university degree were usually forced to pay an excessive "education tax." This was dropped in 1973 when the U.S. secretary of the Treasury, George Shultz, protested to Leonid Brezhnev, general secretary of the Communist Party of the Soviet Union. The Soviet government then began to torment would-be immigrants with punitive legal charges ranging from "hooliganism" to "espionage." A new word, *refusenik*, then entered the English language. Long jail sentences were intended to intimidate would-be immigrants. A growing band including the heroic Natan Sharansky resisted Soviet repression even in prison. He has published the memoirs of his years in a Soviet prison's isolation cell. Today, he holds a seat in the Israeli cabinet and has become a champion of the rights of all recent immigrants.

To rescue those who had lost their employment and income because they awaited a long-delayed visa, foreign Jewish organizations sent as much relief as possible. Young American Jews would travel as tourists to the USSR carrying small objects that could be sold for high prices on the illegal but open free market. An item such as a fake fur garment might be temporarily in demand. American or British Zionist organizations would open clandestine links to the growing Soviet Jewish Zionist underground. Then, as often as the demands of the free market changed, couriers would carry prized sale items to Soviet contacts who could raise money for Jews awaiting their visas to Israel.

In a 1972 visit to the USSR, President Nixon made it a point to advocate the right of Jews to emigrate freely. U.S. Senator Henry Jackson attempted to tie freedom of emigration to a trade bill that was highly sought by the Soviets. In 1973 Henry Kissinger, visiting Moscow, gave the Soviets a list of 738 Jews specifically seeking emigration.

Although the Soviets continued the harassment of Jews seeking visas, the numbers of persons being allowed to leave steadily increased. However, at the moment when Jewish emigration opened dramatically, the Israeli economy was at a low point. Thus, an increasing percentage of Jews arriving in Israel despaired of earning a living there. A disproportionate percentage of the new immigrants were academics, medical personnel, professional musicians, artists, and scientists. Although such new arrivals represented a great boon to Israeli cultural life, the small nation found it hard to absorb them in a hurry. Their mastery of Hebrew, a language entirely new to them, was slow. In addition, because Soviet medicine lagged behind Israeli medical competence, retraining was required.

A growing percentage of Soviet Jews stayed in Israel only long enough to receive an Israeli passport and citizenship, then sought entry to the United States or some other western country. Others skipped even that step and journeyed from Vienna (through which the Jewish Agency routed their departure from the USSR) to Italy. There the American Hebrew Immigrant Aid Society (HIAS) established transient residence facilities for those willing to tolerate the long wait for a visa permitting them to enter the United States. In economically difficult times, the percentage of Soviet Jews going to Israel and striving to create a new life there steadily declined.

However, the great boom in Soviet Jewish settlement in Israel coincided with the somewhat dreary years of the Unity Government. One year after the initiation of that experiment, Mikhail Gorbachev became general secretary of the Communist Party of the Soviet Union—and ultimately its president. His fundamental reforms and the ultimate breakup of the Soviet Union opened the gates to a huge flood of refugees of all ethnic stocks. The United States and other advanced western nations did not close their doors to fleeing Jews, but in 1985 it became increasingly difficult for Soviet Jews to choose a destination other than Israel. Too many of them were becoming applicants for welfare support and U.S. politicians became increasingly reluctant to become burdened with a potentially indigent population.

Suddenly a great flood of immigrants produced more than a million new Israelis. Perhaps as many as one-third of the newcomers had no claim to Jewish ethnicity, except for one parent or grandparent. The Israeli rabbinate was suddenly inundated with candidates for religious conversion, seeking the automatic citizenship that the Israeli Law of Return confers on Jews. Ironically, the Russian Orthodox Church in Israel gained a large new membership of Christians in that flood of humanity.

Having no other place to go, the new immigrants decided to remain in Israel. Although Israel has experience with housing masses of newcomers, there had been nothing like the arrival of the former Soviet Jews since the *maabarot*, or transit camps, of the 1940s and 1950s. The younger immigrants found it easiest to learn Hebrew and to begin the daunting quest for retraining in their old profession. Physicians and dentists performed useful functions by serving in the clinics of small and isolated towns where veteran Israelis did not choose to go. The army remained the great equalizer, as the younger immigrants became conscripts serving the country and learning Hebrew at the same time.

ARRIVAL OF THE BLACK JEWS OF ETHIOPIA

Side-by-side with the Russians, a smaller but very visible immigration of another sort emerged. These are the so-called Black Jews of Ethiopia. Their enemies call them Falashas, or "Strangers." However, they prefer to be called the Beta Yisrael, or "House of Israel." Little was known about them until Jacques Faitlovitch (1881–1955), a French-Jewish anthropologist, entered Gondar and other parts of northern Ethiopia, confirming the existence of these Ethiopian Jews for the first time.

The Black Jews of Ethiopia claim to be descendants of the biblical Tribe of Dan, one of the patriarch Jacob's twelve sons. Modern anthropologists debate their origins but tend to describe them as descendants of Yemenite Jews who intermarried with African converts. They were apparently entirely isolated from other Jews because their Judaism rests solely on a literal reading of the Torah, the Five Books of Moses. They observe the commandments that are clearly prescribed by the Torah. They are unaware of the later books of the Bible and the entire body of rabbinic commentary in the Talmud. Their clergy, the *kessim*, are not associated with the hereditary priesthood (descended from Aaron, the brother of Moses) who enjoy special status among other Jews. The *kessim* are chiefly distinguished by their knowledge of Ghez, an ancient Semitic language not known by the laity. The Torah is read aloud in Ghez by the *kessim* and translated into Amharic, the modern Semitic language that is the vernacular tongue of the Ethiopian masses. Hebrew is not used for prayer or Torah reading.

Prime Minister Menachem Begin was the first Israeli political leader to open regular contact with the lost colony of Jews. The Ashkenazic rabbinate tended to express doubts about their identity as true Jews who would be entitled to Israeli citizenship under the Law of Return. The Sephardic chief rabbis, however, gave them full faith and credit as descendants of Dan.

As early as 1974, the Jewish self-help organization ORT sent agents to northern Ethiopia to compile a census of Jews. It was not until 1984, however, that the Israeli government launched Operation Moses, which undertook to guide Beta Yisrael on an extremely difficult journey by foot to camps in the Sudan from which they could be flown to Israel. However, the news leaked to the press. Arab Sudan, which had been willing to avert its eyes while this traffic in human beings grew, could no longer ignore the pro-Israel activity. The Sudan closed its doors.

The next opportunity to effect an Ethiopian exodus occurred in 1991 when Prime Minister Yitzchak Shamir launched Operation Solomon. The pro-Soviet Ethiopian Communist regime of Mengistu Haile Mariam fell in the spring of 1991, and a new Ethiopian government that was friendly to Israel took office. It then became possible to evacuate all Beta Yisrael who wanted to go to Israel. Massive flights began on May 24, 1991. Since then, regular air traffic has linked Addis Ababa and Israel.

There are now more than 60,000 Beta Yisrael in Israel. Despite their unfamiliarity with modern technology, they are eager to learn and be assimilated. The army, being Israel's great equalizer, has expedited the absorption of their youth. They learn Hebrew quickly because, like their native Amharic, it is a Semitic tongue. The Sephardic rabbinate has been receptive, and those Ethiopians who have settled in the midst of Sephardim have adopted normative Jewish religious practice. Already the first Ethiopian rabbis have been ordained. In the big cities, however, the Beta Yisrael generally are alienated from the *kessim* and the primitive African Judaism of their ancestors, and they have not adopted normative Talmudic Judaism.

Creating schools to absorb them has also been a problem. There is a grave danger that many may miss the benefits of Israeli elementary education and become part of a permanent underclass. Yet some of the children of the earliest arrivals are entering the universities, and one (Addisu Messala) holds a seat in the Knesset.

However, evidences of racial tension give cause for concern. For example, the Red Magen David, Israel's extension of the International Red Cross, had been accepting blood donations from the Beta Yisrael, but it was discovered that a much higher than normal percentage of such blood samples were infected with HIV, the virus that causes AIDS. Red Magen David then began to discard all Beta Yisrael blood donations without telling the donors that their gifts were wasted. When word slipped out, there were large-scale demonstrations; Red Magen David apologized and agreed to process the infected blood stocks in the usual way. It may be hoped that the Beta Yisrael will not bear the scars of a sense of exclusion because of that crisis.

In the meantime, in Ethiopia, tens of thousands of would-be immigrants have inundated the Israeli embassy with applications for transport. Known as the Falash Mura, these are the descendants of Beta Yisrael who accepted conversion to Christianity during the last century under duress, but who now wish to be recognized as Jews. A rabbi and teachers have been sent from Israel to prepare immigrants who seem sincere, rejecting those whose motives seem to be purely economic. The young Falash Mura are studying Hebrew and learning normative Jewish religious practice. A steady stream of these enthusiastic immigrants are regularly transported to join their kinsmen living in Israel.

THE *ACHILLE LAURO* AFFAIR

In the midst of these harbingers of the fulfillment of Theodor Herzl's dream of the ingathering of the exiles, Israel was made aware of danger on the horizon. On October 7, 1985, an Italian cruise ship, the *Achille Lauro*, set sail from Alexandria, Egypt, carrying passengers on a pleasure cruise. It was scheduled to make stops at Port Said, Egypt, and Ashdod, Israel. Aboard the vessel were four terrorists belonging to the Palestine Liberation Front, a faction within Yassir Arafat's PLO. They planned to hijack the ship.

An Italian steward aboard the *Achille Lauro* discovered that the four terrorists were on board and alerted the captain. The four men, realizing that they could not wait until they reached Ashdod to carry out their plot, decided to seize the vessel immediately and force it to head for Syria. However, Yassir Arafat was locked in a quarrel with Hafez el-Assad, the Syrian dictator, who declined to offer a safe harbor to the

PLO terrorists. They then panicked and seized a 69-year-old American tourist, Leon Klinghoffer, who had suffered a stroke and was confined to a wheelchair. The terrorists shot him and threw him and the wheelchair into the sea. After holding the ship's officers at gunpoint, the exhausted terrorists then decided to let the Italian crew sail them to Port Said, where they would take their chances with the Egyptian authorities.

At that juncture Mohammed Abu Abbas, the head of the Palestine Liberation Front, flew from Yassir Arafat's headquarters in Tunisia to Egypt. There he negotiated a deal with the Egyptians that would permit the four terrorists to leave Egypt; they would go to Tunisia, where Yassir Arafat would reputedly punish them. Hosni Mubarak, president of Egypt, was deeply embarrassed by the entire affair because Egypt was at peace with Israel. Mubarak did not want to provoke a quarrel with the United States, which sought justice for the murder of an American citizen. At the same time, Mubarak did not want to seem hostile to any PLO faction that was part of Arafat's forces.

Immediately Mubarak announced that Abu Abbas and the four terrorists had already left Egypt for Tunisia, although in fact they did not leave Egypt (aboard an Egyptian plane) until October 10. Both U.S. and Israeli intelligence services, however, knew exactly where the fugitives were. Fighter planes from the U.S. aircraft carrier *Saratoga* forced the Egyptian plane to land at Sigonella, Italy, where the Italian authorities took them into custody.

Abu Abbas was immediately freed on the grounds that he had not been involved in any crime. The other four were ultimately tried and imprisoned by an Italian court. Their alibi that Klinghoffer had not been murdered but had died of a heart attack did not hold up once the victim's body washed up on Syria's shore and Hafez el-Assad revealed that Klinghoffer had been shot through the head. Yassir Arafat then made a demonstrative public gesture, disassociating himself from Abu Abbas. The terrorists have enjoyed a long career in Italian, Spanish, and Greek prisons, leavened with dramatic and apparently easy escapes. Abu Abbas has recovered the good will of Yassir Arafat and is now a member of his advisory council.

THE POLLARD SPY CASE

Meanwhile the relations of Israel with its closest patron, the United States, fell into quicksand. Jonathan Jay Pollard, a civilian U.S. naval intelligence analyst, was arrested and charged with spying for Israel in

November 1985. It seems that he volunteered to give classified information to an agent at the Israeli Embassy in Washington who paid him
$45,000. Pollard protested that he had merely given the Israelis infor-
mation related to their security and that it ought to have been shared
between two nations pledged to such partnership. U.S. secretary of defense Caspar Weinberger, however, in a confidential message to the court
that tried Pollard, declared that the information shared with Israel was
compromising to the security of the United States. Pollard, who confessed fully the nature of his crime in hopes of winning a lighter sen-
tence, was sent to prison for life. Successive presidents of the United
States since 1985 have declined to pardon him or shorten his imprison-
ment. The exact nature of Pollard's crimes has never been revealed.

THE INTIFADA

Origins

The next crisis to afflict the Unity government was unexpected. On
December 8, 1987, an Israel tank-transport truck crashed into several
Arab cars in Gaza, killing four persons and injuring several others. At
the funerals of the victims, anti-Israel demonstrations began that soon
became riots. Spreading from Israeli-ruled Gaza, disturbances also broke
out in Egyptian-held neighboring Rafah and soon thereafter at scattered
sites in Jordan. The Egyptian and Jordanian armies suppressed disorder
on their side of the border. However, the riots spread in Israel and soon
assumed the appearance of a full-scale rebellion. This came to be called
the Intifada, literally a "shaking off": the Arab rebellion against Israeli
rule.

At this time Gaza contained the greatest Arab population density of
any area under Israeli rule. The Arab refugee camps endured crowded
squalor. Israeli attempts to improve their conditions and to incorporate
their sewer and electrical services into those enjoyed by the existent Arab
municipalities were resisted and blocked by the Arab authorities, who
did not wish to make any change that would render the refugee camps
permanent new municipalities. The Gazans held to their expectation that
when Israel was ultimately destroyed, the refugees would return to their
original homes. Even Anwar Sadat, fighting for Egyptian acquisition of
the Sinai Desert, showed no willingness to assume the burden of ruling
the Gaza Strip, which Egypt had administered from 1948 to 1967. The
Intifada rapidly spread to Arab towns in Judea and Samaria, and there

were public expressions of sympathy for it in prosperous Arab communities in Israel proper, such as Nazareth.

The PLO was caught by surprise by what started as a spontaneous rebellion. It scrambled to catch up to create an infrastructure that would provide some centralized leadership. The matter was rendered more complicated, however, when in February 1988 the Moslem fundamentalist movement called Hamas attempted to capture the rebellion by establishing its center of operations at Gaza. Another group, Islamic Jihad, had urged violent revolt even before the Intifada.

The revolt very quickly developed norms. The traditional leadership of older men was thrust aside and was assumed by activists in their twenties and thirties. The masked leaders organized mobs of Arab adolescents who could be pressed into action to throw stones at Israeli soldiers. Minister of Defense Yitzchak Rabin's first reaction to the news of disorder was to say angrily that the army should break the arms of the stone throwers. However, the situation soon developed the stolid automation of a carefully rehearsed dance. Bands of adolescents would assault Israeli army patrols with stones. The Israelis, most of them 18- and 19-year-old conscripts, would "return fire" with rubber bullets to avoid causing bloodshed. While the older riot leaders stayed safely in the rear, the young rock throwers became more bold. The army's standing orders were to avoid lethal fire, aiming only at the legs of the mob. Thus, this dangerous game gave the rock throwers good reason to stand behind stone walls. Inevitably some of the more daring young Arabs attempted to charge the armed soldiers, and the death toll began to climb.

Because it was far safer to throw stones at passing Israeli autos and buses, the Intifada gave rise to a burgeoning new industry for Israeli mechanics. Everyone whose daily life required driving through Arab towns had the windows of his vehicles plasticized. Thereafter glass struck by rocks no longer shattered but bore a spider web–shaped scar where the rocks had struck. Only the relatively rare use of Molotov cocktails (petrol laced with glue) posed real dangers to the lives of motorists. These confrontations, repeated often enough, became routine.

Effects on Arab Society

Soon competing leaderships began to assert themselves to claim supremacy. The PLO found itself in competition with Hamas and with other splinter groups. They contended with each other to assert their primacy. They would order Arab villagers to close their shops or not to attend school on a particular day, simply to force everyone to recognize their authority. The competition crippled Arab businesses trying to make a living as two or more organizations often commanded the population to close shop on different days. In once-prosperous Arab villages that became ghost towns, the graffiti of Arab organizations in conflict condemned the Israelis but damned each other as well. It wasn't long before the Israeli army commandeered the rooftops of strategically located Arab houses to prevent excessive stone throwing. Through all of the *intifada*, the worst incidental consequence was the race of foreign and domestic television cameramen to show scenes of rock throwing. They were not above inducing groups of youth to stage a rock throwing exercise. If new film was not available, old scenes were sometimes replayed.

One consequence of the Intifada was a frantic search for foreign workers to replace the increasingly undependable Arabs from the territories. Whether from Thailand or Rumania, these newcomers evidently liked what they found because what began as a trickle became a flood. Once in Israel, they rarely wanted to leave. By marrying Israelis or obtaining legal rights to stay and open businesses, their population grew. Israel's Central Bureau of Statistics reported as recently as November 1995 that the country had 60,000 legal workers and some 47,000 "illegals."

Jordanian Reaction

At the heart of the changing political situation lay the position taken by King Hussein of Jordan. Ever since the Arab states declared that the PLO was the only legitimate representative of the Palestinian people, the king had faced an impossible situation. On one hand, he continued to subsidize institutions operated by the Arab inhabitants of the territories known as the West Bank until 1967. Those inhabitants held Jordanian citizenship. Furthermore, since 1971, without a formal treaty, Israel allowed the passage of people and consumer products across the Jordan River. The king's government made a very serious effort to deter terrorists from entering Israel. The king knew well that Israel was his surest guarantee that Hafez el-Assad would not swallow Jordan as a province of "Greater Syria." Furthermore, the Israeli Labor Party still held to the Allon Plan, which offered to cede a large part of the former West Bank to Jordan (although not as much as the king regarded as his due).

Nevertheless the king felt ill-used. The Arab nations and the United

Nations had officially replaced him with Yassir Arafat's PLO. Thus, on July 31, 1988, King Hussein formally renounced all claims to the West Bank and declared that it belonged to the PLO. He offered the reassurance that his subjects there could count on his protection for the time being. However, he hinted that someday they might lose Jordanian citizenship. He canceled a five-year development plan for the West Bank, which spread panic. He also dissolved the Jordanian Parliament and announced that thenceforth residents of the West Bank could not vote or receive representation in the next election. In an additional blow, on August 4 Hussein laid off twenty thousand government employees who lived west of the Jordan River.

In all this posturing the king was gambling that Israel would never recognize the PLO. This would permit him to recognize the PLO while making it clear that Jordan was absolutely necessary to any permanent settlement west of the Jordan River.

THE PLO PROCLAIMS THE "STATE OF PALESTINE"

In November 1988 the PLO's Palestine National Congress, meeting in Algiers, proclaimed the existence of "the State of Palestine, with its capital in the holy Jerusalem." Aware that only such a declaration might win recognition by the United States, the Palestine National Congress (PNC) announced its readiness to negotiate with Israel on the basis of United Nations Resolutions 242 and 238. Resolutions 242 and 238 reaffirm the principle first enunciated in 1967, namely that peace can be achieved only through open negotiations and definitive maps. This meant little because of the interpretation applied to Resolution 242 as a consequence of the difference between the English and French versions of that document. However, even a pretended willingness to recognize Israel marked a major break with the PLO charter, which called for violent struggle against Israel and the destruction of that state. More significant, the PLO declaration called for a confederation between Jordan and a PLO State of Palestine.

The United States Considers Recognition

In December 1988 the PLO gained enormously when U.S. secretary of state George Shultz referred publicly to the PLO Declaration of Palestinian Independence as a concept planned for the future, although he desisted from recognizing it as a fact. Thereafter a dialogue was begun between the U.S. ambassador in Tunis, Robert Pelletreau, Jr., and the PLO, whose headquarters was located there.

What followed was fifteen months of maneuvering on the international scene. Fifty nations of the Third World, the Soviet bloc, and even Greece (a member of NATO) rushed to offer full diplomatic recognition to the newly proclaimed "State of Palestine." Much more threatening to Israel was a shattering of Israeli unity.

Israeli Opinion Is Divided

On the right wing, Prime Minister Shamir offered the Arab inhabitants of Judea, Samaria, and Gaza free elections to determine the direction of their own autonomous self-government. He specifically denied, however, that he would consider an independent Palestinian Arab state or the surrender of Israeli control of security within those territories. Shamir made it clear that the PLO would not be recognized as a partner in such a program.

On the left, the mainstream of the Labor Party as well as the radical far left came to regard it as inevitable that the PLO be recognized and become a party to the creation of an independent Palestinian Arab state.

During that interval of shift within Israel, in January 1989 George Bush became president of the United States and James Baker his secretary of state. Baker, particularly, became increasingly hostile to Israel's rejection of ties with the PLO and its refusal to partition the country. He opposed the residence of Jews in Judea and Samaria, as well as East Jerusalem. It was precisely the right of Jewish residence all over the country that was central to Likud's platform.

BUSH, BAKER, AND RISING HOSTILITY TO ISRAEL

Even before Baker adopted the Arab position, growing Israeli disunity brought on a crisis. On March 15, 1990, Labor's Central Committee decided to quit the beleaguered Unity Government headed by Yitzchak Shamir. To avoid the necessity of new elections, an attempt was made to patch together a new government. Shimon Peres failed to obtain enough support to create a coalition with the necessary support of 61 members of the Knesset. Yitzchak Shamir, with 40 members of his own Likud Party, was able to form an extremely fragile coalition of 62 by gaining the support of the religious parties and two small nationalist parties. In addition, in February 1991 Shamir reluctantly invited Moledet, a most aggressively nationalist party, to join his coalition. This move gave the prime minister more votes to keep his government in power, but it made any kind of concession to the Arabs even more difficult. On the other side of the debate, Hosni Mubarak of Egypt also found himself free to take an increasingly stubborn position owing to the apparent encouragement given him by Secretary of State Baker.

The new right-wing government abandoned Shamir's proposals to schedule elections to attain Arab Palestinian self-government because the entire matter had been foreclosed by Mubarak and Baker. Baker favored partition of the country, recognition of the PLO, and denial of the right of Jewish residence in the disputed territories.

The PLO "Shoots Itself in the Foot"

At that juncture the PLO itself unwittingly helped to rescue Israel and the United States from what had become a hostile impasse. On May 30, 1990, a branch of the PLO launched sixteen terrorists in six speedboats on a projected attack that was intended to strike the Israeli coast at Tel Aviv. The Israeli navy dispatched them quickly. It was proven that the architect of the failed attack was Abu Abbas, the same member of Yassir Arafat's Executive Committee who had tried to enable the *Achille Lauro* hijackers to escape arrest after the murder of Leon Klinghoffer in 1985. It was impossible then to pretend that the PLO had renounced terrorism. Talks between the U.S. ambassador to Tunisia, Robert Pelletreau, and the PLO at Tunis were terminated. At that point, still another event made clear the uselessness of collaborating with the PLO.

THE TEMPLE MOUNT "MASSACRE"

For many years a few dozen eccentric, Jewish enthusiasts calling themselves the Temple Mount Faithful have been in the habit of announcing at major Jewish holidays that they intend to climb the Temple Mount in the Old City of Jerusalem and lay a cornerstone for the construction of the Third Jewish Temple. Their leader, Gershom Salamon, is not recognized by most religious Jews and has been disavowed by the rabbinate. In September 1990 Salamon made his usual announcement at the advent of the Jewish New Year. On that occasion, concerned Jewish citizens brought a suit before the Israel Supreme Court, and a judicial decision barred the Temple Mount Faithful from the Mount. The police announced that they would enforce the ban. On October 1, and during the ensuing week, Teddy Kollek, mayor of Jerusalem, placed paid ads in four Arabic newspapers circulated in Jerusalem, assuring Arabs that the police would bar Gershom Salamon and his followers from ascending the Mount.

Meanwhile the Arab leadership of the Intifada—both from the secularist wing of the PLO and from the Hamas Moslem fundamentalist wing—distributed leaflets to the Arabs in surrounding villages warning the villagers that Jews were plotting to seize El Aqsa, Islam's third holiest shrine, located on the Temple Mount. They were urged to mass on the Mount on Monday, October 8, to prevent the alleged Jewish plot. That morning as Jews were at prayer for the festival of Succot, at the western wall (Kotel) at the bottom of the Mount, an estimated three thousand Arabs began to throw stones, bottles, and other objects at the worshippers below. Security personnel were able to get Jewish worshippers out of harm's way, and only about a dozen persons were hurt. Even as it was apparent that no hostile action had been initiated by Jews, the loudspeakers at the mosques began to urge Arabs to hasten to the Mount to repel the alleged incursion.

The Israeli police took no action for ten minutes until an Arab mob tried to set fire to a small police station on the Mount. After receiving a radio call for help, the Border Police arrived. It was then that the out-of-control mob were met by lethal weapons. Twenty-one of the mob died, and an undetermined number were injured.

The United Nations Security Council then met and passed a censure of Israel. The United States voted for the measure. Perhaps the main reason for the U.S. decision was to build an alliance against Iraq on the eve of the Persian Gulf war. Perhaps it seemed necessary to condemn Israel in order to win the support of such Arab allies as Saudi Arabia, Syria, and Egypt. Among the members of the Security Council who identified themselves as defenders of civil rights and human dignity were China, Yemen, Zaire, and Colombia. Subsequently Israeli prime minister Shamir brought further condemnation on his country by refusing to receive a UN investigative commission because he believed that based on the Security Council's censure, the commission's report was already written. For Israel, this was the background against which a major world crisis erupted.

THE GULF WAR OF 1991

From September 1980 until July 1988, Iran and Iraq had been at war. The struggle derived in part from secularist Iraq fearing the aggressive Shi'ite Islam of Iran's Ayatollah Khomeini. Perhaps more fundamental, Iraq strove to widen its outlet to the sea to ensure control of the mouths of the Tigris and Euphrates Rivers, as well as its ability to export oil without fear of blockade at the Persian Gulf. Iraq had beaten Iran but had not solved any of the basic problems that induced Baghdad's original attack.

On August 2, 1990, Iraq attacked neighboring Kuwait with the dual goal of broadening its strategic seacoast on the Persian Gulf and at the same time forcing Kuwait to cut oil production, as it was a threat to Iraq's profits from that product. It became immediately evident that Saddam Hussein of Iraq intended to annex Kuwait, threatening the entire balance of power in the Persian Gulf. President George Bush and Secretary of State James Baker had miscalculated Saddam Hussein's intentions when he first threatened Kuwait.

Once aware of that oversight, however, the Bush administration moved with skill. The United States was anxious that this should not appear to be a war fought only by Americans. Syria and Egypt agreed to send troops to form a symbolic Arab alliance to defend Kuwait, the United Arab Emirates, and Saudi Arabia. The Americans also sought and obtained European military contingents, although they were essentially token forces. The only nation whose help was rejected was Israel. Evidently President Bush feared that Israel's contribution to a battle for Arab independence would so offend certain Arabs that they would not support this war.

When Saddam Hussein rejected a United Nations resolution to leave Kuwait by January 15, 1991, the Gulf War began. For Israel, the period from January 15 to February 28, 1991, was deeply painful. The Israelis were constrained by the strongest American pressure to do nothing in their own defense. The United States feared any Israeli action that would alienate Arab allies. The Americans sent anti-missile batteries to Israel to attempt to intercept and destroy Scud missiles fired by Iraq at Israel. All Israelis were fitted with gas masks, although Saddam Hussein is not known to have used gas. Most Israelis prepared one sealed room in their home to serve as a shelter if gas was used. The people maintained remarkably good morale despite being subjected to Iraqi missile attacks without being permitted to strike back. Being obliged to keep the Israeli air force on the ground while Iraqi weapons hit much of the Israeli coast induced a strong sense of shame and frustration.

The Bush administration pledged the money needed to repair missile damage. It also proposed to guarantee $10 billion in loan guarantees, helping to make it easier for Israel to borrow the money it needed to settle immigrants from the Soviet Union. However, the United States included a proviso that none of the money thus borrowed could be used to settle Jews in Judea and Samaria.

As the missiles flew over Israel, Arabs in Judea and Samaria held roof-top parties to celebrate Israel's humiliation. Because Jordan and the PLO supported Iraq, Kuwait expelled about 500,000 Palestinians even though these laborers had played no part in the decisions of Yassir Arafat.

To the great disappointment of most Israelis and a good part of world opinion in the West, Iraq was allowed to sue for peace while Saddam Hussein remained in office. For Israelis, it was frustrating to have un-dergone attack without gaining any political, strategic, or moral rewards.

THE MADRID PEACE CONFERENCE

The Bush administration ultimately reached the conclusion that only the acceptance of the PLO as a peace negotiator would end the Arab-Israeli conflict. This was decided in spite of the support given to Iraq during the war by Yassir Arafat and the PLO. Thus, in October 1991 Secretary of State James Baker managed to arrange an international peace conference, convening its opening sessions at Madrid. The ceremonial dignity of the Spanish monarchy acting as host lent the assemblage a certain dignity.

Calling in the favors owed for having rescued the Persian Gulf from Iraqi aggression, the United States was able to seat old enemies at the same table. The Israeli, Egyptian, Syrian, and Lebanese delegations were seated at the horseshoe-shaped table. If nothing else, Syria found itself listening to speeches by Israelis and acknowledging the de facto inde-pendence of a state against which Damascus had fought since 1948. A joint Jordanian-Palestinian delegation was created in order to seat PLO officials at the table without identifying them as such. Also present, though not counted as one of the negotiators, was the Saudi Arabian ambassador to the United States and the secretary-general of the Gulf Cooperation Council.

After the conference concluded its ceremonial initiation at Madrid, it continued meeting at Washington and elsewhere. However, it foundered in pointlessness. Prime Minister Shamir stood against the surrender of land. He seemed firmly opposed to the sort of concessions demanded by all the Arab delegations and the United States.

However, a dramatic development changed the picture. Prime Minister Shamir decided to advance Israel's national election, which had been scheduled for the autumn, to June 23, 1992. The results would determine the future.

12

Meretz Holds the Helm; The Peace Process, 1992–1996

THE ELECTION OF 1992

As the election progressed, the popular mood was quiet as short lines waited outside the polling places. No one seemed to have any inkling of an impending political earthquake. Not even the right-wing parties evinced any fear for the future, though it seemed likely that Yitzchak Rabin would lead the Labor Party to victory. After all, in the months before the election Rabin had beaten Shimon Peres in the battle for party leadership. Peres was regarded as a man held captive by impractical dreams and illusions. Rabin was regarded as rock-solid. Just three weeks before the election he had pledged, publicly, that Israel had no intention of yielding the Golan Heights. He had repeatedly stated that even for peace with the Arabs, Israel ought never to consider returning to the boundaries that had existed until June 4, 1967, on the eve of the Six-Day War. Indeed, Rabin won the election.

Forming a Cabinet

The thirteenth Knesset since the birth of independent Israel contained 10 political parties. Labor had 44 members. Defeated Likud had 32.

Chaim Herzog, president of Israel, would be obliged to invite Yitzchak Rabin, as the leader of Labor, to attempt to build a coalition of the essential minimum of 61 pledged votes. Outside the conservative, capitalist, and nationalist Likud Party, Labor had only a limited set of choices for coalition partners. A unity government encompassing both Labor and Likud would have solved the mathematics of getting a majority of the members of the Knesset to vote for a new government. However, a coalition between Labor and Likud had already been tried from September 1984 to March 1990. Both parties experienced frustration and confusion as their ill-begotten, two-headed horse pulled in different directions. Labor was determined in 1992 to find parties prepared to make peace with the Arabs by yielding land to some sort of Arab governing authority. The official Labor platform was still committed to the twenty-year-old Allon Plan, which would have given King Hussein's Jordan possession of Arab population centers in Judea and Samaria, with a land route to Jordan via Jericho. Israel would have received the Jordan Valley and would also have annexed the Etzion Bloc south of Jerusalem, including a passage to Kiryat Arba and the Tombs of the Patriarchs in Hebron, Judaism's second holiest shrine. The Etzion Bloc is a solid aggregation of Jewish towns south of Jerusalem which were regarded by almost all Israelis as essential for the future security of Israel's capital city.

Most Israelis would have settled for a similar compromise for the sake of peace. Even King Hussein's renunciation of his claims to the West Bank in 1988 did not foreclose the Laborite dream of a settlement with Hussein. Very few Israelis gave serious consideration to the possibility of collaboration with the PLO. To be sure, the United States under the Bush administration was moving closer to that, and a great number of Third World nations had actually recognized Yassir Arafat as president of a Palestinian state. However, in Israel it was still counted as a statutory crime to enter negotiations with terrorists. The PLO certainly fit that description, and Abie Nathan, the most dramatic Israeli peace activist, had actually served a short prison term for his public meetings with Arafat's staff. Therefore, few Israelis regarded the PLO as a serious choice.

However, if Labor was to construct a coalition without Likud, partners would have to be found who were willing to trade land for peace. The third largest party in the Knesset was an amalgam of three disparate factions calling itself Meretz. The twelve Meretz members of the Knesset were united by a common view that Israel must be prepared to give up control of all or most of Judea, Samaria, Gaza, and the Golan—lands that

Israel had administered since the Six-Day War. They believed that only in this way could peace be obtained with the Arabs. Some adherents of Meretz were veterans of Mapam, the Marxist left wing of the old Labor Party. Mapam, before 1948, had believed in a binational state in which Jews and Arabs would share power. Other members of Meretz were primarily devoted to the advancement of civil rights. A few were hostile to Jewish religious orthodoxy and wished to scrap Ben-Gurion's Status Quo agreement that had kept religious peace since the birth of the state. The only thing that held this strongly individualistic group of twelve together was the determination to win peace with the Arabs through the surrender of land.

However, even if Meretz and Labor joined in a coalition of the left, they still did not have sixty-one sure votes in the Knesset. They achieved that by bringing an unlikely partner into their coalition. Shas is a Sephardic religious party led by Rabbi Ovadia Yosef, the former Sephardic chief rabbi. Rabbi Yosef held that Israel could surrender parts of the Holy Land to the Arabs if such a sacrifice would save lives and make peace possible.

By bringing these ill-matched and contentious factions together, Prime Minister Elect Rabin obtained sixty-two votes in the Knesset. In addition, he could count on two Communist Front parties represented by four Arab men and one Jewish woman, all of whom favored land cession and did not demand entry into the cabinet as the price of their support.

The Meretz Key to a Political Revolution

However, Rabin now found himself in an extremely uncomfortable position. He held to the Allon Plan and was deeply offended by the suggestion that Israel might strike a deal with the PLO. However, the twelve members of Meretz who were essential to the survival of his fragile coalition were prepared to retreat to the borders of 1967, although they held to the universal Zionist claim that Jerusalem would have to remain the undivided capital of Israel. Most members of Meretz and a small but growing minority of the Labor Party were prepared to deal with the PLO. After all, even former prime minister Yitzchak Shamir had submitted to entering the Madrid Conference and had sat at the same table as PLO officials thinly disguised as representatives of Jordan.

In the delicate political situation of 1992–1993, the crucial decision would be made by Foreign Minister Shimon Peres, not by Prime Minister Rabin. In Israel's political equation, Rabin needed Peres to keep unity in the party. The Labor Party needed Meretz to remain in office. Rabin was forced to yield precedence to his old political foe, Shimon Peres, or face the collapse of the government. The Meretz-Peres tail was now ready to wag the Israeli dog.

As early as 1991, long before winning office, Peres had begun extremely risky and illegal negotiations with the PLO. Central to the plan to legitimize Yassir Arafat and to bring the PLO to the center of the diplomatic stage were some unusual allies.

BIRTH OF THE OSLO ACCORDS

The foreign minister of Norway, Jorgen Holst, and his wife, Marianne Heiberg, provided discreet and inconspicuous meeting places where Peres's agents could meet with Yassir Arafat's top advisors in order to bring their plans to maturity. Marianne Heiberg played an especially significant role because she was a scholar who had pursued research in Judea and Samaria and who felt a deep and emotional commitment to the Palestinian Arab cause. Dr. Yossi Beilin, who was to become a deputy foreign minister and ultimately a cabinet minister after Labor came to power, probably took the leading role in formulating the *Declaration of Principles* that was the basis of what became known as the Oslo Accords. Joel Singer, a partner in a Washington law firm, was one of the principal architects of those accords. Even before the elections of June 1992, reports appeared in the Israeli press concerning Beilin's not-so-secret illegal meetings with PLO officials. Apparently, by then, most Israelis were prepared emotionally for such conversations. Indeed, in February 1993 the new Kenesset revoked the law prohibiting meetings with the PLO. Thenceforth, anything that had been accomplished clandestinely could be revealed. The gradual leakage of such news created no public shock.

The Political Philosophy of Shimon Peres

Shimon Peres's book, *The New Middle East* (published in 1993) explicitly stated his political philosophy. Its thesis is that the solution to international problems is the generation of prosperity. Peres apparently believed that the nations of the Middle East can become very much like the European Union, whose economies are so bound to one another that old enemies like France and Germany can no longer do without one another. Peres held that when prosperity displaces nationalism, age-old hatreds become obsolete. Everyone would agree that there is an undeniable appeal to such dreams for the future. Peres's admirers would aver that bold risks must be taken to achieve peace. However, his critics would dismiss his ideas as delusions. Some future generation of historians will wrestle with the dramatic shift in Peres's world view, swinging from his hawkish philosophy as a close ally of David Ben-Gurion in the nineteen-fifties, to his adoption of a post-Zionist "little Israel" during the Unity Government of 1984.

The public was not told immediately of the Oslo Accords. The government allowed the impression to be given that nothing startling had taken place, only that (1) Arab-inhabited towns would be self-governing, (2) they would have their own lightly armed police force, and (3) an administrative council, to be known as the Palestine Authority (PA), would be elected by Arab voters. Only after Oslo I was published did the Israeli public learn that the Palestine Authority would enjoy supreme authority in designated areas and that the Israeli army would have no right to enter such areas, even in pursuit of terrorists fleeing arrest.

Oslo and the White House

On September 13, 1993, Prime Minister Rabin, Foreign Minister Peres, and Palestine Authority Chairman Arafat shook hands on the White House lawn under the genial patronage of President Clinton and signed documents formalizing the Oslo pact. Only then was the full nature of the document known. It is unprecedented in the history of democratic governments for a treaty binding a nation to such serious concessions to be signed in so public a manner, without the Israeli legislature having a chance to accept or reject its premises. As long as the Peres-Meretz team held power, all their policies were carried out in secrecy and were revealed only when they were irrevocable.

As long as Shimon Peres held office, he denied that he created an independent Palestinian state whose borders would run within 9 miles of the Mediterranean Sea, capable of cutting Israel in half. Arafat is now styled "Reis," which the Israelis translate as "Chairman" but which Arafat's supporters call "President." Yassir Arafat had made no secret of his intention of being president of Palestine, and in a world where symbols matter a great deal, the logo on his stationery shows the Republic of Palestine encompassing all of Israel. The Israelis still speak of the indivisibility of "Israel's eternal capital, Jerusalem." Reis Arafat speaks of "holy Jerusalem, the Capital of the State of Palestine." Foreign Minister Peres never contradicted top officials of the Palestine Authority who used such language. As long as Peres held office, rumors flew that he had given at least verbal assent to the creation of a sovereign republic of Palestine with its capital in Jerusalem.

Arafat Pledges to Revise the PLO Charter

On September 9, 1993, before the ceremony on the White House lawn, Arafat solemnly wrote to Rabin pledging that he would convene a meeting of the Palestine National Council to repeal all clauses of the PLO charter of 1968 that approve terror as a legitimate weapon or that suggest that Israel must be destroyed. The cogent part of Arafat's letter stated:

> In view of the promise of a new era and the signing of the Declaration of Principles, and based on Palestinian acceptance of Security Council Resolutions 242 and 238, the PLO affirms that those articles of the Palestinian Covenant which deny Israel's right to exist, and the provisions of the Covenant which are inconsistent with the commitment of this letter, are now inoperative and no longer valid. Consequently, the PLO undertakes to submit to the Palestine National Council for formal approval the necessary changes in regard to the Palestinian Covenant.

Reis Arafat must have been aware that such promises go against Article 33 of the Covenant, which states that the "Charter shall not be amended save by a majority of two-thirds of the total membership of the National Congress of the Palestine Liberation Organization at a special session convened for that purpose." Nevertheless, to accommodate a meeting of the PNC the Israelis opened their door to the free entry of all members of the Congress. These included persons who had perpetrated bloody crimes and who had, until 1993, been counted as criminal outlaws.

Yassir Arafat has never carried out his promise to amend the old charter and to write a new one recognizing Israel's legitimacy. Even when the Rabin government completed the negotiation of the final provisions for the partition of Judea, Samaria, and Gaza (known as Oslo II) in 1995, all that could be gotten from Arafat was an assurance that the PNC would, indeed, begin consideration of charter revision. Once the PA actually received possession of eight cities in Judea, Samaria, and Gaza, Reis Arafat dropped the pretense. He said that the PLO does not need a new charter because Israel does not have a written constitution either. The charter of 1968 remains on the record, pledged to the destruction of Israel by means of war and terror.

Ironically, the Nobel Peace Prize Committee had voted to award its highest honor to Prime Minister Rabin, Foreign Minister Peres, and Reis Arafat. One member of the Prize Committee resigned in October 1994 rather than lend his name to a "Peace Prize" honoring the world's best-known terrorist. Kaare Kristiansen, in repudiating the award that included Yassir Arafat, made himself the voice of protest against what seemed to be a determination to win peace at any price.

ISRAELI FULFILLMENT OF THE OSLO ACCORDS

One by one, the Israelis have made irrevocable transfers of Arab-populated lands to the Palestine Authority, holding to the pledges made by Rabin and Peres in Oslo II. Arafat now governs Jericho, Gaza, Jenin, Tulkarm, Kalkilya, Ramallah, Nablus, Bethlehem, and 80 percent of Hebron. Hundreds of Arab villages have been added to the land areas abandoned by Israel. More is destined to be ceded under the terms of Oslo II.

Throughout all this, it appears that Reis Arafat has done little to inform the Palestinian Arab population that a new day has dawned and that it is time to make peace. He has continued to incite violence and hatred. His diatribes have been captured on videotape so that they cannot be denied. Every concession made by Israel has been answered by angry speeches demanding still more.

POSITIVE ACCOMPLISHMENTS OF THE OSLO ACCORDS

From 1993 to 1996, the Oslo Accords could claim some victories for Israel. Most visible, a formal peace treaty was signed between Jordan and Israel. Although a de facto peace has existed between the two neighbors since 1971, beginning in 1993 and continuing through 1994 a series of meetings between King Hussein and the Israeli leadership have settled most outstanding problems. On October 26, 1994 in the presence of 5,000 foreign guests including President Clinton, Prime Minister Rabin and King Hussein signed the most important of the new treaties at the Arava south of the Dead Sea. With formal, mutual recognition, embassies and consulates have been opened. Air, auto, and bus traffic across borders has been facilitated. Foreign tourists may now fly to Aqaba, Jordan, and make a short journey by bus to neighboring Eilat, Israel. Already the Israelis have hastened to visit such historic sites as Petra, Jordan. Israel has ceded a few segments of disputed land to Jordan. In return, Jordan has allowed Israeli farmers to continue to cultivate that land, paying a rental fee to Jordan for the privilege. The two countries have arrived at amicable agreements on the shared use of water resources.

As these agreements were signed, the Arab Gulf Coast states, notably Oman, opened trade missions with Israel, even without formal diplomatic ties. The Arab League terminated its long boycott of Israel and entered mutually successful economic exchanges with Israel. However, the Arab League occasionally threatens a renewal of the boycott in response to apparent instigation by Arafat. Hopefully, however, the Arab States are so fully involved with Israeli trade that it would be hard for them to restore the boycott. In this area, Shimon Peres's *New Middle East* has become a partially vindicated reality.

SYRIA REFUSES TO MAKE PEACE

Israel's relationship with its northern neighbors has been encumbered by seemingly unsolvable problems. Israel still maintains a security zone in southern Lebanon to make it difficult for terrorists to launch missiles at northern Israeli towns. There, guerilla war continues. Iranian-trained and -supported Hezbollah terrorists regularly harass Israel and its Maronite Lebanese allies. In fact, Lebanon today is a province of Greater Syria. The government at Beirut apparently makes no move without the consent of Syria's Hafez el-Assad.

The Rabin-Peres government attempted between 1993 and 1996 to negotiate peace with Syria. U.S. secretary of state Warren Christopher made the advancement of that cause one of his top priorities until he left office at the beginning of President Clinton's second administration. The Israelis made it clear that they would consent to abandon the Golan Heights to Syria in exchange for normalization of relations, meaning diplomatic ties and the unhampered movement of civilian populations across borders. Prime Minister Rabin stated that a treaty involving the retrocession of all or part of the Golan would have to be submitted to a national Israeli plebiscite. He seemed confident, however, that the Israeli public would support such a sacrifice if it meant peace.

However, Hafez el-Assad raised objections on minor matters. He rejected Israel's insistence that electronic early warning lookout stations be erected in the Golan to alert Israel to Syrian surprise attacks. Although such stations have worked smoothly in the Egyptian Sinai, the Syrians demand that similar electronic warning stations be placed on Israeli soil. The Syrians also quibbled about whether the border would be at the water's edge on the eastern side of the Sea of Galilee or a specific number of meters from that point. The precise points of disagreement have not been publicized. However, it is surprising that Syria was prepared to place difficulties in the way of recovering the Golan when dealing with an Israeli government that showed itself ready to surrender that coveted mountain barrier. Perhaps Assad fears the entry of Israeli tourists into his closed society, which might open the way to the overthrow of his dictatorship. Perhaps he fears the intrusion of liberal ideas. Today, Syria remains a refuge for terrorists.

ALIENATION OF JEWS IN THE TERRITORIES

When the 150,000 loyal Israelis living in Judea, Samaria, Gaza, and the Golan begged for reassurances from their government, Prime Minister Rabin referred to them as "crybabies" and as "propellers spinning in the wind." These were Zionists who had settled in the barren mountains of Samaria and the semi-desert lands of Judea to build and populate a Jewish state. They had been encouraged to do so by both Labor and Likud governments. When Rabin and Peres appeared to abandon them, offering no assurance that the government would concern itself with their security, a sense of desperation arose. At least the fears of the Israelis in the Golan could be expressed politically.

The Jewish population of the Golan was mostly secular and had voted for Labor in the 1992 election. Within the Labor Party, members of the Knesset such as Emanuel Zissman and Avigdor Kahalani founded a political movement called the Third Way, which made retention of the Golan central to its efforts. All over the country, banners were suspended from balconies and windows affirming the desire of many Israelis not to budge from the Golan. The new movement also published a *Peace Map* in August 1995, just as Oslo II was being pushed through the Knesset. It identified those Jewish towns in Judea and Samaria that it felt ought never to be surrendered to the Palestine Authority.

Following the basic program of the Allon Plan, which was still officially being maintained by the Labor Party, the *Peace Map* demanded full Israeli sovereignty for such towns as Eilon Moreh, Ariel, Migdalim, Maaleh Ephraim, Shiloh, Ofra, Beit El, Neve Yaakov, Kfar Adumim, Maale Adumim, Tekoah, the Gush Etzion, Kiryat Arba and the portion of Hebron encompassing the restored Jewish neighborhoods there, and the Tombs of the Patriarchs. While Labor remained in power, the Third Way did nothing to undermine the government. As members of the Labor Party, they worked within the system. Even in 1995, when Oslo II was presented to the Knesset for approval, the Third Way did nothing to embarrass the government.

In August 1995 Prime Minister Rabin finally issued a statement to the press admitting, for the first time, that the Golan might be yielded to Syria. Even that did not lead to secession by the Third Way. Foreign Minister Peres presented Oslo II, a document of more than four hundred pages, allowing the Knesset three hours to read it before being asked to vote on it. When it seemed likely that Shas and the Third Way might abstain, Peres counted on the five Communist-line votes, and for good measure persuaded Alex Goldfarb, a member of the nationalist Tsomet Party, to offer his vote in return for subministerial perquisites. Thus, Oslo II was approved by a hairbreadth.

PERES AND MERETZ BECOME DESPERATE

Next in this political drama the government, in its desperation, turned repressive. Over the course of a half-century Israel had witnessed numerous political street protests. For example, during the 1982 war in Lebanon the left had called hundreds of thousands of people into city streets, many of them Israeli Arabs who were bused into town at night. Police force had never before been used to break up peaceful demonstrations.

However, as the Peres-Rabin government pursued its program of conducting its activities in secret, springing each aspect of the "peace process" on an astonished public, police violence grew. Worse, the numbers and kinds of Arab terrorist acts seemed to grow, unchecked, even though Reis Arafat had a large and growing armed police force of his own. At the news of each incident Rabin, Peres, and the other government ministers glossed them over as the inevitable but passing consequence of the "peace process."

The Purim Massacre

At Purim 1994, the most joyous holiday in the Jewish calendar, a young Israeli army doctor, Major Baruch Goldstein, attended services at the Tomb of the Patriarchs in Hebron. In the adjoining room and on the mosque's loudspeakers he could hear anti-Jewish speeches and cries from the Arabs, *Itbach al-Yahud* ("Kill the Jews"). The next morning he returned to the shrine and opened fire on the Arabs at prayer there. Twenty-nine worshippers died. He was killed by the survivors. This act of terrorism by an emotionally disturbed Jew was deeply embarrassing to a government already facing popular demands to take stronger steps to control Arab terrorism.

Belatedly the government did what it ought to have done years before, dividing the schedule of prayers at the Tomb of the Patriarchs so that Jews and Arabs would not come face-to-face. The government created the Shamgar Commission to investigate all aspects of the tragedy. Its conclusion was that the bloodshed was the consequence of an over-wrought man driven to emotional breakdown. But that was not the end of a growing circle of hatred.

ORDER IS THREATENED

Between April 6, 1994, and August 21, 1995, Arab suicide bombers killed sixty-seven Israelis, all but three within the borders of pre-1967 Israel. Israelis who had once held the illusion that they could live peacefully in Jerusalem, Tel Aviv, Ramat Gan, or Afula were awakening to the price of the Oslo Accords. Labor-Meretz popularity was plummeting, and all public opinion polls predicted a Likud victory and a complete revision of Israel's attitude toward the Palestine Authority. Labor turned in desperation to political rallies, concerts, street demonstrations, and other self-assurances that somehow all would yet be well. Within this atmosphere, Prime Minister Rabin was about to become a victim of the domestic fury that the "peace process" had unleashed.

On September 28, 1995, Prime Minister Rabin and Yassir Arafat signed the Interim Agreement, which formally extended Palestine Authority in Jenin, Ramallah, Tulkarm, Kalkilya, and Nablus. Jericho and Gaza had already been surrendered by the Israelis. Of the larger towns destined to be yielded to the PA, only Hebron was still withheld. As Israel had allowed Arafat's police to take control, Israel's security steadily diminished. Hamas and Islamic Jihad enjoyed shelter without harassment within the towns controlled by the Palestine Authority.

The Murder of Yitzchak Rabin

On the night of November 4, 1995, a peace rally was convened in Tel Aviv. Prime Minister Rabin and Foreign Minister Peres lent the affair prestige by attending. As the rally ended, a 25-year-old law student from

Bar Ilan University, Yigal Amir, shot and killed the prime minister at point-blank range. Very likely, before that night a majority of Israelis would have been glad to see Rabin lose office in a normal election. No sane person, however, would have wanted to see him murdered. Certainly, Yigal Amir gave unintended support to Shimon Peres who became acting Prime Minister.

Immediately a wave of revulsion swept through Israel. Thousands of memorial candles were lit by weeping young people. Yitzchak Rabin, who had never drawn public emotion during his life, brought the nation to tears and repentance through his death. Overnight, the peace process became his movement, and it suddenly seemed likely that his memory would carry his party to electoral victory. His funeral in Jerusalem brought the top officials of most world governments to his graveside. President Clinton cried out in Hebrew *Shalom Chaver*, "Farewell, Partner." Even Hosni Mubarak, who had avoided setting foot in Israel's capital, Jerusalem, offered condolences.

Left versus Right

There was a darker side, however, that revealed a long-suppressed hostility between the two Israels. It dated back to the battle cries evoked by the murder of Arlosoroff, the Season, the *Altalena*, and all the other battles between Israel's left and right.

One aftermath of Rabin's assassination was popular revulsion against all religious Jews, regardless of their personal position, simply because Yigal Amir, the assassin, was religious. Secularist politicians, headed by certain Meretz members of the Knesset, went out of their way to attack the Status Quo agreement that David Ben-Gurion had worked out with the chief rabbinate and that had kept the peace for almost fifty years. Suddenly there arose unusual movements such as the Women of the Wall, who persisted in demanding the right to lead innovative religious services within the enclosure at the Kotel even though there is an unenclosed section of the Kotel at its south end, where innovative and pluralistic services have always taken place without protest. The tragic consequence of such challenges to the old status quo is that any threats to the old order have precipitated the danger of violence.

Self-Defense by Jews in the Territories

As the left wing was engaged in efforts to denigrate the right wing, nationalists countered by protesting what appeared to be the government's abandonment of the territories. Some groups, like the Women in Green, worked to affect public opinion. Nadia Mattar highlighted the plight of the 150,000 Jews allegedly abandoned by the government. In the new atmosphere of police repression, the Women in Green were especially effective.

New groups such as Pro Israel or One Israel, led by Yechiel Leiter, worked in the United States and throughout the Diaspora to raise funds to continue building towns in the territories. Other protest groups such as Zo Artzeinu ("This Is Our Land"), being Zionists, occupied hilltops adjacent to Jewish towns that seemed likely to be surrendered to the PA in the government's final settlement. However, sometimes Zo Artzeinu was self-defeating when its supporters sat down in the middle of busy city intersections, blocking traffic and disrupting the normal lives of people who may have been otherwise sympathetic.

The government seemed locked into pretending that the political right was collectively an accomplice to the murder of Yitzchak Rabin. At the unity rally that the government sponsored at Madison Square Garden in New York, no leader of Likud or the political right was invited to speak, even though the government attempted to persuade them to sit on the platform. Orthodox Jews were recruited to sit in the audience.

DECISION TO ADVANCE THE 1996 ELECTIONS

In that hour when Israel had never been so divided, the government decided to advance the date of elections scheduled for the autumn of 1996 to May 29, 1996. Before the assassination, Labor had been slipping badly in all public opinion polls. However, the grief aroused by the death of Yitzchak Rabin evoked a turnabout from which Labor might profit. Moreover, Bill Clinton, president of the United States, seemed prepared to come as close to campaigning actively for Peres as he could without abandoning presidential protocol. Benyamin Netanyahu, the leader of Likud who would surely be prime minister if he beat Peres, was shunned conspicuously. On January 21 the Palestine Authority held elections for its proposed 88-member legislative body. Yassir Arafat was elected chairman of the Council with 90 percent of the vote.

Then followed a series of events that changed the political picture. On February 25 the Arab terrorist organization Hamas launched two suicide bombings directed against Israeli civilian bus traffic, one at Ashkelon and the other in Jerusalem. As a result, 26 people were killed. On March 3 a Hamas suicide bomber in Jerusalem killed 19 people. On April 11, faced with Hezbollah bombings in northern Israel, the Israeli government launched Operation Grapes of Wrath, which ended with the death of 91 Lebanese civilians in whose midst the Hezbollah terrorists were entrenched. The United Nations condemned Israel for the act without a word of sympathy for the victims of Hezbollah bombings in the Galilee.

Shimon Peres's government was suddenly losing popularity at the public opinion polls. It still seemed, however, that Labor would win the May 29 election—although with steadily diminishing margins.

On April 24 the Palestine National Council voted to examine the PLO charter and undertake to amend portions that called for the destruction of Israel. Because it had not carried out that intention since 1993, the Israeli public did not take it seriously even though Prime Minister Peres pronounced it the greatest event in the Middle East in a century. President Clinton invited Yassir Arafat to the White House to celebrate it.

The Election of 1996

The election was indeed close. Israeli voters went to bed that night thinking that Labor had won. They awoke in the morning to learn that Benyamin Netanyahu was the prime-minister-elect by a bare majority of 51 percent of the vote. Fifty-five percent of the Jewish vote had supported the Likud candidate, but Israel's Arabs had overwhelmingly supported Peres.

Nevertheless a political revolution was complete. The question now was how the new government would respond to Peres's peace process. The Arab cities held by Reis Arafat were an unreversible reality. Only Hebron awaited disposition. It would be a burning hot coal that might scorch the hands of anyone who grasped it.

Epilogue

NEW ELECTORAL RULES

The election for the fourteenth Knesset on May 29, 1996, involved an experiment. In all previous elections, voters cast a single ballot for the party of their choice. The president of Israel then called on the leader of the largest party to attempt to forge a coalition with other compatible alignments to create a government binding at least sixty-one members of the Knesset to support him or her as prime minister.

In the election of 1996, however, for the first time each voter cast two ballots. The first ballot was to designate the chosen prime minister. In this case, there were two choices: Shimon Peres of Labor, and Benyamin Netanyahu of Likud. The second ballot was for the voter's preferred party list. The leaders of the thirteenth Knesset who designed the two-ballot system assumed that this experiment would eliminate the numerous small, one-issue parties that had made previous Knessets a jigsaw puzzle to be fitted together to create a coalition. The election of May 29, 1996, however, proved them to be wrong.

As it turned out, after Israeli voters cast their ballot for a prime ministerial candidate, they felt free to vote for one of the small parties, rather than the large party to which their top choice belonged. Thus, on the morning of May 30, the public learned that Netanyahu had been elected. However, his party had won only 32 seats. Shimon Peres's defeated Labor Party had won 34 seats, two more than those of Likud.

ELEMENTS OF NETANYAHU'S COALITION

President Ezer Weizman was required to call on the winning prime-ministerial candidate to form a coalition because he had won a majority of the popular vote, even though his party was slightly smaller than Labor. Benyamin Netanyahu had no trouble in piecing together a coalition. However, he was obliged to make promises to each of his willing partners that reduced his freedom of action. Shas (10 seats) pressed the religious and ethnic goals of the Sephardim. The National Religious Party (9 seats) was interested in obtaining support for its schools and institutions, and particularly the settlement of Jews in Judea and Samaria. Yisrael Ba'aliya (7 seats) was led by Natan Sharansky, the most celebrated of the Russian Refuseniks, who fought for the benefits owed to recent immigrants. The Third Way (4 seats) was made up of former Laborites who were determined not to surrender the Golan to Syria. United Torah Judaism (4 seats) was devoted to deeply religious Jews who are most interested in building their schools and institutions.

DILEMMAS FACING THE NEW GOVERNMENT

In a general sense the new prime minister was sympathetic to all these causes, but every concession he made to any of them constrained his freedom of action. In the world of political reality, Netanyahu has had to deal with an overwhelmingly large set of challenges. He has had to face the fact that the ousted Labor government has already handed over a large part of Judea, Samaria, and Gaza to the Palestine Authority. The last of the big Arab-inhabited towns, Hebron, still awaited a partial withdrawal of the Israeli army, and it was necessary to partition the town so as to ensure the safety of its Jewish community. Hebron contains the tombs of the biblical patriarchs and matriarchs and is, next to the Kotel, the second holiest Jewish shrine. Israelis have painful memories of the Arab massacre of the Hebron Jews in 1929 and do not wish to see it repeated. Thus, Netanyahu drew a partition map designed to offer as much security as possible for the Jews of divided Hebron. However, in the long run, security will also require the Palestine Authority's commitment to peace.

Oslo II also provided for even more Israeli evacuation of Judea and Samaria, every mile of which would be contested by Arabs and Jews. The language of the pact was sufficiently unclear that the three subsequent withdrawals were likely to create angry dissatisfaction, regardless of what Israel might consent to surrender. (See Map 13.1.)

Netanyahu also had to test President Clinton's attitudes, because the White House had supported Shimon Peres during the election. Netanyahu must also address the fact that the European Common Market and the Third World now recognize the PLO. The belligerence of Egyptian president Hosni Mubarak is another challenge as well.

DEFIANCE OF ORDERLY NEGOTIATION

The entire system called for in Oslo II can succeed only if both sides fulfill their obligations. Yassir Arafat seems to have concluded that he may attain victory by continuing a state of belligerence. Exercising sovereign power in the large segment of land once administered by Israel, perhaps he expects world support if Israel should take military action against him. He seems to ignore his repeated pledges to revise the 1968 PLO charter and write a new one.

Israel's formal charges against the Palestine Authority for its breaches of Oslo II state that the PA has:

1. built a police force of 34,000 members without submitting a list of their names to Israel, even though the Oslo Accords allow for only 24,000. Beyond that, officials of the PA have boasted that they intend to build a National Guard of 80,000 conscripts, even though such a force is prohibited by Oslo II.

2. imported heavy weapons from Egypt; these include artillery pieces in excess of the light weapons allowed to a police force.

3. allowed its police to open fire on Israeli police and soldiers.

4. failed to confiscate weapons and disarm the private militias run by Hamas and other anti-Israel groups.

5. failed to extradite suspected terrorists sought by Israel.

6. failed to use the PA court system to punish terrorists and others who incite violence. Suspects are usually arrested and then freed, except in rare cases when the United States demands more action.

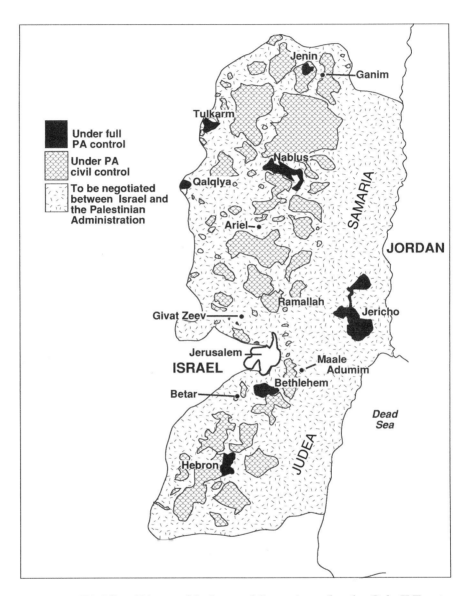

Map 13.1. Dividing Disputed Judea and Samaria under the Oslo II Treaty Agreements. Within the land under full control of the Palestine Authority the Israeli army and police have no authority and do not enter. In the areas under Palestine Authority Civil Control, the Israeli police and army share power to protect life and property with the Palestine Authority Police.

7. harassed Arabs who have collaborated with Israel in the past. The PA court system has sentenced to death any Arab who would sell land to a Jew, and an increasing number of Arab landowners have been murdered under suspicious circumstances.

8. allowed a large number of buildings to operate as Palestine Authority government offices in Jerusalem, including at least one that has essentially become a foreign ministry dealing with representatives of foreign nations. PA police also operate in Jerusalem, arresting persons known to disagree with Yassir Arafat.

9. closed down Arab newspapers that are critical of Arafat.

Israel's principal failures to continue the fulfillment of Oslo II have been in response to the Palestine Authority's refusal to continue normative negotiations whenever Israel declined Arafat's demands. Israel, for example, has delayed giving approval for the construction of an airport and port facilities at Gaza because the PA has declined to offer assurances that such means for importing foreign weapons would not inundate Israel with more hostile weaponry than is allowed to the PA by Oslo II. In the face of Reis Arafat's behavior, Netanyahu has adopted new tactics. He is now insistent that a complete and final settlement be reached immediately, ending the piecemeal partition of the disputed territories. In this, Arafat accuses Israel of breaching the Oslo II agreement because the original plan called for the partition of Judea and Samaria in three phases. Moreover, Netanyahu has problems in pacifying his coalition partners who worry that his secretiveness masks a weakness that could end by giving the PA everything that it wants.

THE PLOY OF A UNITY GOVERNMENT

Netanyahu cannot fulfill the program of Likud, a party to which he has been devoted all his life. Moreover, if he attempts to govern in unity with the Labor Party, both partners will likely frustrate one another. At the same time, Shimon Peres's career as a prime minister is over. Yet Netanyahu derives no benefit from magnifying the prestige of Ehud Barak, Labor's presumptive new leader. As the year 2000 and the next election approach, the chief function of threatening to create a national unity government would be to frighten Netanyahu's colleagues in Likud, and his coalition partners, to join him in absolutely necessary concessions to the Palestine Authority. In that difficult political game, he must work assiduously to deter any of the coalition partners from abandoning him to pursue their own political ambitions.

While they have been preoccupied with domestic issues, Israel's leaders—regardless of party—have also been facing the opportunities and threats implicit in a new world order. The Soviet Union no longer exists. Thus, the long-time danger that the USSR might aid Israel's Arab enemies is gone. The Russian Republic hovers near bankruptcy. However, in Russia's very weakness a danger lurks. Russia is still capable of producing atomic weapons and long-range missiles. It is becoming a potential supplier of dangerous weapons to numerous states, many of them in the Arab world. Israel is faced with the question of whether the United States, the only superpower today, is prepared to police the proliferation of potentially dangerous arsenals.

On the positive side, Israel has entered a brave new economic world. The long-frustrated ambition of the Likud Party has been to privatize Israeli industry. The old socialist tradition of the early Zionists has been superseded. Today, as never before, Israel is moving aggressively to sell its advanced technology throughout the world. Minister of Communications Limor Livnat, the only woman in the cabinet, has opened telephone, radio, and television to private enterprise. Natan Sharansky, as minister of trade, has journeyed around the world to sell Israeli expertise to the nations of the Third World. A vital new industrial aristocracy has emerged.

The diplomatic theater awaits the next act, in which we will learn how Benyamin Netanyahu and the State of Israel will weather the storm.

Notable People in the History of Israel

Agnon, Shmuel Yosef (Samuel Joseph Czaczkes), 1888–1970. A central figure in modern Hebrew literature. Born in Buczacz, Galicia, he moved to Palestine in 1907 but spent significant parts of his life in pre-Nazi Germany. He returned to Palestine in 1924. He received the Israel Prize for Literature in 1954 and 1958, and the Nobel Prize for Literature in 1966—the first awarded to a Hebrew writer.

Ahad Ha-Am (Asher Hirsch Ginsberg), 1856–1927. Emphasized the vitality of the Hebrew language as a unifying force for all Jews. Born near Skvira in Ukraine, he became a permanent resident of Tel Aviv in 1921. He was the greatest of the Maskilim. Until his death at Tel Aviv, he remained uncertain about the wisdom of striving to create a Jewish state.

Allon, Yigal (Yigal Pascovich), 1918–1980. Creator of the Allon Plan, the Labor Party's official platform as late as 1993. Born in the Lower Galilee but residing at Afula, he served in the Palmach during the War of Independence. Entering politics in 1950, he won a seat in the Knesset in 1954 and became deputy prime minister in 1968 after the Six-Day War. He urged that Israel retain united Jerusalem and the lowlands near the Jordan River but yield the heavily Arab-populated Judean and Samarian mountains to the kingdom of Jordan, thereby creating a land link between the East and West Banks through Jericho.

Begin, Menachem Wolfovitch, 1913–1983. Prime minister of Israel, 1977–1983. Born at Brest-Litovsk, he earned a degree in law at Warsaw University. With Poland's defeat in 1939, he was arrested by the Soviets for his outspoken anti-Communist Zionism. When Nazi Germany and the USSR went to war in 1941, Begin was freed from prison to enter the Free Polish Army. Having been stationed in Palestine, he entered the Irgun Zvai Leumi (IZL) and became its commander, battling the British who intended to surrender all of Palestine to the Arabs. After the creation of the independent State of Israel he entered political life, leading parties known variously as Herut, Gahal, and Likud. He attained political triumph in 1977 and, while encouraging Jewish settlement in Judea and Samaria, negotiated the Camp David agreements that ended in peace with Egypt and the return of the Sinai to Egypt. After 1982 Begin attempted to pacify Lebanon, but his efforts ended only with perpetuating disorder there and the ultimate domination of that country by Syria.

Ben-Gurion, David (David Gruen), 1886–1973. At the establishment of the State of Israel he became the country's first prime minister, leading the country through its War of Independence. Born at Plonsk in Russian Poland, he settled in Palestine in 1906. During much of World War I he was in exile in Egypt and the United States. After the issuance of the Balfour Declaration, he volunteered for the British army as part of the Jewish Legion. Beginning in 1920 he served as secretary-general of the Histadrut labor movement for fourteen years. He was chairman of the Jewish Agency Executive from 1935 to 1948, becoming the de facto head of Palestine's Jewish government. His last years were somewhat clouded by his inability to make RAFI, the political party that he founded, a dominant factor in politics.

Ben-Yehuda, Eliezer (Eliezer Yizchak Perelman), 1858–1922. The father of modern Hebrew. Born at Luzhky in Russian Lithuania, he entered a French medical school in 1878 but moved to Palestine in 1881, undertaking to speak only Hebrew thereafter. Once he married, his wife took the same pledge. Although he was employed by the French-speaking Alliance Israélite Universelle, he received permission to teach all Jewish subjects in Hebrew. He began the publication of two Hebrew magazines and after 1891 traveled extensively to raise money for the compilation of his multivolume Hebrew dictionary. By 1910, drawing on ancient and medieval Hebrew, he was able to create a modern Hebrew lexicon; he invented words of Hebrew origin to fit the needs of twentieth-century technology. In 1890 he founded the Vaad ha-Lashon, or Academy of the Hebrew Language. He and Menachem Mendel Ussishkin took the leading role in persuading British high commissioner Sir Herbert Samuel to recognize Hebrew, Arabic, and English as the three official languages of Palestine, later Israel. He also took a leading role in the Planning Committee of the Hebrew University. After his death his widow, Hemdah, and his son, Ehud, published a seventeen-volume dictionary in 1959.

Ben-Zvi, Yitzchak (Shimshelevich), 1884–1963. Second president of Israel. Born at Poltava in the Russian Ukraine, he was involved in early revolutionary activities but finally settled in Palestine in 1907. During World War I he was exiled to New York but returned as a volunteer for the Jewish Legion, recruited for British service. He was active in the Hagana during the Arab riots that preceded World War II. After the creation of the State of Israel, he served in the first and second Knessets (1949 and 1951). He earned a distinguished reputation as a scholar of obscure Jewish sects throughout the Near East. At the death of Chaim Weizmann in 1952, Ben-Zvi was elected second president of Israel. He served a second term (1957–1962) and was elected to a third term in 1962 but died in office on April 23, 1963. The Ben Zvi Institute in Jerusalem is committed to publishing the historical studies that are most associated with his name.

Bialik, Chaim Nachman, 1873–1934. Poet laureate of Zionism. Born in Ukraine, he moved to Tel Aviv in 1924 and died there in 1934. He was one of the most expressive of the Maskilim, who used Hebrew as the heart of philosophical Zionism.

Dayan, Moshe, 1915–1981. Israeli general. Born in Deganya Aleph, the oldest of the Kibbutzim, he served in the Haganah during the Arab riots (1936–1939) under the orders of British colonel Orde Wingate. He lost an eye while fighting the Vichy French in 1941. He served as commander-in-chief of the Israel Defense Forces from 1953 to 1958, directing the forces that conquered the Egyptian Sinai in 1956. In 1959 he entered the Knesset as a Mapai member. He remained loyal to Ben-Gurion during the prolonged Lavon Affair (1960–1961 and 1964–1965) and continued to support the dissident RAFT party. At the outbreak of the Six-Day War in June 1967 he entered the National Unity Government as minister of defense, sharing credit for the defeat of Egypt, Syria, and Jordan. In 1970–1971 he played a major role in opening the borders of Israel and Jordan to trade and tourist traffic, even though no peace treaty had been signed. In 1977 he joined Menachem Begin's Likud government, supporting the Camp David peace treaty with Egypt. He broke with Begin, as too aggressive, shortly before his own death in 1981. Despite hawkish origins, he became one of Israel's classic doves.

Eban, Abba (Aubrey Even), 1915– . Long-time Israeli ambassador to the United Nations. Born in Capetown, South Africa, and educated at Cambridge University, he became a lecturer in Arabic from 1938 to 1940. He took up residence in Jerusalem in 1945 and served as a member of the Jewish Agency's delegation to the UN General Assembly. After 1948 he was Israel's ambassador to the UN and headed Israel's embassies to both the UN and the United States from 1950 to 1959. Elected to the Knesset in 1959 as a Mapai member, he became foreign minister in February 1966. His defense of Israel's legal position made him Israel's most eloquent voice following the Six-Day War. However, like Golda Meir, he suffered popular blame for Israel's failures in preventing the Yom Kippur War of 1973. Thereafter he found himself losing support in his own party and moving steadily toward a dove-like position. He moved so far to the left that he could not recapture his once-dominant position, even when the Oslo Accords (1993–1995) rendered his ideas one again mainstream. He has been in semi-retirement since then.

Eshkol, Levi (Shkolnick), 1895–1969. Prime minister of Israel, 1963–1969. Born in Oratova near Kiev, he settled in Palestine in 1914. He served in the British-commanded Jewish Legion from 1918 to 1920. In his youth he was a kibbutz laborer and an activist in the growth of the Histadrut. He began to play a major role when he became the first director of the Mekorot Water Company, which provided Israel with a dependable water supply originating in the Sea of Galilee. From 1948 to 1963 he was at the center of the Jewish Agency's Land Settlement Department. A member of the Knesset as early as 1951, in 1963 he became prime minister and minister of defense. In 1967, when RAFI joined the National Unity Government at the advent of the Six-Day War, Eshkol named Moshe Dayan minister of defense. Eshkol played a critical role in obtaining U.S. military aircraft when France ceased supply services to Israel. Prime Minister Eshkol died of a heart attack on February 26, 1969.

Gordon, Aharon David (known by his Hebrew initials as Aleph Daled Gordon), 1856–1922. Pioneer settler and socialist philosopher. Born at Troyanov, Russia, he lived in modest seclusion for the first forty-eight years of his life, serving as an estate steward for his distant kinsmen, the Barons de Günzburg. In 1904, facing possible unemployment and distressed by the Kishinev pogrom, he left for Palestine. In his new home he threw himself into hard manual labor, developing the philosophy of the "Conquest of Labor." Not religious in a standard sense, he argued that Zionism would not succeed unless Jews performed all work required for the maintenance of a state. Though not a Marxist he held to a socialist philosophy, which he viewed as the only means of rendering the Jewish people capable of self-redemption.

Herzl, Theodor, 1860–1904. Father of Zionism. Born at Budapest, he and his family moved to Vienna in 1878. Although he received a superficial Reform Jewish education, his mother, Jeanette Diamant Herzl, pressed him to become an "enlightened German Jew." In his youth he urged mass conversion to Christianity as a solution to the Jewish problem. He received his law doctorate but became a journalist, serving Vienna's *Neue Freie Presse* as its Paris correspondent from 1891 to 1895. As a reporter observing the trial of Captain Alfred Dreyfus, he concluded that anti-Semitism would remain an unsolvable problem until a majority of the world's Jewish population resided in a Jewish state. In June 1895 he completed the first draft of *Die Judenstaat (The Jewish State).*

His life's work began with his battle to convene World Zionist Congresses to raise money to finance his goals and to win the support of wealthy patrons and statesmen. Very few wealthy Jews took him seriously. Among world statesmen his principal encouragement came from Joseph Chamberlain, the British colonial secretary, who offered land to the Zionists in Kenya (the so-called Uganda Plan) as well as a portion of the Sinai Desert. The Zionists rejected the Uganda Plan, and the Egyptians refused to provide irrigation for Jewish settlement in the Sinai. Herzl's greatest success lay in building Zionist Congresses dominated by Eastern European Jews who would not settle for anything less than a Jewish state in Palestine. Despite his sudden death from a heart attack in 1904 and fears that all his work would be in vain, the Kishinev pogroms of that year had the result of building a strong resource of young Jews who refused to accept a passive response to anti-Semitism.

Herzog, Chaim, 1918–1997. President of Israel, 1983–1993. Born in Belfast,

Ireland, the son of Isaac Halevy Herzog, chief rabbi of Ireland and ultimately the Ashkenazic chief rabbi of Israel. Prior to attaining the presidency Chaim Herzog was an Israeli army general, director of military intelligence, envoy to the United Nations, and governor of Judea and Samaria. He also served as a Labor Party Knesset member, an attorney, and a businessman. He served two terms as president (1983–1993), following Yitzchak Navon and succeeded by Ezer Weizman.

Hess, Moses, 1812–1875. Advocate of Zionism. Born in Bonn, he was educated by his religious grandfather. A short stint at the University of Bonn and occasional work as a newspaper correspondent persuaded him that the solution to the Jewish problem would ultimately require the triumph of socialism and the correction of the economic ills of all society. However, over time he gradually moved back to his Jewish religious loyalties and the conviction that only a Jewish state could provide solutions for Jews whose problems were not exclusively economic. In 1862 he published the seminal work *Rome and Jerusalem*, which Theodor Herzl later acknowledged inspired his own Zionist philosophy.

Jabotinsky, Ze'ev Vladimir, 1860–1940. Zionist pioneer. Born in Odessa, he earned enthusiastic popular support through his brilliant oratory in Hebrew, Yiddish, Russian, English, French, and German. He took particular pride in his Hebrew prose and poetry. Working as a correspondent for two Russian newspapers, he adopted the pen name Altalena. At the outbreak of World War I he worked with Josef Trumpeldor to recruit a Jewish Legion, as he had worked originally to create a Zion Mule Corps. By 1918 he had created the First Judean Regiment, which was composed of British, American, and Palestinian Jewish volunteers. Opposed to Socialism, he formed the Revisionist Zionist Organization when the British awarded Trans-Jordan to an Arab Hashemite kingdom, closing it to Zionist settlement. Jabotinsky always maintained that both banks of the Jordan ought to have been part of Zionism's license under the Balfour Declaration. With his very military demeanor he was subject to criticism by the Socialist Zionists because he was willing to work with the authoritarian regimes of eastern Europe to help expedite the migration of Jews to Palestine. He was willing to cooperate with Nazi Germany in order to evacuate Jews but refused to give the Nazis any money. Thus, the Jewish Agency's active support of Haavara led to conflict with Jabotinsky. Dismissed as a Jewish Fascist by the Socialists, Jabotinsky became one of the models for the modern Likud Party.

Kook, Abraham Isaac, 1865–1935. Chief Ashkenazic rabbi of Palestine. Born in Greiva, Russian Latvia. After a distinguished early career in Europe, Rabbi Kook moved to Palestine in 1904. He spent the years of World War I in a rabbinic post in London, winning influential friends for the concepts of orthodox religion in general and Zionist orthodoxy in particular. Following his return to Palestine after the war, he was named chief rabbi of Jerusalem and in 1921 became chief Ashkenazic rabbi of Palestine. Although Rabbi Shmuel Salant had been the head of the Palestinian Ashkenazim until his death in 1909, prior to 1921 only the Sephardic chief rabbi or *Rishon le-Zion* had held that title officially. Rabbi Kook's effectiveness built a philosophic movement centered in a religious nationalism that was determined to build Jewish residence in all parts of Palestine. In 1924 he established a Jerusalem yeshiva known to this day as Merkaz Ha-Ray Kook, or Rabbi Kook's Center. He was never entirely at ease with Mizrachi Zionism, which he regarded as primarily political.

Meir, Golda (Mabovitch), 1898–1978. Prime minister of Israel, 1969–1974. Born at Kiev, Ukraine. The family moved to Milwaukee, Wisconsin, in 1906. Following her marriage to Morris Myerson, the young bride adopted the name Golda Meir when the couple settled in the Palestinian kibbutz Merhavia. She rose in the ranks of Labor Zionists, and because she spoke English fluently and was a persuasive orator, she was sent to the United States to organize support for the movement. During the years of increasing conflict with the British as it became likely that London intended to transfer Palestine to the Arabs, Golda Meir moved steadily upward in the ranks of the Jewish Agency leadership. On May 10, 1948, just before Israel declared its independence, Golda Meir was sent in disguise to visit King Abdullah in Trans-Jordan, in an attempt to persuade him not to make war on Israel. She was not successful, but she earned his respect and made useful contacts with potential enemies. As war began, she was sent briefly as Israel's first ambassador to the USSR. In the years before the Six-Day War she played a significant role at the United Nations and in world diplomacy. She was particularly active in opening contacts in Africa and other former colonial territories, encouraging young people to study in Israel. Following the death of Levi Eshkol in 1969, she became the fourth prime minister of Israel. Until the Yom Kippur War of 1973, Meir presided over what appeared to be a growing acceptance of Israel worldwide. Although Israel recovered from the shock of the Arab surprise attack and actually won the war from a military viewpoint, the Arab oil powers were able to threaten the world's great industrial powers with the loss of essential oil supplies. The Meir government was blamed for failing to anticipate the Arab attack and was forced out of power. She did enjoy the satisfaction of participating in the peace settlement with Egypt and developed a warm and confidential relationship with Anwar Sadat.

Netanyahu, Benyamin, 1949– . Prime minister of Israel, 1995– . Born in Israel. His father, Ben-Zion Netanyahu, temporarily settled his family in suburban Philadelphia when Benyamin was 14 years old because the senior Netanyahu had been named professor of Jewish history at Philadelphia's Dropsie College. During his four years in American schools, Benyamin mastered colloquial English. At the outbreak of the Six-Day War the young man returned to Israel. Although the war ended before he could don uniform, he soon accepted a commission in an elite combat unit. Concurrent with his military service, he completed his bachelor's and master's degrees at two universities. His life and attitudes were profoundly affected by the death of his older brother, Yonathan, the only military casualty suffered by Israel in the Entebbe raid conducted against PLO terrorists in Uganda in July 1976.

The triumph of the Likud Party in 1977 opened a political career to Benyamin. His special interest was in combating terrorism, and he earned a name for himself by publishing works dealing with that subject. His true career in politics became meaningful when, although Labor won the election of 1992, Netanyahu was placed fifth on his party's electoral list. At the time of the 1995 election, following the withdrawal of Yitzchak Shamir from party leadership, Netanyahu headed the Likud list. Upon winning election, he became prime minister.

Nordau, Max (Simon Maximilian Suedfeld), 1849–1923. Co-founder of World Zionist Organization. Born in Budapest, Hungary, the son of an orthodox rabbi, Nordau went through phases of hostility to religion but returned to it as he matured. A physician by profession, he was interested in analyzing all aspects of human thought. He and Theodor Herzl were co-founders of the World Zionist Organization. He was strongly opposed to the so-called Uganda Plan but defended it publicly as part of his loyalty to Herzl. He referred to it as a *Nachtasyl*, or a "night's rest," but opposed any abandonment of a Palestinian Jewish state. It is typical of him that when an assassin tried to murder him for supporting the Uganda Plan, Nordau defended him in court. He was equally opposed to Ahad Ha-Am's Cultural Zionism and Chaim Weizmann's gradualist construction of a Jewish state, settlement by settlement. Nordau pressed for the immigration of 600,000 eastern European Jews to create an undeniable presence in Palestine. Nordau died in Paris and is buried in Tel Aviv.

Oz, Amos, 1939– . Noted Israeli writer. Born in Jerusalem, Oz is one of Israel's most respected, though most controversial, authors. He holds the chair in modern Hebrew literature at Ben-Gurion University in Beer Sheva, as well as numerous honorary doctorates and other awards. Since the Six-Day War he has been active in the peace movement, and he has been a leader of Peace Now since its founding in 1977.

Peres, Shimon (Shimon Persky), 1923– . Prime minister of Israel, 1984–1986 and 1995–1996. Born in Vishneva, White Russia, he settled in Palestine in 1934. He served as foreign minister and prime minister of Israel. See lengthy treatments in the latter chapters of this book, the bibliography, and earlier chapters as well.

Rabin, Yitzchak, 1922–1995. Prime minister of Israel, 1974–1977 and 1992–1995. Born in Jerusalem, his earliest career was as a professional soldier, culminating in his role as chief of staff during the Six-Day War of 1967. He then enjoyed success as Israel's ambassador to the United States, followed by his years in parliament and his service in successive cabinets—usually as minister of defense, foreign minister, or prime minister. See lengthy treatments in this book. His assassination on November 4, 1995, led to Shimon Peres attaining the prime ministership.

Reines, Isaac Jacob, 1839–1915. Founder of Religious Zionism. Born in Karolin, White Russia. Rabbi Reines served in a series of major rabbinical posts and created considerable controversy in orthodox circles by his use of Maimonides's logical system to explain talmudic positions. He also distressed traditionalists by introducing secular studies into the yeshiva curriculum. Before Herzl published *Die Judenstaat*, Rabbi Reines became an ally of Rabbi Samuel Mohilever, who urged through the Hibat Zion movement that religious Jews should settle in Palestine and join in physical labor to rebuild the land. He became the first prominent rabbi to offer support to Herzl, who was shunned by the rabbinate as irrevocably secularist. As a mark of loyalty to Herzl he even supported the so-called Uganda Plan, although the concept of an African Zionism seemed to be

in conflict with his religious program. Because he mistrusted the secularist cultural program of Zionism, he founded the Religious Zionist, or
Mizrachi, movement in 1902 at a meeting of religious leaders in Vilna.
His dream of building a Mizrachist yeshiva was frustrated by the outbreak of World War I. Nevertheless the Religious Zionist movement continued.

Rothschild, Baron Edmond James de, 1845–1934. Supporter of Israel.
Born in Paris. Unlike his older brothers, he was barely interested in the
financial ventures of the French banking house of which he was an heir.
Married to a devoutly religious cousin, he devoted his life to building
the security of the Jewish community of Palestine. At his own expense
he established a Palestinian wine industry, thereby creating a bureaucracy whose expenses he absorbed. He visited the country frequently,
emphasizing not only the central sectors at Ekron, Rishon l'Zion, and
Zichron Yaakov but also Samaria, the Golan, and the Hauran. He made
significant contributions to the establishment of water supply and electric
power, as well as the foundation of the Hebrew University. He belatedly
accepted ideological Zionism but had the grace to yield to ideologues
such as Ahad Ha-Am and to political leaders like Chaim Weizmann and
David Ben-Gurion. In 1954, after the birth of the State of Israel, the baron
and baroness were reinterred in a garden overlooking the sea at Ramat
Ha-Nadiv, "the Philanthropist's Heights," near Zichron Yaakov.

Szold, Henrietta, 1860–1945. Founder of Hadassah. Born in Baltimore,
Maryland. Until 1909 she was known as a linguist and translator, an
employee of the Jewish Publication Society, and the able assistant of
Professor Louis Ginzberg, whose great work was *The Legends of the Jews*.
In 1909–1910 she and her mother made a visit to Palestine that prompted
the work for which she is known. For the remaining thirty-five years of
her life she built the Hadassah Organization, attempted to improve the
health of all Palestinian residents, and began the systematic training of
health professionals. At the rise of Nazism she courageously entered Germany and began to rescue young Jews, bringing them to Palestine. She
never believed that the creation of a Jewish state was a practical goal,
and she died before it was achieved.

Weizman, Ezer, 1924–   . President of Israel, 1993–   . Born at Tel Aviv,
he served in the British Royal Air Force in World War II and subse-

quently helped to found the Israeli air corps. In the course of a varied career he has been active as a member of the Knesset, defending the policies of both Labor and Likud governments. He played a particularly important role in negotiating the Camp David treaties that led to peace with Egypt. As long as Anwar Sadat lived, the two men remained good friends. He broke with Menachem Begin over the results of the Lebanon campaign in 1982. However, he was elected president of Israel in 1993 and has enjoyed reelection. He has not hesitated to criticize Israeli governments, regardless of party.

Weizmann, Chaim, 1874–1952. First president of Israel. Born at Motol, near Pinsk, Russia. In 1892, being barred from university studies in Russia, he moved to Germany and entered the Darmstadt Polytechnic. Two years later he moved to Berlin to study biochemistry at the Institute of Technology at nearby Charlottenburg. He completed his doctorate at Fribourg in 1898. The publication of Herzl's *Die Judenstaat* was electrifying for Weizmann and the circle of Zionists residing in Germany. He became an activist immediately. When in 1903 Lord Lansdowne, Britain's foreign secretary, formally proposed the so-called Uganda Plan, Weizmann made the crucial decision to oppose it, urging Palestine as the only Zionist homeland. However, the British proposal probably played a large role in making Weizmann the devoted Anglophile that he remained throughout his life. In 1896 Weizmann won the admiration and friendship of Prime Minister Arthur James Balfour, convincing him that Palestine was essential to Zionism. In 1907, after the Eighth Zionist Congress, he made his first visit to Palestine.

The advent of World War I brought Weizmann into contact with influential people in all classes. In 1916 he was able to win a particularly large circle of new friends when he established a process that yielded acetone, a solvent essential to the manufacture of munitions. Through those contacts he was able to win the support of the British government for the Balfour Declaration, which appeared to offer the support of the British government for Zionism and its goals. This launched his career as president of the World Zionist Organization (1920–1931 and 1935–1946). In the end, more aggressive Palestinian Zionist leaders such as David Ben-Gurion bypassed him. When the State of Israel came into being in May 1948, it was assumed that Weizmann would be its first president. He held that office until he died on November 9, 1952. As long as his eyesight permitted, he continued to pursue pure scientific research. His ongoing interest in the Weizmann Institute, where he lived his last years and where he is buried, remains his memorial. Within his lifetime he made preparations for the publication of his diaries and other papers, which are in print today.

Selected Annotated Bibliography

Arens, Moshe. *American Foreign Policy and the Crisis between the U.S. and Israel.* New York: Simon & Schuster, 1995. A former Israeli foreign minister castigates President Bush and Secretary of State Baker for their alleged hostility toward Israel.

Aumann, Moshe. *Land Ownership in Palestine, 1880–1948.* Jerusalem: Israel Academic Committee on the Middle East, undated. An Israeli diplomat discusses the problems posed by Ottoman Turkish laws on land ownership, which still creates problems in modern Israel.

Begin, Menachem. *The Revolt.* New York: Dell, 1977. An autobiographical account of the author's battle to combat British closure of Palestine to Jewish immigration, and his leadership of the IZL.

Beilin, Yossi. *Israel: A Concise Political History.* New York: St. Martin's Press, 1994. Beilin was one of the architects of the Oslo Accords and a major director of foreign policy during Shimon Peres's government until 1996. He is frank about his motives for surrendering land to the Arabs.

Bein, Alex. *Theodore Herzl.* Philadelphia: Jewish Publication Society, 1962. The late state archivist of Israel wrote a masterful biography of the founder of political Zionism.

Ben-Arieh, Yehoshua. *Jerusalem in the Nineteenth Century: Emergence of the New City.* New York: St. Martin's Press, 1986. Describes the development of a Jewish majority within the walls of the Old City, and the expansion of the city westward beyond the walls.

Ben-Gurion, David. *Israel: A Personal History.* New York: Funk and Wagnalls,

1971. Israel's first prime minister offers an autobiographical account of his political life through 1967.

Blumberg, Arnold. *Zion before Zionism, 1838–1880.* New York: Syracuse University Press, 1985. Describes the means whereby the pre-Zionist Old Yishuv laid the foundation for the New Yishuv.

Dayan, Moshe. *Breakthrough: A Personal Account of the Egypt-Israeli Peace Negotiations.* New York: Alfred A. Knopf, 1981. General Dayan twice held command positions as Israel conquered the Sinai Desert, and he was a member of the Begin cabinet when Israel returned the Sinai to Egypt following the Camp David negotiations.

Finerman, Irving. *Woman of Valor: The Story of Henrietta Szold.* New York: Simon & Schuster, 1961. An excellent study of the life of the founder of Hadassah and the creator of Youth Aliyah.

Gilbert, Martin. *Jerusalem: Rebirth of a City.* New York: Viking Press, 1985. Describes the tremendous growth of Jerusalem since the reunification of the city following the Six-Day War.

Herzl, Theodor. *The Jewish State.* New York: Herzl Press, 1970. This translation of *Die Judenstaat* is essential background for understanding what Herzl believed.

Hurewitz, J. C. *Diplomacy in the Near and Middle East: A Documentary Record, 1535–1956* (2 vols.). New York: AMS Press, 1975. A valuable source about the role of diplomacy in the affairs of Palestinian Jewry.

Kark, Ruth. *American Consuls in the Holy Land, 1832–1914.* Detroit: Wayne State University Press, 1994. A study of the means whereby a representative diplomatic power built its role in Palestine through the extension of protection to persons having no claim to U.S. citizenship.

———. (ed.). *The Land That Became Israel.* Jerusalem: Magnes Press, 1990. A well-edited collection of studies touching all elements of the population from Zionist settlements, through Arab villages, and even such small groups as the Baha'i.

Konovsky, Eliahu. *The Economy of the Israeli Kibbutz.* Cambridge, MA: Harvard University Press, 1968. A scholarly description of the unique Israeli kibbutz system.

Kornberg, Jacques. *Theodor Herzl: From Assimilation to Zionism.* Bloomington: Indiana University Press, 1993. An excellent treatment of Herzl's evolution from assimilation to passionate Zionism.

Landau, Jacob M. *The Arab Minority in Israel, 1967–1991: Political Aspects.* New York: Oxford University Press, 1993. Describes the role of Arabs as Israeli citizens, their relation to other Arab populations, and their problems with self-concept.

Laqueur, Walter. *A History of Zionism.* New York: Holt, Rinehart, and Winston, 1972. An excellent and accessible discussion of Zionism and Israel.

Near, Henry. *The Kibbutz Movement: A History.* New York: Oxford University Press, 1992. The first of two volumes describing the way in which the kibbutz made it possible for an urban population to build a country that became self-sufficient in the production of basic foods.

Netanyahu, Benyamin. *A Place among the Nations: Israel and the World.* New York:

Bantam Books, 1993. Published three years before the author became prime minister in 1996, this work sets forth his philosophy as a Likud leader.

O'Brien, Conor Cruise. *The Siege: The Saga of Israel and Zionism*. New York: Simon & Schuster, 1986. A former Irish diplomat who knew intimately many of the historic figures whom he describes over a forty-year period. His printed sources are meticulously documented. He is sympathetic to Israel but presents the Arab case fairly.

Oz, Amos. *Israel, Palestine, and Peace*. New York: Harcourt Brace, 1995. A respected author presents his Peace Now philosophy as a vision of Israel's future with the Arabs.

Penslar, Derek J. *Zionism and Technocracy: The Engineering of Jewish Settlement in Palestine*. Bloomington: Indiana University Press, 1991. Gives appropriate credit to the engineers, such as Arthur Ruppin, who made Jewish settlement possible in Palestine.

Peres, Shimon, with Arye Naor. *The New Middle East*. New York: Henry Holt, 1993. Written when the author was foreign minister, the book describes Peres's belief that Israel's Arab neighbors will become peaceful if a Middle Eastern Common Market with open borders and free trade is created. He asserts the necessity of ceding land to create a peaceful environment.

Rabin, Yitzchak. *The Rabin Memoirs*. Bnei Brak: Steimatzky, 1994. The greater part of this book was published in 1977, but this edition carries the narrative up to the meeting with Arafat at the White House in 1993 and offers some insights into Prime Minister Rabin's feelings about the PLO.

Sachar, Howard M., et al. (eds.). *The Rise of Israel: A Documentary Record from the Nineteenth Century to 1948* (39 vols.). New York: Garland Publishing, 1987–1988. This massive collection in three series is invaluable as an archival and bibliographic guide.

Shafir, Gershon. *Land, Labor, and the Origins of the Israeli-Palestinian Conflict, 1882–1914*. Cambridge: Cambridge University Press, 1989. A well-documented and scholarly study of all the factors that made possible the birth of Israel, as well as the interaction of Jews and Arabs.

Shamir, Yitzchak. *Summing Up: An Autobiography*. Boston: Little, Brown, 1994. Describes the author's career from his days as leader of the IZL and his work as head of the Mossad, or Secret Service, through his years as prime minister until he lost the election of 1992.

Shapiro, Yonathan. *The Road to Power: The Herut Party in Israel*. Albany: State University of New York Press, 1991. A good study of the evolution of the party that is Israel's modern Likud.

Tessler, Mark A. *The History of the Israeli-Palestinian Conflict*. Bloomington: Indiana University Press, 1994. This well-documented work tends to be somewhat more sympathetic to the Arab cause than such works as that of Conor Cruise O'Brien.

Tinken, Marie. *Golda Meir: Woman with a Cause*. New York: Putnam, 1963. A popular study of the life and career of the woman who subsequently became prime minister.

Vital, David. *The Origins of Zionism*. New York: Oxford University Press, 1975.

The first of a three-volume series; the two others are not cited here, but all are equally valuable for the author's balanced views on the history of Zionism and the condition of world Jewry since 1881.

Wasserstein, Bernard. *The British in Palestine.* London: Royal Historical Society, Studies in History Series, 1978. Based on British and Israeli archives, this excellent study describes the decline of British-Zionist relations from 1919 to 1948, and the ultimate struggle to expel the British when it became obvious that they intended to make Palestine an Arab state barring Jews from entry.

Weizmann, Chaim. *The Letters and Papers of Chaim Weizmann.* Meyer Weisgal, ed. London: Butler and Tanner, 1973–1980. This multivolume work comprises the invaluable papers of a founder of Israel and its first president.

Zipperstein, Steven J. *Elusive Prophet: Ahad Ha'am and the Origins of Zionism.* London: Peter Halban Publishers, 1993. A valuable study of one of the greatest Maskilim.

Index

About the Author

ARNOLD BLUMBERG is Professor of History at Towson University in Towson, Maryland. He was honored by the University in 1995 as its Distinguished Scholar. Blumberg is the editor of *Great Leaders, Great Tyrants? Contemporary Views of World Rulers Who Made History* (Greenwood, 1995), and other books and articles on diplomatic history.